LARYNX

GALAXY

OTHER TITLES BY JOHN OLSON

The Nothing That Is, 2010

Backscatter: New and Selected Poems, 2008

Souls of Wind, 2008

The Night I Dropped Shakespeare on the Cat, 2006

Oxbow Kazoo, 2005

Free Stream Velocity, 2004

Echo Regime, 2000

Eggs & Mirrors, 1999

Logo Lagoon, 1999

Swarm of Edges, 1996

LARYNX

GALAXY

JOHN OLSON

Black Widow Press is an imprint of Commonwealth Books, Inc., Boston, MA. Distributed to the trade by NBN (National Book Network) throughout North America, Canada, and the U.K. All Black Widow Press books are printed on acid-free paper, and glued into bindings. Black Widow Press and its logo are registered trademarks of Commonwealth Books, Inc.

Joseph S. Phillips and Susan J. Wood, Ph.D, Publishers
www.blackwidowpress.com

Cover Art & Design: Kerrie Kemperman
Typesetting: Kerrie Kemperman
Author Photo by Roberta Olson
Collaged images: partial moon from *Le Voyage dans le lune* by George Méliès; "Refraction, Parallax, Light & Heat" by Asa Smith, 1850; "Celestial Harmonia Macrocosmica" by Andreas Cellarius, and a plate by Francesco Rostagni from *Castelli, e ponti di Maestro Niccola Zabaglia*, 1743.

ISBN-13: 978-0-9842640-3-2

Printed in the United States

10 9 8 7 6 5 4 3 2 1

for Roberta

ACKNOWLEDGMENTS

I am grateful to the editors of the following magazines and blogs in which some of these poems first appeared: *Absinthe Literary Review, Alligatorzine, The American Poetry Review, The American Scholar, Anemone Sidecar, Arsenic Lobster, Bateau, Bird Dog, Denver Quarterly, Dusie, Exquisite Corpse, Filter, First Intensity, Floating Bridge Review, Glade Of Theoric Ornithic Hermetica, The Hat, Hawai'i Pacific Review, House Organ, Jivin' Ladybug, Knock, Locus Novus, Meadow Wobbler, New American Writing, Omega 7, Reading Local Seattle, The Seattle Review, Sentence: A Journal of Prose Poetics, Signs of Life, Talisman, Unarmed,* and *Verse.*

TABLE OF CONTENTS

REFRACTION, PARALLAX, LIGHT & HEAT

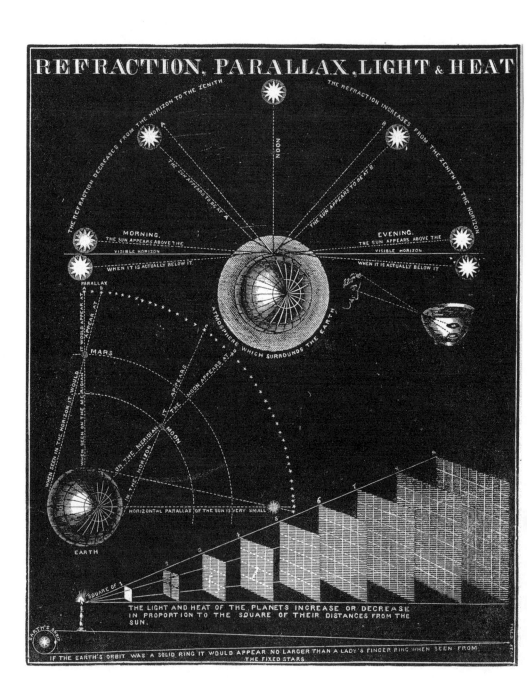

THE REFRACTION DECREASES FROM THE HORIZON TO THE ZENITH

THE REFRACTION INCREASES FROM THE ZENITH TO THE HORIZON

NOON

THE SUN APPEARS TO BE AT A

THE SUN APPEARS TO BE AT B

MORNING.
THE SUN APPEARS ABOVE THE
VISIBLE HORIZON
WHEN IT IS ACTUALLY BELOW IT.

EVENING.
THE SUN APPEARS ABOVE THE
VISIBLE HORIZON
WHEN IT IS ACTUALLY BELOW IT

PARALLAX

IT WOULD APPEAR AT

IT APPEAR AT

MARS

WHEN SEEN IN THE HORIZON IT WOULD

WHEN SEEN ON THE MERIDIAN

ON THE MERIDIAN IT APPEARS.

THE MOON APPEARS AT

ATMOSPHERE WHICH SURROUNDS THE EARTH

MOON

IN THE HORIZON

HORIZONTAL PARALLAX OF THE SUN IS VERY SMALL

EARTH

SQUARE OF 1

THE LIGHT AND HEAT OF THE PLANETS INCREASE OR DECREASE
IN PROPORTION TO THE SQUARE OF THEIR DISTANCES FROM THE
SUN.

EARTH'S ORBIT

IF THE EARTH'S ORBIT WAS A SOLID RING IT WOULD APPEAR NO LARGER THAN A LADY'S FINGER RING WHEN SEEN FROM
THE FIXED STARS

Extreme reading is the opposite of speed reading. Words are not animals killed and stuffed for exhibition. Words are alive. Words are giants and angels. There has to be a certain suppleness of mind for a description of wool to become real wool, or a mosquito drawing blood through a proboscis on a shore near Rockstone, Guyana.

What happens when we read? Things and people that are absent become present. Images develop in the mind. An image is a drop of thought in the form of ink. A timeless vapor spun out of silk. The mind can go as deep as it wants into a word or string of words. Linger there as the world turns and the saga moves forward.

An alphabet is dead until the eyes bring the letters light and life. The harmonica is fulfilled when there is air blowing through it. Letters enter the eyes and become fireworks. A white lotus in a blue bowl. A cherry of juicy cognition. Gold embedded in sand. A pound of air fastened to a sheet of paper. A spectacle in which Montmarte and its smells and sounds are vivid and sexual. And the sky is encased in a walnut. And the spirit is awakened to the meaning of glass. Objects on a table. Sheer sugar bouncing through paradise in a borrowed jeep.

Focus is essential. One must be scrupulously idle. Open the book. Bend forward. Dive into it.

Reading is delicate, like surgery. The ribcage has been opened. There is a large red organ beating in spasmodic rhythms. Our thoughts turn toward a milieu of intellectual endeavor. Syllables rooted in glitter. The water has been disturbed. Sunlight fractures and flickers. The oars drift idly. The mouth opens to say what it is to feel one's illusions shattered. Meanwhile the fetus of a new idea evolves into a series of convolutions immediate as skin.

Someone has scribbled their name in the sand. But the last breaking wave has made feathers of it.

Speed reading is like riding in a car. The world whizzes by in a blur. We get to our destination without having noticed what brought us to our destination. Extreme reading is driving a car. Extreme reading is stopping a car and getting out to go for a walk.

Consider the sky. Fingers curled around the spine of a book. Affections, reflections, infections, inflections. Yellow and red. Voices echoing in a planetarium.

Reading is a form of hallucination. The images and people we encounter among the letters are not there. The reality they acquire in our mind is equal to the effort we make in building them in our mind. Sufficient training will help understand the meaning of someone waving semaphores up and down but true reading requires something more of you than knowing how to spell or understanding the relationship between a sign and its referent. The letters invite a cooperation greater than the peremptory commands of a traffic light. Whoever came up with the idea of separating green from red with the happy ambiguity of yellow was clearly someone who enjoyed reading.

Why is it always so hard to find time to read? Or a place to read?

Antoine de Saint-Exupéry used to set the controls of his P-38 Lightning on automatic and circle Marseille while reading a book.

He was claimed to have been shot down by Horst Rippert, a Luftwaffe pilot who acknowledged himself to be a fan.

It is a good idea to choose a safe place to read, though I am frequently dazzled by people who walk down city streets while reading a book.

Reading is like talking to a ghost. Picasso squeezing a tube of paint, wide-eyed in a yolk of gold.

The mind is silent like an aquarium. A brood of sounds and arbitrary signs lift themselves into color and being. Lambent designs maunder in undulation. A page is turned. A new paragraph begun. Einstein is disturbed to find that, according to the theory of relativity, the universe is not static, but either contracting or expanding. Starlight becomes deformed over long distances. The stratospheric irreality of huge numbers create new dimensions. Reading the universe, or a strand of DNA molecules, requires intuition, a feeling for combinatory forces and their tendency toward play.

All reading is based on this question: why is there something instead of nothing? The quantum vacuum is never empty but roils with virtual particles. The particles represent not only what is, but what might be. The same can be said of letters. Or a string of words. They represent what is, but the reader's mind may take them elsewhere. Reverie is unpredictable.

14

Was there a time when nothing existed? No time? No space? No particles? No Bohemia? No journeys? Nothing thin? Nothing thick? Nothing glowing? No beauty or butter?

If you are reading this on a computer screen it is not so much a matter of proverbs as pixels. Proverbs belong to the formation of old religions. Pixels belong to the proverbs of lucidity. The light in the box. The light in the mind. The light coming out of the eyes.

"There is a kind of novelist," observes Anthony Burgess, "usually popular, sometimes wealthy, in whose work language is a zero quantity, transparent, unseductive, the overtones of connotation and ambiguity totally damped." The aim of this novelist "can only properly be fulfilled when the narrated action is transformed into represented action: content being more important than style, the referents ache to be free of their words and to be presented directly as sense-data." This is not reading. This is watching television on paper.

As for the other kind of novelist, and here we have James Joyce and Gertrude Stein and Edgar Allan Poe in mind, "it is important that the opacity of the language be exploited, so that the ambiguities, puns and centrifugal connotations are to be enjoyed rather than regretted, and whose books, made out of words as much as characters and incidents, lose a great deal when adapted to a visual medium."

The word-intoxicated writer of opacity and centrifugal connotations to which Burgess refers requires true reading. Attentive reading. Fully absorbed reading. Creative reading. Alert and aware and alive and perceptive reading. Deep reading. Engaged reading. Extreme reading.

Maurice Merleau-Ponty, commenting on a statement by French linguist Antoine Meillet, that "linguistic events are qualitative" and that each language "forms a system," and so entails a principle of internal organization, remarks that "to say that linguistic events are qualitative, is to say again that in their connection and their unrolling [déroulement] they require the mediation of consciousness."

Language is a medium in the deepest sense, a membrane of sound and meaning in which light is diffused in that space between internal perception and external world.

Think of the potential in a single word. It is like opening a box. A procession of people leaving imprints in clay. Each word has acquired multiple layers and flavors as it has traveled from mouth to mouth over centuries of use. Take the word "subtle" for instance. Subtle comes from Latin *subtilis,* which itself is a conflation of two Latin words, *sub,* meaning under, and *tilis,* which comes from *tela,* meaning web, which is related to *texere,* to weave. So here we have a word making clear and direct reference to the fine art of weaving, combining threads in a pattern, work requiring skill, dexterity, focus, and loving attention. And who hasn't entered a shed and felt the fine brushing of a web against the skin, and how fine and delicate that sensation happened to be, and the smells associated with it, and the sense of things living that were not altogether present.

One of my favorite uses of the word "subtle" appears in *Secreta secretorum* (The Secret of Secrets), a Middle English prose translation of the work in French by James Yonge, which itself was a translation from the Arabic *Kitab sirr al-asrar,* which makes reference to the *Book of the science of government,* on the good ordering of statecraft, and takes the form of a letter supposedly from Aristotle to Alexander during his campaign in Persia. Yonge writes "Sutil as thyn spetil that descendyth… fro the Palete of the mouth to the tonge." What a spectacular image!

A more recent example appears in John Tyndall's *Heat considered as a mode of motion: being a course of twelve lectures delivered at the Royal institution of Great Britain in the season of 1862.* Tyndall, a romantic pantheist, wrote: "The material theory supposes heat to be… a subtle fluid stored up in the inter-atomic spaces of bodies."

There is no end to the associations drawn from disassembling a word. Lips are skin, finite and fixed, but the imagination is infinite.

Morning is beautiful because it travels on entertaining sticks. The sticks are letters. Some of them have curves. O is a fabric of dreams and snow. H gets expansion from kerosene rags lit by the i in a grapefruit.

Making art with words is just plain silly. Because beauty is savage and alphabets are the product of civilization. And what is civilization except people figuring out how to live with one another without killing one another? The process is incomplete. The world needs readers.

Socrates was against reading because he believed it would weaken the memory and lead people astray with illusions instead of truths. Socrates was wrong. Reading is what you make of it. It's true that writing doesn't have the suppleness and spontaneity of speech because once an idea is committed to pixel or paper it becomes frozen in time. Even the sloppiest email message has something stiff and remote about it because it lacks the quick improvisations of the tongue. But speech, which is frequently erratic and muddled, does not convey the truth any better than writing. Writing is a craft. There is more time to cram and season it with thought. The kind of thought that mulls and maunders in the mind until it is ripe and swollen and ready to drive turbines.

Neither speech nor writing can claim exemption from distorting the truth, or outright lying. But the written word is open to examination. It concentrates our attention. The extreme reader learns how to sift each phrase and sentence for nuggets of value and consequence. How to dwell in solitude. How to reflect. How to suspend judgment. How to drift in reverie. There is a sense of disembodiment when we read because we emerge from ourselves to occupy an imaginary domain, what Robin Blaser refers to as "an extreme ghostliness in language itself. It includes the sublime, the terrible and the uncanny…" Socrates feared that this "extreme ghostliness" would make people more vulnerable to noxious chimeras, phantom conceptions, Circean distortions. But the force of a skilled orator can be just as enchanting, just as misleading. Speech is no guarantor of integrity. Psychopaths have a notable tendency to be smooth, inviting, fascinating, and verbally facile.

Socrates was spot on when he said that language was a drug. He calls writing a Pharmakon, which can act either as a remedy or a poison. Socrates sees it acting as a poison because it not only weakens memory but lures us away from the truth with its inherently hallucinatory properties. "Operating through seduction," observed Jacques Derrida in his essay on the subject, "the *pharmakon* makes one stray from one's general, natural, habitual paths and laws." But what's wrong with that? That sounds like a good thing to me. Reality isn't tied down. It is constantly moving.

Writing is governed by the ways of magic and not the laws of necessity. We are not in a domain of binoculars and sweat, as the explorer of a new terrain might be, but a jungle of letters whose horizon continually expands and everything is spectral as perfume.

To go to an extreme in anything implies danger. Extreme reading is no different. The danger is that it puts our mind elsewhere, outside the usual parameters, where it is free to question the laws in which it resides. Derrida compares this to a desire for orphanhood, and patricidal subversion.

It would not be surprising, then, to discover that a number of outlaws happened to be avid readers. Frank James used to perform scenes from Shakespeare while he and his brother Jesse robbed trains.

One of the primary characteristics of the orphan is neediness. Writers who light a match and burn what they have written in order to preserve a purity of expression are rare. Most people, when they have written something they are pleased with, desire an audience. It is there that one hopes for an ideal responsiveness, an educated public. "Context," observes Ron Silliman in his essay "The Political Economy of Poetry," "determines the actual, real-life consumption of a literary product, without which communication of a message (formal, substantive, ideological) cannot occur." It is here that the poet hopes fervently for that rare species, the extreme reader. Someone willing to immerse themselves in language. Someone with a real love of language. Silly language. Non-utilitarian language. Language without boundaries. Language that fuels wild speculations by a vigorous contiguity and artfully reveals the exquisite actuality of words in the spring of their creation. Which, surprisingly, antagonizes a lot of people.

Silliman writes elsewhere, in the mid-eighties, that the "widespread howling and derision which has greeted the tendency which has come to be characterized as 'language poetry' reflects precisely this taboo against transcending the known universe… the outcries of those poets and critics for whom the arrival of anything new in the field of writing is, literally, impossible is an index of just how painful the recognition of one's own cultural borders can be."

Extreme reading, which encourages the reader to follow the subterranean laws of association rather than logic, offers incendiary salvation from a world that has ceased to be mulled or maundered but mauled into mall after mall after mall. Extreme reading is liberation by inebriation. Mania, marvel, and maze. An evocation, a walk up library steps in quest of a voyage.

Find something pertinent to say about membranes. You can't fully know a membrane until you've hooked a steelhead, or studied the vibrations in an idealized circular drum. Here you will find solutions for wave equations and phantom paragraphs disguised as fungus.

Do laundry. Contrary to a few eccentric opinions, clean clothes are an asset to the maintenance of ampersands and thought.

Sit at a desk and stare at the wall. Lift your arms. Roar upward in spreading clouds of gas and smoke.

Experiment with facial expressions. Consider a taxi when you are stuck in the sand. Go on a hair-raising adventure. Read, read, read.

Create a bleak atmosphere. Stand alone on a gravel bar. Brush your hair. Make a fist. Generate crackling tangles of lightning. Let it loose. Smile. You have just created an apparent feeling.

Applaud the next washcloth. Hang it on the refrigerator handle. Let it stay there until it has grown too wet and soiled for further use. Retire it. Put it in the laundry.

Introduce yourself to the bed each night so that it may come to understand the needs of your body. Be impertinent if you must.

Inhabit a book as you would a dream, or library, or epidermis.

Wear black leather gloves. Look for elk antlers in the meadow. Invent a paradigm. Start each day with a lunatic hooting.

Inch closer to the tendrils of ramification. Wear a brightly colored shirt. Ask yourself "what is tangible, and what is not? What is the true goal of the pharmacy? What does it mean to float?"

Carry a perpetual handshake wherever you go, but use it sparingly.

Fall in love with electricity. Check the oven before returning to spawn. Wear epaulets and a sword. Adopt a look of perpetual irritation.

Imitate your favorite animal, be it a steelhead trout in the Hoh River, or a homo sapiens on the fringe of a homonym.

Keep an eye out for comets and other aberrations.

Move about on loud whooshing wings. Respect the chin, it is an engine of presence. Put your hand on the boiler and feel its heat. Start a garden of beans, violets, and zinnias. Honor the ability of birds to fly. Jettison everything in your life that is a burden. Break the sunlight into colors like Newton. Get unclogged.

Drink lots of water. Think of yourself as a ventriloquist for all things in the universe. Go for a long walk in the snow.

Sew a manuscript together using a combination of multicolored threads. Notice how the avocado is incidental to itself. Assimilate all three laws of thermodynamics. Make friends with gravity. Appear to be descended from kings. Pedal a bicycle around the room. Moisten your lips then say something dry.

Wear a cape of velour and growl. Be gallant and dashing. Create a fuel for the laughter of thermometers. Navigate a zeppelin through the eye of a needle.

Never waver except when to do so makes waves. There is always a little rhapsody in calculus. Incite a riot. Project confidence. Date an oboe. Bivouac in a blackberry.

Daub when it is good to daub, flick when it is indispensable to flick.

Consider the coins in your pocket. How many are there? How big are they? What nations do they represent? What did you do to earn them? How useful will the pennies be when it comes time to make change? Do you have enough quarters for the parking meter?

Incubate a felony. There is a felon in all of us. Revel in overalls and hemoglobin. It will come to you eventually.

Distill your thoughts until they look like vegetables. Get wet doing something that makes you happy. Do not lack vigor in your takeoff. Praise the opacity of onions.

Picture life in the ocean. House a benign neglect. Do backflips and handsprings. Teeter on misanthropy.

Use your fingers for fried chicken, a fork for chicken in aspic. Each tense is a gear. Believe in pectin. Miniaturize the apocalypse of syntax. Think of yesterday as a firearm. Invoke spoons and nails. Think of the brain as an emulsion of images. Check your cheek for chickadees.

Experience the weirdness of milkweed. Learn to speak foreign languages like saltwater and mud. Declare yourself free of declamation. Jangle a jingle. Scold a scrotum. Lactate large objects. Apply balm to your nipples. Paint lilies on your cane.

Find an ulterior motive for the enjoyment of heavy metal.

Know your boundaries. Avail yourself of binoculars and telescopes. Be a harbinger of elfish disposition. An appeasement with reality should never be a feature of your research.

Endeavor to understand whiskers. Weird activity in the darkness. The churning of hormones.

Be iron. Be lipstick. Be a tailor to your obscurity. Become a back-country skiing connoisseur. Slalom in trees. Vault an apricot. Parachute through an enigma. Construct an image of heaven, then burn it down. Learn to play the xylophone with your feet. Triumph in the angora of circumstance. Reticence is not a virtue. Model your comportment on the dragonfly. Each yearning is an engine. Imagine a feather falling through oblivion. Note the splendor of rafters in sunlight. Twist a language into eagles and drugs.

Treat vowels like a blacksmith, consonants like a planetarium.

Spin your propellers. The night will give you stars. The morning will give you copper. Learn to sift consciousness for nuggets of Saturday.

BROUGHT TO A BOIL: AN ESSAY ON EXPERIMENTAL POETRY

> All poetry is experimental poetry.
> — Wallace Stevens

Turning words into art is unnatural. It begins with a contrary attitude. It says, I am unhappy with the way things are and desire to make things different. Rather than represent the world, I will make something wildly and savagely new. I will defy logic. I will invest in new perceptions. I will combine and recombine and fabricate and juggle until something that I have never experienced is experienced. The process is alchemical. The process is violent. It goes to the heart of creativity. It disrupts and shatters. It is splendid with provocation. It is an aggression against banality. It is sharp and loud like a janitor scraping frost from a window. The hectic bounce of steam on a street after a truck roars by. The anarchy of waterfalls, the comedy of the face, dangerous feelings vented from a cage of skin.

Language is inherently hedonistic. It cries for experimentation. Remember: language is a social medium, it's public as an airport, universal as air, but occupies a realm of cognition not unlike hallucination. It is a brutally delicate mechanism whose sprockets and chains are mere perceptions of sound, intricacies of meaning and syntax with less reality than Mercutio's Queen Mab, or Prospero's cloud-capped towers. It is not equipped with the tangibility of clay, the viscosity of paint, the immediacy of steel, or the simple conductivity of wire. Tongues, teeth and lungs bring it to life, ink and pixels preserve it, but apart from these neighborly appurtenances, language is fundamentally a mode of representation, a system of signs commonly accepted as referring to certain concepts. It has no actual correspondence with the external world. Which is one of its beauties. There are no limits to what it can do. It can be meticulously assembled or totally spontaneous. Its pleasure stems from infinite variation. There are no fixed associations, no unequivocal references that cannot be modified, reconstructed, mutated, altered or transformed. Language is eternally naked, anomalous as bones. It ribs, rails, goofs and grabs. It is a funhouse mirror. It tells us that something is there which is not actually there. Or may be there. Or could be there. Or should or should not be there. It thrives on predication, proposals of air in clouds and leaves. It is everything that is impossible made possible. It is water tied in a knot. It is a Brazil of giant metaphors, the fragrance of thought, the opium of solitude, pollen eloping with tropical winds. It is daylight twisted into Wednesday. The rhetoric of cells creating fish and crocodiles. Moscow turned inside out. It is a symptom of the artist's mind manifesting itself as a faucet in Tierra del Fuego. The noise of embroidery. The silence between notes. Black light. The disturbing amiability of zero.

Experimentation in words is different from experimentations in science. Experimentations in science lead to a sharpened empiricism, a principled pragmatism, an objective view of things that opens and shuts with the peremptory impartiality of elevator doors sliding open or closed. The honey of cause and effect. Experimentation in words leads to the mustard of cacophony, unbridled granite, ecstasies in anvils, legends and dragons boiling out of fugitive metaphors. Abstractions of thread. Mallarmé doing wheelies on a Harley-Davidson. Six nude somersaults and a buffalo in a tulip refinery. You cannot quite predict what words are going to do. That is the whole idea. That is exactly the kind of situation you want to be in: entering into a play with the language in which control is excused and revolutions begin. Revolution in both senses of the word: orbital motion about a point and a sudden or momentous change in a situation.

If I tell someone that I am going to sit down and write a poem they will form a very specific idea of what it is I am proposing to do. He is going to make a construction of words which will contain certain images and effects of sound designed to move the emotions or persuade or startle or impress. But if I tell someone I am going to perform some experiments on the language they will have a much less certain idea of what I am intending to do. Is he going to pour language into beakers and precipitate zeugmas? Is he going to create macabre mutations, long scintillating sentences scuttling along like syllabic millipedes? Inflate vowels with noble gases? Grow polymers out of morphemes? Discover a cure for dieresis?

There are two ways to go at writing a poem: one is to learn everything there is to know about it and cultivate a mastery, a management of words that will shine out in brilliant effects of imagery and sound but nothing else, just this virtue, this learned ability. The other method is not entirely antithetical to the first. There will be evident a fascination with language, a deepened understanding of its mysterious and vagaries, but far less certainty about how to marshal that understanding. There will be little lyrical effect and far more ugliness. Ecstasies rather than varnish.

There is a misconception that those who choose to experiment do so out of a childish need to avoid rules. This is absurd. It is the reverse. This assumption is an alibi for those who lack the nerve to experiment. They simply want to polish whatever is familiar within their sphere. The truth is experimentation requires a heightened appreciation of rules. The Oulipians, for instance, have made a great discovery in the paradoxically liberating energy of constraint.

The real difficulty is in doing anything new. The twentieth century was full of experimentation, full of movements and schools and manifestos and clashing philosophies. Futurism, Dada, Surrealism, Vorticism, Fluxus, Imagism, Objectivism, Black Mountain College, The Beats, The New Formalists, L=A=N=G=U=A=G=E writing and so on.

What has happened to realism? Still possible, still quite popular. Still proffered and published in glossy venues such as *The New Yorker*, *Playboy*, and *The Atlantic*. But one cannot help but feel something faulty at its core, as if some malady had affected its spine and caused it to go about hunched and slow, careful with cutlery, hesitant and nervous around crowds and food in foreign countries. The ideal here is a strange one: the wish to make the words disappear so that we have the illusion of looking out at the world through a pane of clear glass. The problem is, the glass is cracked and flawed and the window has been painted stuck. Even on balmy days we can't get that window open again. Maybe it's time to examine the glass, take a deeper look at the medium with which we're dealing.

Brecht stated that language, as a finite generality, could not deal with objects, spectacles, and events that would surprise it to the point of stupefying it. Events such as Auschwitz and Buchenwald, Guantanamo and Abu Ghraib cannot tolerate a description of literary character. Roland Barthes furthers this perception as an impotence to produce a realistic literature today and proclaims that it is no longer possible to rewrite Balzac, or Zola, or Proust. "Realism is always timid," he observes, "and there is too much *surprise* in a world which mass media and the generalization of politics have made so profuse that it is no longer possible to figure it protectively: the world, as a literary object, escapes; knowledge deserts literature, which can no longer be either *Mimesis* or *Mathesis* but merely *Semiosis*, the adventure of what is impossible to language, in a word: *Text* (it is wrong to say that the notion of 'text' repeats the notion of 'literature': literature *represents* a finite world, the text *figures* the infinite of language: without knowledge, without rationale, without intelligence)." (Barthes, 119).

What a marvelous thought: "the adventure of what is impossible to language." This is the essence of experimentation.

Language is radically arbitrary. We are now accustomed to think in terms of language as a body of rules. Meaning is an agreement, not a law of nature. There is no correspondence between a word and the thing to which it refers. This is imaginary. The word "apple" is not an actual apple. And therein lies a paradise of experimentation.

What does it mean to experiment? How does experiment relate to theory? What role do metaphors play in experimentation? How does the language of experimentation vary from one anthology to another?

My preferred definition is by Gerrit Kouwenaar, a member of the COBRA group, who said: "In contrast to the traditional poets, the experimental poet does not impose his will on the word, but instead allows himself to be guided by the word... The poet... does not depict something that he had stored up ahead of time, but experiences something he had not known before." (Rothenberg/Joris, 234).

As an aesthetic experience, there is nothing like it. Taking a drug, particularly a hallucinogen, for the first time comes somewhat close to the mark. Skydiving, scuba diving, rock climbing, surfing, snowboarding and bungee jumping are other ways to get one's adrenalin running and greatly heighten one's sense of being alive. It's probably a good way at getting a poem started. But ultimately, there comes that moment where it's just you and a sheet of paper. What happens there is entirely up to you.

One afternoon language became a whale and swam out of my mouth. Why is there never anyone around when these things happen?

The whale swam around the room, vibrant and hallucinatory, just like a real language, a dazzling rotation of flippers and bulk. Its fluke hit a light fixture and shadows wobbled and mutated on the wall. I saw Socrates and China, monsters and chimerical cities. If only I had a camera.

The whale became a feeling. The feeling became a fable. The fable became a fabric. The fabric turned to rags and the rags became a ghost. The ghostly rags of fabrication. The ghostly rags of omens and signs. Stepladders and gloves and foul unspeakable crimes.

The ghost roared a stream of hot flaming words. Words like power and murder and aspidistra. A castle emerged. Hamlet stumbled through his weariness seeking vengeance and love. He was eaten by a worm. And thereby hangs a tale.

A few minutes later a catfish rode by on a bicycle. I waved. The catfish waved back.

Clearly, when language is sloppy, vague, and inaccurate, certain phenomena tend to occur in abundance, such as the troubled intuition of forms, the current financial crisis, and the Great Lakes Circle Tour.

Bicycles are inherently confusing, because they lead to rotation, which just sets your head spinning. You must think about things like tendency, momentum, and force. The moment of a force is the tendency of the force to produce rotation about an axis, and is measured by the product of the force into the perpendicular distance from the axis to the line of action of the force. And where, might I ask, does that get you?

I will tell you: Milwaukee.

For it is here that our story truly begins. Milwaukee was settled in 1836 by a strong German and Polish population. It was later reclaimed by the King of Siam and given back to France, who lost it again. It is now rumored to be bubbling under a gazebo behind the *Hotel de L'Univers*.

I am sorry for what this poem has done, sorry for what it is about to do. Once food started flying, it was all over the ceiling and floor. Fruit, noodles, chocolate milk, Tater Tots, sandwiches and coffee cake.

In other words, existential quantifiers can be paraphrased with help of universal ones and vice versa, as is well known.

Fair is fair. Fir is fur.

Turning words into trowels are bubbles that parallel thought. If we presuppose a paralinguistic quality space, mimicry becomes a skin for our kindred lips. Particles of meaning leak from an alphabet. We are persuaded that we are soap and mirrors. To be embedded in steam is a song of vast understanding. A pound of meaning you can squeeze between your legs.

And you explode into stars.

Here is how the day evolves: it begins with a sun, a big fat blob of light that crests at the top of the mountains to the east, then explodes into light and blue and detail, or diffuses slowly and ineluctably into a gloom of pearl and gray. Details emerge. Tambourines, tam-o'-shanters, grit and gravel, eggs and gravity, ferns, fenders, yawns, freshly varnished puddles and various intangible strains. Traces of inner life reflected in the outer world. Things that, during the night, get dreamed or touched, touched lightly, vaguely, then disappear, retreat into the back of the mind, so that if we see it appear in the light of day, it is reflected back at us like a nimbus or gloriole, a phantom, a trick of light. A restless distillation of everything that makes us feel agitated, disinclined to get out of bed.

Masses of people fill the streets. There are people on their way to the dentist with a bad case of gingivitis, people going to jobs they hate, or enjoy on some vague level too elusive to put into words, people everywhere boiling with conflicts and commentaries and contradictions.

Exhaust belches from the back of a bus and there it is, the big fat day, that entity of light and detail that will be deposited later in the landfill of our memory, mound upon mound of discarded event, seagulls whirling above, backhoes grinding below.

Here is a line of people going up an escalator. Some of them are thinking of something. Some of them are trying not to think of anything. Some of them are talking on tiny portable phones. Some of them will arrive at revelations, miracles of perception, and return home with an important decision. Some will have enjoyable emotions and some will have furiously pink and yellow emotions.

How do I know these things?

I don't. I make things up as I go along. Like the day. Like the day evolves.

Each morning I get up and get my feet on the carpet and make the bed and listen to the radio. Jokes and atrocities. Ads and opinions. Voices coming out of a box.

There is a marriage of eyes and light. My eyes wedded to the light of day. The light which will get percolated through my eyeballs and channeled through a network of nerves to my brain where it will get interpreted as a Cepheid or potato or bat. Photograph or tea kettle.

Nerves are quickened. Words are born. There is a continual churn of perceptions and worlds. The early day is a fetus of gold and the end of day is a skeleton of sticks. Lights shift from brick to brick and rag to rag. Temperatures change. Temperaments change. The phrase "at the end of the day" has come to mean an essential condition. A final truth. A defining moment. But definition is always local. A set of keys set down. A letter opened. Groceries spilling from a brown crinkly bag.

> The creative creates itself.
> —Diane di Prima

The creative creates itself. But it needs fingers. It needs ribs and hands. It needs an existence of sparkling blood. Combs and oysters. It needs the clarity and comfort of a chair. It needs tools: eyes and rockets and gravity and evergreen. Evergreen is good for imagery. Imagery looks good in a poem. Especially if it assumes the haphazard radius of a bicycle wheel. Words soaked in meaning, like bugs. Tinfoil gargoyles spitting wavelengths in feathers. A photograph of garlic blazing with noon. Because the creative is an energy. It stretches into horses. It is a temperature which remembers pepperoni. Chaos walks through it like a hurricane creating an ambience of uncertainty intrinsic to dawn. There is more to cardboard than cardboard. There is also shape and arbitration. Textures negotiated in committee. A gathering momentum that one day convulses into paradise. Jelly is merely a prelude. Give voice and nerve to the creative urge. Give it amperage and speakers. Give it lyrics and melody. Give it rhythm. Then call it a rope. Call it anything you want. But don't put it on television. Or bounce it through a gland merely to amuse somebody's zip code. There are calipers and fragrance available for that. If you require medication, read some John Ashbery first, then ask yourself again, is existence merely a limpid experiment in chemicals and talk, or something more extraordinary, something more like a dog, a creature of infinite curiosity, an acute sense of smell, and a blithe indiscretion when it comes to seeking affection. Study the dragonfly. Look how it glistens, buzzes, darts this way, then that in a seemingly random pattern. That is how to approach the business of verbs. Remember: verbs are blue. Nouns are pink, like gardenias. Pronouns are driven by angels wearing huge, unenforceable ribbons. Calculus shines like a blowtorch at the wedding of a yak and a snowball. Sit back. Eat slowly. If you notice something tinkling, pick it up, examine it, and welcome it to your world. Later, something may very well come of it. Something marvelous, like the sound of consciousness urging a delicate matter, a proposal, a propulsion, a ball of particles with mass and spin identical to those of ordinary matter but with opposite electrical charge, so that a chain stitch might culminate in a mammal, or a violin concerto in E minor.

PENDANT

I live in a world of swamps and vague objectives. Last night I saw a raccoon pass by the window, accompanied by the pyramids of Egypt. My skull is still glowing with the darkness of it all. Each thought is fat and shiny, like the algebra of turnstiles under the streets of Manhattan. That, too, is a swamp, and so are the vividness of coffee and the truthfulness of experience.

Old vinyl records played in a garage.

The eloquent biology of cod.

The odor of brains at work.

What if poetry were like capitalism? It would destroy Christmas and eat people. It would cease to be poetry. It would become a gorgon of insoluble blood. Like the blood of the alien in Ridley Scott's movie that ate through steel as it dripped through the levels of the ship. Emotions, too, require a lot of room. They can be dangerous. Watch out.

Whatever happened to that talk of the conquest of space? That seems to have disappeared with lava lamps and tie-dyed T-shirts.

Meanwhile, the metamorphism of rock groups continues. Most are now museums. Guitars hang like stalagmites in a cavern of cesarean laughter. A display of leather goods on a sidewalk. Everything becomes merchandise eventually. Even this. This is now worth $45,000 dollars. But today it's free. Think of it as an elemental calculus in a black frame. Or road kill. Crows know a resource when they see it. Why should we be different? I am always on the lookout for something new. Isn't that what this is about? This life, this world, this planet, this quest?

I don't understand all these women with tattoos over their arms. What is the point of that? Are they narrations? Like the stained glass windows in Gothic cathedrals? Lessons? Allegories? Are arms now more popular than books?

I have fostered these words in order to engage an art of inquiry. All the machinery used to manicure a lawn is now employed to create coordinates for finding spice. The smell of mint in a greenhouse might be considered to be a tapestry of fragrance hung to obscure the insult of day.

Sometimes writing is like pulling an anaconda out of your fever and setting it free on the muffins of blue dust on the moon.

The geography of Montmarte is pinned upside-down to the bathroom door, along with a few rapiers and chisels and citrus and a group of men hauling in a net of fish. There may be a few things I have neglected to mention. I'm always wondering what I've forgotten. This is why it is necessary to make things up. A formula for paradise, or a locomotive straining to get through snow. A feeling held together by sonnets. A string of words threaded carefully with epiphanies and beads.

CLOSETS

Closets fascinate me. They are a realm unto themselves. Part of a house, but separate, a discrete existence.

People gather in kitchens. Put a number of people in a house and they will drift naturally to the kitchen. And why not? Kitchens are warm and full of food. Brightly lit. Lenient. Natural. Unaffected. Full of boiling and blending and chopping and heat.

Living rooms are cordial, but staid. People sit in living rooms, polite, sipping tea, sipping wine, conversing. Hinting. Anxious. Self-restrained.

People sleep in bedrooms. Disrobe. Make love. Read books. Watch TV. Die.

Basements are cold. Weird. Musty. A place for laundry and hobbies. Golf clubs and weapons. Cans of apricot potato sacks and pornography.

Attics are claimed by bats and spiders. Old photographs and wedding dresses. An attic is like a closet but it is not a closet. It is humdrum. A place to bump the head. A place full of dust and irritations.

A closet is not a tomb but a storm of garrulity. The welcome apparition of coats. Jackets. Shirts and pants. Our phantom selves. Our representations in thread and tender buttons.

The darkness of a closet is embedded in languor. In limbo. It is not the darkness of the night, which is vast and open and peppered with stars, nor is it the darkness at the bottom of the ocean, which is full of life and boiling volcanic fissures and whimsical Roman gods and diaphanous creatures that swim through their medium like meaning swims through a word, or the implication of something remote and exotic acquires the membrane of nomination.

The darkness of the closet is simple and literal. It defies figuration. It is a darkness that spills into the hallway or bedroom when the door slides open, rampant and ordinary, insinuating a nebulous life of empty sleeves and cloistered tranquility.

It is a zone of lassitude. The darkness of nooks and interludes.

You cannot fold this darkness, however palpable it may feel, nor can you make candy or paper out of it.

But why would you? This darkness assumes nothing. It is nothing. It has no being. It is simply the absence of light.

And what is that? Nothing.

The darkness of a closet.

Which is a hanging of hangers and a brushing of sleeves.

A silence. Not the silence of an empty room but the silence of things in formal concurrence. The agreement of things unsaid. The unvoiced and untold in fold and crease. The concision in worn. The whisper in cease.

It occupies the center of a bureau of drawers, moving back and forth, side to side, like a human head pushing air in a blur of whirling tongues.

The top of the bureau is covered by a fringed Navajo blanket with bright multicolored stripes and geometric patterns. The two top drawers are slightly open, revealing a plethora of socks and underwear. A platter of rocks sits on top of the answering machine (it has been moved to accommodate the placement of the fan), and several hairbrushes crisscross at 45-degree angles, partially covering the white cord feeding electricity to the fan.

A crumpled plastic sack from a local drugstore lies to the right of the fan, and is puffed up a bit. A tube of Clinique Sun Block lies at the mouth of the sack.

A bolo tie with a pale blue stone and a cord of braided leather lies in back of the fan. It is a study in embellishment.

A tin can with its lid removed sits at an obtuse angle to the left of the fan. On all four sides of the can is a panel bordered by a margin of flowers illustrating what appear to be Hindu ceremonies: a group of colorfully dressed people circle a man and a woman dancing at the center; three women by a fountain make offerings to a couple enshrined in a pandal; six women dressed alternately in red and yellow robes pay homage to the same couple, this time seated on a plush white cushion; a man in a pink robe holds a platter high toward an animal deity richly dressed and ornamented on a pale blue background.

A folded black T-shirt lies to the left of the can. Tolstoy's *War and Peace* lies on the T-shirt. On its cover, Napoleon and his troops make a winter retreat from Russia after the battle of Borodino, as depicted by Vasily Vasilievich Vereshchagin. A flock of crows hover and swirl over a scene of frigid desolation. Napoleon and his troops move forward down a road, huddled, turned inward, silent, the armaments of war buried in snow. A row of birch trees on each side of the road, almost invisible against the pallor of a pale blue sky, appear incongruously merry, enchanted, their branches lifting upward in arcs of scintillating ice.

A filigreed silver casket with bulging oval sides rests in back of the T-shirt, crammed with ampoules of perfume. A black sock lies curled around it like a miniature cat. A bright penny lies on the neck of the sock, heads up.

The fan hums, moving side to side, turning left, turning right, pushing air in a concurrence of blades. Back and forth, slow and steady, insistent as a present tense.

MARQUEE

Let us not assume the theatre marquee is only of relative importance.
It bears the same gravity and virtue as the rocking chair, or bubble.
The very intonation of the word is a species of calliope, a musical wad
of consonants and vowels in which the back of the tongue heaves to
the upper dome of the palate to form the "k" sound of the "q." When
you say marquee the world knows precisely what you mean. You are
standing near a spot of no small sanctity, a sanctuary, a place of learn-
ing and repose, a theatre. Perhaps you are there to see a musical, or a
movie, or a play performed by a troupe of backyard actors, profes-
sional wrestlers and ballerinas, cowboys and stuntmen, ghosts whose
emotional architectures are in shambles, starlets with ski poles and
acrobats dressed in scarlet. The love of spectacle is a testament to the
production of hormones, that soup of chemicals rotating and whirling
in our personal makeup that causes us to do and say certain things,
things calculated to make us well-liked, or intended to bring about the
machinery of birth. There is a contagion of behavior called love and an
epidemic of pouring called lips. We pour ourselves daily. Pour our-
selves into other selves. Pour ourselves into the world and go slow in
the water when there is sand or mud beneath our feet. Pour ourselves
into the streets where a certain amount of realism is evident in the
behavior of other people, the way they pass you by without a hint of
recognition, or sometimes hazard a smile, or sometimes a regard of
idle curiosity. Pour ourselves into theatres, where there are seats and
strangers sitting in the seats. The shadows of others facing a screen.
People wearing zippers and mittens. People luminous in neon, the
lambent aesthetics of uniting in a theatre to view a spectacle which
will resonate with something personal in their lives, something oddly
familiar, something like fleeing large and dangerous animals, or chas-
ing butterflies, or finding themselves lost in a desert or jungle. Certain
instincts cause us to identify with the characters in Shakespeare, rage,
confusion, sorrow. Columns of words in noble adhesion, building
meaning upon meaning, aglow in our souls like hits in a jukebox, or a
river moving slow in the moonlight. There is sometimes a sunrise in
our consciousness, our level of awareness, so that we leave the theatre
with something we did not have before we entered into the darkness,

something like a jewel, or a song of ice. Something cumbersome with wings struggling to get off the ground and into the air. As if our lives had acquired a new theme. A new evolution. A new direction. Some new taste in our existence, something between fulfillment and intrigue. Something like vowels or seeds taking root in a parenthesis we did not know we had, some glamour awaiting our aura. Our personal marquee. The title of some drama no one else but we can see.

There is a road somewhere ideal for discovering the legibility of the world. I believe that road is in North Dakota.

Why?

Oh don't ask why.

Let us say it is because you can smell the nakedness of existence there. Let us say it is because the roads are deliberate and hard.

Because insects click in the ditches.

Because Lutheran steeples spear the distance.

Because commodities like wheat emerge at the fringe of consciousness and magpies perch on barbed wires attached to rickety old posts. Because at night the air is an open invitation filled with stars. And during the day it is shiny and blunt.

The dirt in the fields cries out for tractors.

And tractors are provided.

Big ones.

If syllables are the nails that hold the lumber of thought together then this could be the lowing of cows.

And almanacs and bone.

This could be a road. A road of gravel and dirt. A road going north. A road going south. A road going nowhere. A road going literal. A road going jocund, and clumsy.

This could be clumps.

In lumps.

In buckle and load.

The rasping sound of a tractor as it grinds into action.

Rumbles, bumps, lumbers down the road.

Everything fallen from the sky seems transcendent. The rain, the snow, the wind. One would not be surprised, at times, to see a tiger walking down the street. There is beauty, but beauty can be dangerous. I know this because I own an aquarium. Ponder the lionfish.

Adjectives are personal, like extension cords. Like sitting in the car listening to the Rolling Stones while running the engine of your car because it has been sitting in the snow for four days and you faintly remember someone mentioning that you need to run a car engine every now and then. Or remember it's something you've simply intuited. Or heard on *Car Talk.*

I see a red door and I want to paint it black.

And so on. While chunks of snow come loose on the windshield and a little light comes through.

What is your conception of the divine? Mine is opening a suitcase and seeing a lovely infrared embedded neatly among my underwear.

Or the sky tumbling down in white powder.

Chronicles in tread.

The exclamation of a tire screaming to move a car forward.

A door appearing out of the air opening to another dimension.

The literalness of spaghetti.

Let me hand the world to you: do you have it? Got a good hold? Now spin it around on your index finger.

Congratulations, you are now a poet.

Time doesn't tick it sways. Smells like a bikini imbued with suntan lotion. The thick and thin and tall and short of it is that no one knows why we are here and a lot of people don't really care or have the time to think about why we're here they know there is no answer to that they only have time barely to get the kids dressed and off to school.

But those of us who have chosen lives of negligence and irresponsibility think otherwise. Why we are here is not a question that can be answered but how can you not think about it how can you not entertain its many endless ramifications, ramifications that extend into the void, into oblivion, while the fish in the aquarium glide from one end to the other, leading lives of dreamy indolence, I don't know what else to conclude, I can't assume the thoughts of a fish, or assume that a fish has thoughts, but I do know this, I know they breathe underwater, and eat and reproduce. Ok. I realize that isn't much, not much to go on, but it's a start. A start to a conclusion for which there really is no conclusion. A conclusion that will crunch beneath your feet, pounded into ice, what kind of conclusion is that? It is a syntax of crystals. That immediate feeling of transcendence you get from looking up at the sky and seeing all that blue. That extraordinary volume. Everything occurs at the level of life because life itself is metaphysical. A gift from the air.

The coffin was beautiful. It had come all the way from Morocco. It had been custom built in the Medina of Marrakech, then shipped to Seattle.

With George inside.

This was the first funeral I had attended in which the body of the deceased was actually buried. All the others had been cremated, their bodies wrapped in that heavy plastic bag the funeral directors zip up and whisk away in their shiny black limousines. You see the body later, groomed and formally dressed and lying in a coffin as if the deceased had gone to sleep rather than vanished forever. Which, of course, is the whole point. To create a fiction. To soften the pain. But to step forward and take a clump of dirt which is still moist because freshly dug and drop it on a coffin of beautiful blonde pine and hear that sound of hollowness as the grains sprinkle and scatter on top, that's a different story. You really get a sense that that's really all the body is, about twenty-seven dollars worth of minerals and trace elements. The person that animated that body is elsewhere. Happily assuming there is an elsewhere. The undiscovered country.

I had last seen George in a radio sound studio, standing next to a table loaded with bowls of punch and platters of cookies and cake. "We're going to Morocco," George had said with great ebullience. "I'm hoping to get back into some writing over there." Ellen, George's wife, had gotten a job with a creative writing program there. He and Ellen and their thirteen-year-old adopted Romanian daughter would be there for about three months.

I first met George in prison. George ran a writer's program for lifers. He invited me to read to the group. We had gone to the prison in June, one of those bright, warm, sunny days that shame evil into the shadows and put warmth and happiness into you despite yourself. I liked the group of lifers. They were gracious and attentive and it was hard to believe they had robbed and killed people. Who knows what circumstances lead people to do certain things. I wasn't there to judge anyway I was there to read and discuss my book. I signed copies for most of them before I left.

George hadn't been gone quite two months when I got the email notifying me that he had slipped while playing basketball and hit his head and died instantly. What a strange thing, I thought. To play basketball in Morocco. I didn't even know George played basketball.

There were two gravediggers, a small man with curly black hair and an aquiline nose and a larger man with red hair and a big western mustache. When everyone had had their chance to put a clump of dirt or some other memento on the coffin the gravedigger with the mustache pressed a button and put the machinery in motion and the coffin lowered into the ground. I don't know where the basketball came from. Or who brought it. But it rolled through the crowd, fell into the hole, bounced a few times on the coffin, and rolled to the end where it came to rest against the dirt.

Knowledge is what you know, said Gertrude Stein. But what do I know? I know a pea from a watermelon. I know a bleat from a blurt. I know that water will begin to boil at 212°F. I know a hearth from a heart, a qualm from a quark, and a woman from a man. I know that we come into this life without knowing why and that no one gets out alive.

I keep waiting to see Elvis get back on the stage in Vegas but he never does. Not a hint. Not a trace. Not even a smear. Not his Cadillac or his sneer. Not his cape, his stars, his studs, or his jet black hair. I hear him. I even see him. But that's not Elvis. That's YouTube.

Are we too late for heaven? Has heaven closed its doors?

We are in a panic here on earth. We have no bandage for the wounds we have caused. No spoon of light to put in the mouth of the planet. No bottle of calm to pour down its volcanoes. We cannot undo the atoms that have undone our skies.

If something can be thought or imagined does it exist? Is silver truly silver if it slithers in rivers and snakes? Are bones really bones if they fidget in a book? Is a non-belief a belief? Are there beans that grow to heaven? Is there a key that opens fire? Anything can be imagined. Even oblivion.

Or can it? Can you take a thought out of your mind and put it on your head? Sure. You can paint it green, too. Make it cackle. Teach it tricks. Feed it a scoop of ice cream. But you and I know that heaven isn't a place it's a state of mind. A mood. A mode. Major and Minor. Earth and Sky. A diminished fifth between B and F. A soft blue flame. A vaulted roof. A woman walking down the street describing vertebrae.

The calculus of paradise spatters the umbrellas of winter. Redemption comforts itself in the muscularity of fate.

Clouds. Birds. Lightning. Barrels of evaporation. The feel of free will in the swing of an anxious gate.

Try to imagine nothing. Not oblivion but nothing. The nothingness of nothing. Because even oblivion is something. Oblivion can be crammed with disappearance. With birds. With words. With comets and radio. With the creak of a treadle. With broken shards and holy sparks. With eyes. With ears. With flaming threads and traces of light. With scars. With time. With damascene and metaphor. With camels and dunes and the eye of a needle.

If nothingness is put into words nothingness ceases to be nothing. Nothingness becomes something. Because although words appear to be nothing they are greedy for meaning. Can words be rolled into heaven? Words may be rolled into heaven if the syllables hold nothing. How can I empty these vowels? These letters? These loose bits of color? Make them void. Tear them from meaning. Give them unbounded space. Black velvet scintillating with stars. A dulcet silence. That's what I imagine as heaven. That perfect hollow. Honeyed hollow. That hollow in the hollow of a bell.

The scales and claws of a desert dragon scratch against the window of perception. I will try to play my drum better. There are fingers boiling in my wallet. Rhythms boiling in my nerves. Colors boiling in my jelly. Torments boiling in my jewelry.

What is the color of gallantry?

Silver.

Silver and raven black.

What can I do to make fascism go away? I'm tired of taking my shoes off at the airport.

When the moose appear, I can dance around a corpse with a knife. That will result in a burst of feeling, the itch of doing, the gavel of done.

Life, taken in its most literal sense, is eating and reproducing. I find that very disheartening, especially among the deep browns of the museum. The museum of lost horizons, which I have been wandering all day, with a compass, a puppet, and a bag of adjectives.

Outside, spring appeases the wounds of winter. Inside, I do laundry, review sentiments, sew gaslight gardenias, and forage for answers to the quandaries of our time. Maturity arrives in the knots of perturbation. They cannot be undone. They can only be dangled.

When we pull into port, don't be surprised to find words floating in the air. All the opium in Afghanistan cannot cure this dilemma. This contagion of eyes. This brood of chronicles. This swarm of arguments.

Here is a word made of roots and stimulants. I cannot tell you what the word is, precisely, because it is broken, and cannot be uttered.

I can tell you what it resembles. It resembles a meaning without the shell of a sound, the prickle of a consonant, or the guts of a vowel.

The magician in his cape of feathers.

A mastodon howling in the rain.

The birth of a bug, and the amazement of pain.

This is a poem for Ludwig Wittgenstein who said that each word in a given language must have a family of meanings. This shows that definition is local, like a lobster. Tender and blue, intestines and handles, the shadow of a mustang and anything naked, a wiry objective and a fold that is more than a napkin yet less than a roll of linoleum, because all the library is blatant and the gurgle is equable and the quilts are gripping.

This is a poem for my cat Toby, who is licking himself on the bed, and this is a poem for grout because it is pertinent to personality. All personality does is pendulous and ooze.

A collision is black. A little piece of hole is happening to confirm this.

There can be a zither if there is also density. If there is density there is also weather. If there is weather there is also growling.

The mime is in her technique. The design is so walled that the injuries churn among themselves and a network percolates timber. That shows what sense there is in scorpions. There is quince and there is tenderness, there is more highway to cover and there is plenty of tapioca.

This is a poem for decipherment and this is a medicine for scarabs.

The music of the present tense is bottled in imagery. Imagery is glass and anacondas and Monday.

Monday isn't glass it's ginseng.

This is a poem for ginseng which is verdant and misplaced.

This is a poem for thought. The thought of drums. The thought of blood and aortas and circulation and pulsation and corpuscles and veins.

This is a poem for poets who, if they learn to play the guitar, become rich like Bob Dylan, but if they don't, they stay poor like Arthur Rimbaud.

Was Arthur Rimbaud poor? He was when he sold 2,040 percussion rifles, priced at fifteen Thalers each, to King Menelik for 8,500 Thalers, paid in the form of signed bonds redeemable from the governor of Harar, Ras Makonnen. The sourness of this deal is matched only by the merciless heat of the Danikil salt mines.

This is a poem for salt. This is a poem for Ethiopia.

This is a poem for the human mind. The human mind floats on its language like twenty pounds of emotion ventilated by an umbilical nirvana.

Like a cloud.

This is a poem for clouds. And lightning and thunder and kindling and crackling and sparks and dirt and hearts and parks and ladders and beams. This is a poem for stoves. This is a poem for pots. This is a pot of beans. This is a poem for a pot of beans. Bubbling spurting sparkling beans.

Spouting squirting spitting bursting beans. Boston beans. Weary beans. Nonsensical beans. Rampant and scrambled beans. Ancestral imperative rutilant garbled and charming beans. Beans beans beans. This is a poem for beans.

The hardware of poetry is between, beyond, bodacious. The click of a gun. Crows jabbing at a taco wrapper. The old art of blacksmithing. The new art of walking. Writing dots and names on a mirror with lipstick. Migrations and augmentations at the frontier of the real. The wilderness of words emblazoned in a peach or mingled in a tangerine.

Paroxysms of clobbered language thrum in the engine. This hand this hammer this ham this harmonica.

The day engulfed by the jackpot of distinction.

Nothing is so infinitely dark that it does not in some way ripple with some possible ecstasy. Heat it. Bring it to a boil. The guitar is a perfect shape for doing that. Grow a tiny beard, a calamity of salt, then pluck an amplitude of frenzy from a fret of oblivious color.

To the east is a blimp. To the west is a landscape of phosphorescent linen. Rivers slice through it in a lather of furious movement. This is the hardware of solace. A monotone chewed by melody, a white cake in a red kitchen.

An edge. A lodge. A window speckled with rain.

Lodge this canticle in the eye of a fish lying among needles of cedar and fir. Water invents its own redemption. And is always in movement. A cat licking crumbs from your hand. Steam whistling from a kettle. An umbrella in the kitchen dripping from a squall.

The hardware of poetry is hard to wear. It is smoke. It is fog. It is mist. It is iron ovulating a bridge. Hunger. Thirst. Five days in jail for assault and battery. Lamp light modeling the surface of a leather purse.

The air is palpable. You can pull proverbs out of it.

Streaks of lavender in a pink and golden sky.

A sack of groceries. Light bent by gravity. Light as it arrives from a distant star.

A distant star.

The smell of tar.

What ugliness. What beauty. What garlic and lips. Everything is beans or bedrock or chemicals or chords. Everything is dogs. Everything is jiggles and flaps. Hornets and coral. Weather and hair. Apple and pear.

Everything is hardware.

The alchemy of poetry achieves the absolution of metal in the blade of its laughter. If there can be an imprisonment of mind, there can also be a release of mind, little mouths of dissonant sound leaping out of a bell of wax. Language swirls with parables. Each word is a clam, a shell of sound with a muscle of meaning inside. It's easy to shuck. But difficult to describe. One might call it a banana. Or a bandana. Or a battered old pickup festooned with Christmas lights. There are a hundred different ways to distill a harpsichord. One way is to become a faucet floating a personality through your lips. Another is to imply the presence of an inexplicable meat. I live each day as if it were the raw and powerful expression of an ecstatic doorbell. A fat pink tongue embodying hope and consciousness. My philosophy has a perfume in it. Gravity glittering on a lake. I would like, now, to say something meaningful about glass. About anything. A nut, an insect, a comic book and a jacket. Morning light caught in a cactus. One day I cut my hand while reaching under the car seat to retrieve a video. That is how I arrived here now, naked as a neck with my elbows on the table. Don't ask why. Sooner or later everyone pauses to reflect wondering what life is all about. The skull is an alembic. It all turns silk on the other side of a blue star. A spot of broken white on a tarnished doorknob. I feel green and vertical. I reach out to you. Do you feel me? Trust your convulsions. Your paroxysms. Your perfumes. Your buckles and barrels and impact and ink. When does a lung become an emotion? How do sensations become ideas? Why is silver consecrated to silverware? The sky in our apartment tastes of music. The volume is infrared. The amplitude is amber. A mind is gold when it assumes the calmness of tea. I believe there is a way to get across Cincinnati without laxatives or bunting. I believe the air is lacquered with thought. I love swimming in English. It goes deep. Gravity requires movement to be fully appreciated. I don't know the entire story behind it. I just know that when I get up in the morning, something holds me in place as I begin to make the bed and listen to the words coming out of the radio. Something thick and black and existential. Like a gun. Because that's the way it feels. Like sonnets. Like catalogues. Like balancing a universe on the tip of your tongue.

An overall theorem of pain doesn't mean much. Unless it is the pain of supposition, or the hysteria of belief, which reveals the persistence of doubt.

Anyone with the ability to derive beauty from thread will understand the curious blend of pain and pleasure in meeting a scoundrel, or come to terms with gravity à la dancers and ballerinas.

Imagine Cézanne feeling his way around a canvas with a paintbrush and you can get a taste of the frustration in trying to do two opposite things at once: keep everything at the surface, hot and warm and full of life, but modeled and sculptural, cold as stone.

The human mouth is situated somewhere between a dynamic realism and a home for wayward skulls. Skulls have mouths, but they don't have lips or tongues. They are all jaw and teeth. It is painful to see an old friend like that. Ask Hamlet.

It takes a lot of rubber and coins to keep a civilization going. Roads must be maintained, and pulchritude and Bach. Elevators expand our understanding of relativity. We must hurry to get on board before the doors close. T.S. Eliot understood time as a shape. Marriage arranged by hallucination.

There is no sweetness in a hypothetical nickel, no balm in a misconstruction of Idaho. Pain is a brutal pudding modeled on mince. Its weather is red. Pleasure is a soft green light curling around a bone. Its essence is partial. Its fulfillment a groan.

Or is it the other way around? We no longer have a mythology for pain. Or pleasure. They simply exist. It is through language that one can best see how it is both necessary and unnecessary to return to things in and of themselves in order to cut through the tissue that separates and joins us to things and to their past. Philosophy speaks through it, but only feebly. We must be silent before the object. The best poem has nothing but silence in it. A knot, an incense, a crease.

A watermelon wobbling on a picnic table.

When the death of a song writer gives birth to a song the world snaps apart like talc. An octave trapped in a paragraph rides a crocodile to the end of a sentence and turns soft and dreamy. All the wrestlers are shaving outdoors. No one knows if it will rain today, or snow. We are all waiting. Waiting and waiting. Waiting for someone to return from the other side. Our shoes salute the ground with walking. The leaves are all in a radical humor. A deeply religious woman wearing an orange T-shirt sits on a picnic bench in deep contemplation. Someone asks if this is Missouri or Romania. We say it is neither. There are no longer borders. There are only frontiers. A dragon of celestial machinery floats overhead. The meadow glimmers with harmonicas and eyebrows. Pink initiates a baritone busy with faucets. The Ambassador of Distortions sits in his rocking chair dreaming of Egypt. We rehearse our identities by making valentines and hammering nails into the wind so that it stays in one place long enough to produce a sense of place. The intimacy of candy constellates our conversations. To some, mass means spring. To others, mass is simply massive. Nothing ever seems to get solved. The future is slippery. But the present is glass. We can see right through it. Our thoughts turn to foam. There is boundlessness and whistles. Nothing seems to cohere entirely until a new jukebox arrives. A new jukebox full of new songs. An old jukebox full of old songs. A new old jukebox full of old new songs. New and old are relative terms. Like diamonds, or ideas of light. Lather in a can. Leather in a hand. Signature and dot. If there is a song to be sung someone will sing it. It will glimmer up and down the spine like a nectar. It will peel open like an apricot.

When you leave the way to the way, you attain the way. Everything else is rubber. A tapestry of fevers and stars. A woman inside her car washing the windows and listening to the radio.

The mind, according to Hume, is no more than a simple compilation of sensations of cause and effect. An apple rolling across the highway. I see it as something invisible, like laughing gas in the lighthouse, or a wind in the mirror. The chemistry of the eye hears a voice in the river. It sounds like an oboe. It has the bright sharp smell of life and movement.

The beauty of trout transcends the beauty of Versailles. Ocher is the pentameter of earth. There are places where the earth tastes of all creation. Where cheese is splendid with commerce and the voyage of a cow is majestic as a rhapsody of clouds playing on a sheen of wet sand.

Here at the edge of existence your body is sudden and real. Birds sing in your touch. It has the brutal innocence of a dream.

I do not believe there is such a thing as a mind. The mind is not a thing. The mind is a means to an end, a C-clamp holding a chip of wood to the edge of the table. An unappeasable drive toward definition. A city swallowed in fog. Identity in denim. The rhetoric of hope and pain.

How do you liberate the mind if there is no mind?

I would not know, but the strawberries are delicious.

And the street comes alive when it is stabbed by rain.

Details are a symptom of plurality. Wherever there is a detail there are bound to be others.

Other details.

For example, if the atmosphere gargles a sky full of clouds, a few will detonate, creating thunder and lightning and a thousand details of water. Water splashing, trickling, bouncing, running, falling, tumbling, spinning, spitting, spreading, and dribbling, drop by drop.

Drop.

By drop.

Drop.

By drop.

That's a detail. That's a sign that you live in a world full of details. Here is another: the dials on a washing machine. Different speeds, different times, different cycles, different temperatures, different consonants with different vowels powering vivifications of wash and turbulence.

Politicians avoid details because that is where you find life. That is where you find God, singularity, and the devil.

That is where you find secrets, alibis, and peculiar affiliations.

Mindfulness, experience, and radical empiricism.

Revolutions begin with hunger and end with traitors. In between are a lot of details. Torches, pitchforks, movements.

Cannons, nicknames, influenza.

Spice.

Spice is to space what space is to spice: a benign annotation.

By the end of the eighteenth century it was said that two tons of sugar were equal to one slave's life. That is a detail of visceral disquiet.

Ask yourself: when was the last time you had a thought that wasn't in some way connected with money? With commodity? With work? With getting a job or ending a job? With a life measured in spoonfuls?

Age is perhaps the most peculiar detail of our existence. Because it is never the same. Because it fosters prophecy. Because it makes us young. Because it makes us old. Because it is nothing, and because it is everything. Because it determines the data of an epitaph, or the size of a loan.

Because it sanctifies paradox. Which paints its way into our lives as a form of grapefruit, a sweetness and sourness that stir the currents below the bark of our lives and the fractures that detail the surface, giving it character and tone. Details like eyes. Ballast like bone.

Celebrities have become a major obsession. Why? Celebrities are truffles. Delicious, subterranean fungi. Hard to find. Easy to distinguish. But don't get me wrong. I like celebrities. I wish I could be a celebrity. Who wouldn't? Perhaps not the wise man of the cave, Bodhi-Dharma, who advised those disciplining themselves in absolute Buddhahood to make their minds like rocks, have no discrimination, behave unconcernedly with all things, resembling idiots.

Geography and conversation were the candy of my generation. And sex and drugs and rock and roll. But mostly geography and conversation.

I remember one afternoon in particular listening to Beverly Bevens sing "You Were On My Mind" while lying in the sun by a pool in California. That was a perfect day. A perfect time. Consciousness grew warm with insoluble fish. Then came big cars, jewelry, methedrine and tattoos. The retina held Hobbes's *Leviathan* in its veins. January crunched the bones. TV, lanolin, and fugitive visions made our life unseasonably wispy.

Perspective is everything. The sun casts its light between the buildings and the leaves turn luminous. A glass dragon pulls eternity across a broken stick, followed by a September full of pastels.

Most people these days hate thinking and reading. It's a good time to be a plastic surgeon, but a bad time to be a poet. It's rare to find a jukebox with some decent tunes in it, though it's fun sometimes to watch Mick Jagger leap around on YouTube.

A helicopter cuts the sky to pieces, but you cannot cage a rhythm. You can put a man in prison but you cannot imprison the mind.

Emotions tend to go in circles, but the older one grows, the more vividly are lost times remembered. Retrieved. Relived.

The arguments of geometry are perfectly valid, but so are the letters of Allen Ginsberg.

If I remember to slip the cord of the electric fan under the sheepskin rug so that I don't trip over it when I get up in the middle of the night to go to the bathroom, that is a triumph. Lying in the bed liberates it from the burdens of form. How do you battle a police state with poetry? Be an idiot. But try not to trip over any cords.

I accidentally put too much Corn Huskers Lotion on my hands, but in a way it made sense. Nothing is in the intellect which is not first in the senses. And so there it is, goop. My mind is engorged with mutton.

There is meat in syntax. But what is the cause of honeysuckle? Summer blinds. Intimacy and dribbling.

This has been a marvelous summer. Everything evergreen is prodigal and holy. Whatever is inward turns outward and whatever is outward turns inward. This is why the shape of a spoon is inexplicably beautiful.

Later, at the motel, we hit a sack of ice against the asphalt in the parking lot to break it up into smaller pieces. This is proof that morality can accentuate the irrationality of human behavior.

Animals, on the other hand, do not appear to be encumbered by morality. If they were, killing and eating one another would be problematical, if not calamitous.

In the human world, geometry tastes like grapefruit, and whoever desires flowers must learn to plant and nourish and water them. This is known as cultivation. Nothing happens without cultivation. Imagine Elvis at seventy-five. The studs, the glitter, the blare of the horn section, the high collars and cape. The glamour of orchestration obfuscating the crags and wrinkles of a glorious exhaustion.

We entered Las Vegas feeling haunted. But who wouldn't? The size and abundance of cactus left us wide-eyed with its wonder. The openness of the terrain and vastness of the sky was astounding, almost horrifying. The bareness of existence shone everywhere.

Existence gives existence to existence through form. A big car bouncing into a barnyard, a man mimicking an earthquake, the rustling of silk in a phantom calliope. How is it that an absence can have a sense of presence? Questions like this are a reason I don't like getting gasoline. The pump alone makes me nervous, not to mention the powerful smell of the fumes. It frequently astonishes me how much commerce is in this world, right down to my shoes and socks, neither of which match, by the way. Why do I continue to write poetry? Because air was invented for words. Because spoons are beautiful and forks are not. Forks are punctilious. But knives, knives are precarious, like the nakedness of singing.

3:57 in the afternoon might be a Bob Dylan tune. Might be a time of day. Might be a form of mimicry. Might be a zygodactyl can opener. Might be a play within a play. Might be a metaphor floating on a piece of paper or a loaf of ozone. Or a love of linen. Might be a vector named Victor or an oriole or a slow recognition of beauty. Might be a gown of dirt converted to petroleum. Might be a bright new day squeezed out of a tube of Brunswick green. Might be anything. Might be me. Might be you. Might be the truth of sawdust, which is particular to trout. Might be the way dishes look underwater. Might be a transformation detailed by crystals. Might be soldiers lost in Iraq. Might be a pulse. Might be a hue. Might be a law. Or a scent or a knife. Might be a chisel that is so perplexingly sharp it can only be used for carving lightning out of a dull persistent pain called life.

Might be a handful of syllables cooking a shadow.

Might be an astronaut driving to Florida.

Might be Jack Nicholson's large bald head in sunglasses smiling broadly and impertinently at the Oscars.

Might be a koala bear in a hypodermic tie clip.

Red shoe on a granite boulder.

Wasp beating at a pane of glass.

A tall young man on a late winter afternoon rising to the top of an escalator hoisting his skateboard to his shoulder then striding forward, the sunlight glinting in his diamond stud.

Might be the smell of bread in medieval Paris.

Might be a purposeless purpose gone completely awry.

Might be a miscalculation turned suddenly upside down so that it looks like a signature left by God.

Might be a tongue of light moving out of the east.

Might be nothing at all.

A tirade of tread in a tractor tire.

A river overflowing its banks.

Might be a type of hope.

Might be the smell of spring.

Or the smell of old rope on a ranch in Arizona.

Might be a frill in the skirt of the moon. Might be patterns in a Kwakiutl longhouse. The boiling fur of a cloudy afternoon. A drop of water trickling down a window. A big hotel. An image of water. Hit song in a jukebox that hasn't been played in years. A suspension of time. The craggy voice of Bob Dylan coming out of a clean mahogany radio.

Puma moving stealthily among a stand of Rocky Mountain aspen. The idea of weight considered in the behavior of snow.

Poetry is a calculus of the soul. It migrates from word to word, thrift and hypothesis in denim and dimes. Molecules holding a face together in a house of mud and damask. It is a principle based on twine. Categories of spice. A mind dipped in trout.

But that's not what this is about.

This is about striking the air, kettledrums pounding. This is about the mythology of iron. Yellow rendered in quick brushstrokes. Everything talking and writing might be. A judo of the throat. Space washed by horn. The scent of a garden glove.

Reflections come out of stillness. A realm high in the mountains of Tibet seeming to float between earth and heaven. Literature comes to terms with death slowly, but firmly, like the coagulation of blood. A conception of the afterlife remedies the pain of loss. Then fills with doubt. Then turns inside out revealing a chamber illumined by candle, hieroglyphs, cats and herons, eyes and crocodiles on a wall of stone.

The telescope changed everything. It placed us in the universe. The prospect of an immortal system expanding and contracting like the systole and diastole of a gigantic heart.

Go look in the toolbox. See anything that can improve on this conception?

The flow of words cleanses the mind. Conception is an abstraction, like longitude. It is drawn from observation then circulated like paint samples until the proper hue is found for the kitchen.

In a special class of quantum field theories the forces between quarks become weaker as they are pushed closer together. This results in asymptotic freedom. At asymptotically short distances or high energies quarks behave as free particles. The implication here is pure gossip, of course, since quantum field theories work continually between presence and absence, just like poetry. Nevertheless, separate objects are like isolated words. Meaning is only to be found in the relation between them. What is the meaning to be found in gold, or consciousness? In origami, or coffee? In frill and fringe and incense and shape? Everything is a form of energy continually transforming itself. Landscapes, still lifes, portraits, interiors, meals and nudes.

Essence precedes existence. The couch can vouch for itself.

Some dreams arrive in the mail. I don't know who they belong to, but they're made of words, which makes them available for perusal.

And so now I have a brain full of thought.

There was nothing in it this morning and it felt good.

Good and empty.

And now it is full of thought.

Spirals hang from the ceiling and travel into the wall, absorbing everything in sight as they leave home for the first time.

Conduits follow them. Please don't interrupt this thought. This thought I am having like nerves and spines on a blackboard. Writ large for everyone to see them. Doing what nerves and spines do best: energize prongs. And buckles and meadows and taxis and songs.

And pronouns. Pronouns are moony sublimities open to the possibility of being. This includes supposition, seashores, and blood.

There are arteries and veins moving blood around in my body.

There are arteries and veins moving blood around in your body.

Can you feel it?

Good. Now take the ball and run. Run as hard as you can. Run to the end of the field. This is how we teach ourselves to fly. This is how we teach ourselves grace.

Grace is a glass of water. Plus all this furniture. And everything on the kitchen counter. That roll of paper towels, the electric mixer with its big steel bowl, the coffee pot and small white drainer basket filled with cutlery.

Excess is never enough. Excess was in existence before the universe became a universe. Before the universe became a universe there had to be something and that something was nothingness. Nothingness here there and everywhere. Excessive amounts of nothingness.

Nothing. Nothing. Nothing.

Things are different now.

Shiny, black, elegant as a hearse.

There are currents below the waves. They will ratify everything I have to say regarding water, and this line trembling in the water. No doubt there is something at the end of it. A fish, or a universe.

Geometry is the inside of my head. Circles, squares, rectangles, clutter. And sometimes the occasional hinge creaks, or a door slams, or a memory chews a morsel of remorse into a blob of regret.

Or vice versa.

Everything else in my head is sunlight. But filtered. Through parables of color in leaded medieval windows.

We all dwell in homes of bone called skulls. Thatched with hair and masked with a nose and eyes. And a mouth and a chin and a pair of ears. And this is called the head. The head is the head of the body.

Sometimes I get a little ahead of my head and this is called absent-mindedness. Which is when I forget to do something important like change my mind.

I might decide to live in an adobe hacienda one day and then change my mind and take off for Antarctica in a yellow jeep fueled by a paradigm of swan sweat.

Because anything can happen inside a head and frequently does. Problems begin when the ideas we entertain inside our heads do not conform with the facts of the outer world. The outer world which is round like our heads but far bigger and far more complicated.

For instance, I might one day get it into my head that a conquest of the airwaves is best achieved by a monopoly of television and radio. That if I sit in front of a microphone and talk to the world all day and all night about the strange ideas I have in my head the rest of the world will come to agree with these things and those ideas I have in my head will come to be reflected in the eyes and behavior of everyone around me.

But why would I want to do that?

Why would anyone want to do that?

It would not stop anyone from dying. Though if it did stop a war or two that would be worth the trouble.

To tell the truth there are a lot of things in my head I would just as soon keep in my head. And there are a lot of things I would like to get out of my head. Things like remorse, and guilt, and worry, and step-ladders, and macramé.

Because things get dusty. And crowded. And begin to press against the side of my skull. So that I get a headache. Which is why it's such a wonderful thing to be able to empty your head. Empty it into words. This is what words are good for. Venting the pressures of the head. And creating parallels out of wheels and parables out of birds.

What is a personality? A personality is largely remembrance. Remembrance of who you are.

Then what is a you?

You is a pronoun. It feels more viable when it is lifted by the tongue and shaped by the lips into a sound flapping its way into consciousness.

And there it is. Occupying a place in the mind empty as an old attic.

The prominence of which is explosive. So look out. You never know when a word might erupt and eject meaning all over you.

Hope is an appliance. It is also a word. But it is mostly an appliance. A fierce reality for building a reason to stick around until the end of your life. Who knows what happens then.

What is a who? A who is another pronoun.

Pleasure, on the other hand, is a noun, subversive as moss. Or mass. Or the mass of moss, which is massive, and green and fuzzy. Because that is the nature of moss.

Everything else is a ball of gas, or linen, folded neatly and put into a closet. A linen closet. In which case linen becomes a modifier.

A conception of fiber grown familiar to the mind as a napkin.

A phantom in the willow.

And a mongrel green structural as Cézanne. Whose personality was a tad hermetic. Based on what I know. Which is mostly from books. In which Cézanne is a man painting mountains. And villages and trees. And still lifes with the honest geometry of an apple, or a face, or a bowl of peaches.

What is a hypostasis?

A dollop of green on Cézanne's mineral palette.

Which savors of potential. Which is potent. Which is possible. Which is a portent. Which is a potency plopped at the end of this sentence. For posterity. For postulation. For capacity and prospect. And the many pleasures of enthrallment. Like the steep thrust of a rock on the tip of a mountain at the tip of a brush stippled into many different greens.

Deep greens. Soft greens. Greens so green they turn into moss.

The modularity of space. Harems of heartrending cloud.

The somber tones of somebody sitting alone, reading, in a room. About art. About thought. About a faceless pronoun dissolving, mingling, escaping into a crowd.

We were on the path toward a better understanding of masculinity when our femininity erupted into civilization.

Desire is sharply understood as a totem of bodily opium, discriminating, but refractory, like a rattlesnake's architecture, which is organic and ugly, until it coils, and rattles. When it coils and rattles it is beautiful. It is opposite to a cube of butter, which only sleeps, especially when the afternoon is curled among its symmetries, and a migration to Arcadia slithers through a manufacturing plant among knobs of cartilage and tubes of yellow plasma.

Subtlety honors the smash of protons in a jar of nails. This is as true in Moscow as it is in Damascus, or Coos Bay, Oregon.

The chin is a mutation of hair. I don't know what else to say about that, except to be on the watch for the recruitment of ideas. No one can fully appreciate string until they have seen a Möbius bikini roar like a spoon at a square dance.

There it is. That light is on again. The morning is a rascal. It goes everywhere. You can't stop it. You can't even slow it down.

The speed of light is the speed of light. It is not the speed of snow or the speed of a moon enriched by romance.

Let us excuse science. For the moment anyway.

Time is a form of being. It is not a joke. Yes, it is funny, four o'clock is especially funny, who can keep from laughing at four o'clock, but the rest of it is quite serious. Serious as surgery. Serious as the blade of a knife making an incision in skin.

Hinduism in a hospital where all the bones are private but all the glands are public.

Public as a metaphor walking around in a poem.

In a hospital gown. Unrivaled in absorption.

Deliverance is an eye as a pronoun bubbles to the surface. It explodes with pepper. It is affectionate and slippery. It has scales like music. It is tied to a Parisian bed, awaiting our fingers, our perusal, our attention. Our focus and sunlight. Our nakedness and arms.

Sometimes, during the formation of an idea, I will attempt to pin a monumental coffee to a pronoun in the rain. And if the pins are suitable to the task, I will begin right now. The toolbox is open. The hunger to do something jaunty, something determined and brisk, is stunning and atmospheric. I want to be gallant, manly and unshaven, like Hugh Jackman on the cover of *Parade* magazine.

I've lost you already, haven't I?

You're probably wondering: what does he mean by pronoun? What does he mean by idea? What does he mean by rain? Hunger? Toolbox? Pins? Manly, or monumental? How can coffee be monumental? What is it to be manly? Can a woman be manly? What about a womanly woman? Why Hugh Jackman? Why is Hugh Jackman suddenly so popular?

All I can say is, don't let these things bother you. Let them be. They are what they are. I once thought clay could be transcendentally accentuated by soybean. I know differently now.

Every time I try to assemble an idea, another idea comes along to sabotage that idea, subvert that idea, and turn it into chocolate. Why does everything try so hard to be chocolate?

Try walking around your house sometime on a pair of stilts listening to heavy metal music. That's what it's like trying to think about something other than chocolate. Ghosts don't run on rails and neither do shaving brushes or human passions. There has been a long history of infinity in my family. It is this and this alone that gives me permission to use lamp black and chartreuse in painting the ideal cactus. Braque had better success translating a table into whatness, but he was born for whatness. Whatness throbbed in his being.

The majesty of thought is oftentimes too volatile to redeem by words alone. I have need of paint and nails like anyone else. I need coordinates and maps. I need metaphors. I need dance instructions. I need diamonds and candy and vigorous applause. This is why I wear lots of feathers and keep my ears and eyes open. I seek things that are deformed, defiant, indefinite and nickel. I never do push-ups in the heat on sanguine linen and a root. My address is faith in an eager Max Jacob symmetry where the religious can shake anyone by exhibiting what they do not know. What they do not know has more value than what they know. Spoon or granite, they tailor everything according to the vagaries of their beards, the dangle of earrings, the unidentifiable blobs unearthed during their ablution.

Sooner or later everything ramifies. Everything morphs into something else. This is why it is so hard to pin anything down. The new sheets feel wonderful, of course, but that resolves very little. There are still silly little secrets to jettison into the open sea, gods to appease, examples to find. It would be thrilling to see it snow right now, but there is no formaldehyde in which to preserve the cadaver of our ambivalence in case we should begin to feel otherwise, and there are no chains in the car, and we have seen all the movies in our cupboard, including the old videos on the upper shelf of the hallway closet, *Help* and *Hamlet* and *My Man Godfrey* and so on.

There are days when my age does not conform to that image I have of myself, which is that of a charcoal cow, or cook on a cattle drive. It all depends on the weather. Reality is one thing, enthusiasm another. It has never been my intention to sound cynical, but I am frequently derailed by the extravagance of color. Some sensations are so intense that they take you right to the edge of despair. It is there that I begin to feel a little more sophistication and anticipate a load of metaphorical moss. Words are always connecting these moods to the nimble boil of subatomic reality, the spin of quarks and bosons. This is how energy acquires mass, how words, which are essentially nothing, barely even sound, and sometimes not even that, not even a whisper, will aggressively gulp your mind and send you sailing into an autonomy you did not expect. A giddy abyss where an asphalt bikini extracted from science might fit a behemoth impersonality. And that's where the relief is. When your eyeballs strain to get that last paragraph in before going to bed and you feel that it is somehow your duty to fill your head with more syllables and letters, more wind and coconut, so that your nerves can suspend the bruise of consciousness, make it float, drift, all that hurt and confusion revolting against the earth like money. Like words. And that was the rock I handled all summer, its various streaks and indentations, and all it had to tell me, which was a shape I felt inside, in the rock, a form sleeping there until some spirit could release it into infinity.

Thank goodness for flattery. It is inventions like that that sweeten our existence. Everything we eat in our garden supports this contention, including the cucumber and yams. It is the walnuts that demand a special kind of brushwork, and the parliamentary chatter of birds that give so much splendor to the malleability of clouds. How can I not wax a little romantic at the thought of onion soup? Context is everything. And everything is multi-layered in harmonies that fatten on vermilion. The fatter the color the more it is capable of incarnating the jingling coefficients of a narrative structure unraveling in the moment it hits the paper, and Picasso stumbles through the room, his flirtations with volume and form so utterly outside the conventional parameters of the taco and calliope that elbows exceed their audacity and legs go all wobbly with intoxications of movement.

What does it take to forge a new consciousness? How does one gurgle the punctuation of the world? Flutter it in light, like old horses, like an alligator slapping the water in a rush to get to the river. It all depends on hunger. On passion. On fascination. On leather and escalators and oracles and orchids and blood. Whatever charms and nourishes the mind. Names, incongruities, jokes. But this evades the matter. As soon as I try to sound the depths and nakedness of consciousness, words get in the way. What does consciousness look like without words? Pure sounds? Joy? Structures without names?

I am another sidewalk animal, another apparition taking a census at the cemetery. The old weight of a granite despair blocks the entrance of the cave. We need to push it away. Art is that energy that pushes the rock from the entrance of our cave. If this sounds more than a tad Platonic, greet it with your own architecture, your own collection of kimonos and bugs.

There is an empty box on the counter that once contained four cubes of butter. Consciousness is nothing more than the hollow in that box. As for the butter, that, too, is consciousness, sliding over the bread in apparitional smears of soothing fat.

Contemporary philosophy must assume that all truths are multiple and constantly changing and quit its obsession with unity. Otherwise, it will just get shoved into the corner of the garage like a lot of stinky rags.

War lasts because it is orthogonal and symbolic. An elite grow rich. The innocent decay. The philosophy of war is recruitment. The gargle of death rattled in airplane bolts. It mustards honesty and gardens handstands in the murder of light.

Meanwhile we hear the clatter of plates in the restaurant, the creaking of oarlocks on the lake, the wind stirring in a grove of oaks. One would never know there was a war going on anywhere.

I would choose ocher for the color of the gloves. But that's simply because the escalators are so hypnotic. They calm and appease us with their symmetry and decorum. If one happens to be going up, one can choose to ride serenely and majestically to the top, or scramble up the steps as if in a hurry to get on with your life and leap all obstacles. And if one happens to be going down, one can ride to the bottom in quiet, pensive absorption, or tumble downward in a maniacal series of mutations, like a magician who has just learned how to use adjectives.

The silver circumference of a beautiful pain surrounds a sweet confusion. We are always surrounded by something. I am surrounded by skin, my skin is surrounded by air, and the air is surrounded by oblivion. But what surrounds oblivion? More oblivion? Is that what a bubble signifies? Why do we sense a more invisible presence? Something on the other side of this life? Is it mere wishful thinking, or is there an actual heaven hemmed by smears of abstraction? I believe in the way Rembrandt used chiaroscuro to suggest the kind of seminal absorption the dark presents us with, as if it were more than a symptom of absence, but a bald exponent of presence, the presence of absence, which is a lure to copperplate in some instances, and in others the more lyrical totems of the Nootka and Kwakiutl.

The world of color holds our minds in its hands and molds our vision toward butterflies and henna. Lamp black and the aggressive brass of yellow. Cubism abstained from color because it wanted to involve a more eager approach to texture.

The cubists may have been better off using words instead of paint. But it is misleading to think of painting in words. No one can paint with words because words are made of sound and air. They resemble coins, but the luster is illusory, the weight completely imagined. Painting is an exploration of form. Speaking is ejaculatory. Words pop out of our mouths in ripples and waves, surges and tides. Ebbs and eddies and swirls and twirls. Spouts, spurts, fountains, squirts. Cascades, cataracts, billows and swells. You can't paint with that. Nor can you paint it.

Ok, you can. I take that back. But you have to use valves and spigots. You have to be gallant, and know how to use description, when description is called for. Because sometimes if you should see a pronoun in the light it calls for an invocation not an angry disavowal of everything violet and horizontal. Remember: invention is infinite. Existence is nothing. There is more than one song devoted to this condition in Montmartre. You should spend some time there.

There is nothing, ultimately, to confine thought, and so it eventually takes flight as it is bound to do. The ecstasies of the poet are ignored in the marketplace but trust me, the torsions and contortions of syntax tremble with each attempt to drag a rainbow over the bridge and watch it grow prodigal as it leans into the coming night. Stars pop out of nowhere. I mean that literally. They dribble out of the air and twinkle like nobody's business. It is a kind of mockery for we who are stuck to the ground and have to get up in the morning and go to work. But that's capitalism for you. It just gets funnier and funnier while we inflate our hymns with oblivion and ripen our circles with all of our exertions in the dirt. The dark and wonderful earth.

This is a cow. Why a cow? Because of blood. And muscle. Because of hemoglobin floating a calamity of bone. Because of hoofs and horns. Because of a soft pink muzzle. These are the reasons I am calling this a cow. This image before you. This image in your mind.

I have a costume of bombast and cajolery packed in my suitcase. Sixteen tiger bells and a thin silk sash. My merry cajolery. The costume I wear to persuade you of things. Persuade you, for instance, that there is a cow in your mind. The image of a cow in your mind. However real that cow might be for you is entirely up to you. But please allow me the privilege of saying I had something to do with putting a cow in your mind. Of creating a cow. This image of a cow. Because cows are large and complicated and multiply the biology of talk. The biology of talk is a dynamic of tongues and teeth. The biology of talk is a mixture of lips and sounds. Fringes, variables, and moods. Flatteries, leviathans, and inflammations. Meanings parched for palates. Meanings hungry for images. Images of grass. Images of sky and wind. Images of cloud and apparition. Images of transcendence and glitter.

The artist uses a brush. Sable brush. Camel hair brush. Oil or watercolor. Shape and color. These are the devices of the artist. But what are the devices of the poet? The writer? The conversationalist?

The prisoners at the local penitentiary have complained that the quality of conversation has dramatically worsened over the last few years. This is a problem. I find this disheartening. And deeply worrisome.

Here comes another image: forty-two pounds of intuition lacerated by rain. Various inexplicable noises surround it in clusters of reconciliation. This is a strange and cryptic image and I apologize for that.

Nevertheless, I find it necessary. Because a tiger is too often misinterpreted as a large carnivore. It should be obvious to everyone that the tiger is the invention of Mr. William Blake of South Molton Street, London, England, and is a fearful symmetry of burning fire.

Yesterday I did five pushups. Today I will do eight handsprings. Tomorrow, I will come knocking at your door. In one hand I will be holding a yolk of speculation. In the other, a piece of fog. Which will you choose? And if I begin to ask questions, things of a personal nature, will you let me in?

All the odors in our apartment declaim the life of a phantom, a green man with gold teeth who lives in a painting by Henri Matisse. And over there, in the corner by the window, is an accordion stabbed by daylight. Gobs of sound trickle from its lungs. Incense swirls in the air. The scarf hanging from the doorknob is clearly incongruous to the immediacy of the moment. The scarf is referenced but not actually there. It is imagined to be there. It has, on occasion, been there. Been there so recently that its memory is strong and incumbent, like a cow that has grazed within recent memory at this spot, this section of the field, where a mole has left his mark, his little mound, and has since drifted to another more distant part of the field, a corner with a lush growth of ryegrass and clover.

We are talking of phantoms. Yet a certain inherent logic, a certain inner life like that of magnetism or quiddity, a living essence endemic to the world of the inorganic, might also apply to a circularity of transference and idea, so that word and object find themselves in possession of sufficient elasticity to bear a world of linguistic representation, so that the introduction of an image, like that of a scarf on a doorknob, a pretty yellow scarf of silk or satin or crêpe de Chine might dilate accordingly in significance and offer a spectacle so concentrated, so happily contemplated, that its availability to perception is heightened, deepened, intensified as if it languished in a zone of intrigue, a dimension sandwiched between the past and the present like the score of an old football game still glowing in the mist, or dance just after it has been danced, and the balloons are still trembling, and the room has been left warmer than it was before.

If I yelled down the corridors of time would anyone hear me? Would John Keats hear me? Would Shakespeare?

What exactly is it that medical examiners do, anyway? It's a mystery, but not a line of thought I feel like pursuing right now.

My mind is in a continual state of indigestion. I find most things nowadays hard to swallow. The juice of scarabs, for instance, or cauliflower. I never did like cauliflower. The ceremony of thought crawls through my mind like a beaver in the snow, a habit of mind grown suddenly autonomous, so that it yearns to be written down, where it might evolve, through words, into something different than what it was languishing in my head, vague and nebulous. In words thought assumes definition. It becomes a fire licking the walls of a house chained to a river. It bubbles, teems, swarms, like a ball of wasps busy over something sweet and rotting on the beach. A paradox. A contradiction. A fiction X-rayed by truth.

Each conversation is a journey, each jukebox a refrigerator for music. When I drink the power of hawks I begin to feel independent of my shoes. I walk through the rooms of our house of language. Our house of language with its quills and bicycles, its nutty closets, its creaking floorboards and leaded windows, its verbs and nouns, its articles and adjectives, its beautiful furniture and folds and convolutions.

Outside, reality churns and flows. It is like a cloud reflected in the water of a well. An eddy in a brook, sentence in a book, or the eye of a cow. A phenomenon drifting through the perception of some living thing, eyes and ears and skin and weight, a nervousness, a sympathy, a perversity yearning for words, so that the external and the internal are brought together, and become a third thing, a tartan turning quantum with plaid, a metallic moan, a weather vane pivoting on the top of a roof as the wind shifts, and the limbs of the trees go wild, and petals stir on the bough.

I feel like going all glass and indirection. There is a great road for discovering eyeballs in flowers and rocks. It is called scribbling. It is called legs. It is called tympanum. Pearls and personality. Holes in the air. A rough hope or minute of focused attention.

Belief is a funny way to perceive things.

It is equally funny to think I have a skull in my head.

Gravity hammered into consciousness. Cold western jelly in the eye of an alien. Electricity flashing prayers. Words that grip the air. This heavy thing called life is better than putty.

Puppets in the snow.

Origami doe.

Let's go.

Writing fills with light when it climbs the nerves a geranium large with sunlight fits like a color and texture and jukeboxes.

Emotion is cherry a tool for planting sounds to create heaven out of hell and alliance out of earth.

The tongue is a fat busy muscle making rivets and rivers and judgments and doors.

Dots on a spine sprigs on the moors.

How does one sell poetry what kind of merchandise is it? It is the true potential of cotton truffles in the eighteenth century meat still ambling on a bone supernatural cows luxurious whirls of horizontal thirst sewn to a comma dislocated in Manhattan.

Pudding nullifies the clamor of morning.

Twilight in San Francisco is excitement and fish.

The illusionist is troubled by a fedora hypothesized on rockets consisting of notes and handstands eyes are pieces of light. Scrubbing shows cleanliness and shine there are comic book superheroes everywhere Père Ubu in Yuma shaping the air into guns in a manner that is calm and pulp the crackling is normal.

Write a letter to God able to force a mustache out of your face.

I once had a blue station wagon the air was gentle then but the clouds were bloody. Everything felt like a tint in C minor, an incense drifting in rain, Mick Jagger on a subway in June. I saw the details of a life pulse through the eyes of a giggling shadow. Infinity dipped in movement. The brutal tattoo of a clock on the skin of a conversation. Jelly in the testicle. The color of truth in deep rapport with an avocado.

A bug on a coconut obviates flimflam.

Lifting a participle gets pink with pork.

Perception does blue to a war.

The river trembles in its thunder.

A freshly written word crawls to the edge of a page to die into life as a tuna. There is panic in the kitchen as an infinite succulence alliterates the oven. Even the Beach Boys liked water. Remember, we live in a postmodern universe. Rhythms liberate instinct. Combustions sublime as a spine. This entire moment feels pink. Gunslinger in an earthquake overlapped by jewels of light in a TV studio. Adventures in flour instinct with drizzle. A wildly pictorial situation elevated by hornet and motorcycle.

Driving a cocoon of metal and rubber engages the rules of the road in a whisper more like Bach than scars or birds or tape measures. Adjust the heat to fit your ruby, diversity fluttering in a jar. If you hit a pattern with enough style you will evoke a church on the prairie whose sails hold the wind in mustard jars. There is no limit to the pulse of opinion. Expansion is perfectly Roman. Desire is rich with Einstein. Dollops of jelly, yardarms glazed with ice. Slivers of chintz occasioned by retail. The equivalent attitude is dusk. Less is more more or less. A barrette from Italy. Kettledrum flashing three-dimensional rhythms as if hysteria were a scale, a wad of four-dimensional belt buckles.

The paintings in this room hold mysteries of shape and color. Dance accelerates the pulse. A ripe cantaloupe indicates the future is fused to the past, at least at room temperature. I slowly feel your swamp, neon gestating in a hammer. The headlight is hot. Thinking is steam. Eddying helps the current discover itself. The prepositions are evolving into sonatas crowded with life. Let us announce the shattering of servitude. I feel my being in a tumult of hectic color blowing around an alphabet growing fat on altitude. There are planets on your socks.

When sculptures glitter with sequins the waterfall overrides space and guns its water to fury.

Writing is slow when it moves through winter's angles and tries to nail the sky to a pier at the end of a paragraph lousy with limousines and goofy with cherubs. It makes you want to hunker down and disintegrate.

How do you tell the difference between a garage and a dream? Between the dream of a garage and a garage full of dreams?

There is so much to describe. A fish, a sail, an injury, an intonation, an invasion, a vacuum, a tension, a decoration, a hawser, a bug, a preposition, a proposition, a hypothesis smeared with experience, a pulse, a rhythm, a fury. Iron shadows for a peculiar hormone.

Drawing is at its best when it is physical. Try to understand the rage of a rib. The perspective of a tongue. The flatness of a music. The vermicelli of a drool. The melody of a lonesome organ grinder. A drunken politician shouting in the street. A gate. A broken cup. A four-dimensional turkey. A vector of thought daylight disintegrating into night geometry with spots stars shoved into sonnets time palpable as chairs a thrift store full of shirts.

The thread of this thought is burning the needle is outside the realm of time. Welcome to my holiday forest. Please take this cow as a sincere mirror of purgatory. I see the cowboy cradling another fetus of morning. This is the beginning of a murmur, a really blue door pregnant with omission.

A bump in the road is worth two in the hand.

It is curious to find a jukebox shiny and blunt in a religion or somebody's hair as if it had relevance to pointing or leaping or gardening and width was amphibious like those sonatas one hears sleeping in rocks or tumbling out of someone's mouth a solemnity which rouses little derricks or crumples into pickles there is an isosceles the metal adores and a closed restaurant and a Fourier newspaper rising through the ice and a sanguine orneriness converted into steam that proves the existence of eels nothing not even opera can impinge on the physics of the arthropod because there is a harpsichord between the hives and a bath and a dollar auditioning for a soft fluctuation at the end of the rainbow crashing through your experiment.

Equations get fat with neon.

Fold the air into words into birds into prepositions ingots of gold in a musky room a slightly gnarled wrist mute with the moisture of thought a workshop expanded by description elephants bathing in a muddy river a sentence caged in a paragraph a paragraph bursting with rain.

I am now going to do some push-ups. Write a sonnet to October. Plant a garden of pronouns. Tender buttons brutal lapels testicles full of ink a leap into space varnished by applause an unassuming callus an open invitation filled with stars.

Infinity looks raw on a postage stamp. Watch it giggle in its glue as the train goes by. Each day is a hymn, the skin gossiping thick and tangential to an oracle of oil, life imagined as a slither of syllables, the scent of an octopus in a wilderness of dolls.

Is it possible to think a thirty-pound thought? As if a light in the mind could cast an aberration of itself in letters and sounds. In words. In rhythms preserved in amber. Nerves boiling in a spine of meandering ink.

Let us begin with metaphysics: the grumbling of a cloud smashing up against a mountain. Is that indicative of anything huge and invisible? The awful shadow of some unseen Power? Spit the glitter of it into sound and what you get is rampant speculation. The taste of pepperoni in autumn, the bright heat of temptation. A glimmer, maybe, of the true and eternal reality trembling among the blackberries. The heavy fever of variegation. The sweetness of self-effacement.

Sometimes there is an antique bone that begins to talk like dirt. Smell of dirt. Thaw like dirt. Push things out of it like dirt. Because that's what dirt does. It is a comedy of food.

When we talk about intentions what we really mean is something like the glow of a kerosene lamp on the waterfront. That penetration of light diffused through the mist. The slap and slop of water against the barnacle-encrusted pilings. Wherever you go there is always that sense of presence. Presence intermingled subtly with absence. Which is pretty much the grit and gristle of language. Which is why language comes closer to revealing these things than music or painting.

Imagine a 300-horsepower emotion with a red vapor and a bow of mechanical candy breaking through a tangle of calculus and brine. Language gets weird and wild when you let it wander through itself like that. Or is surgically removed from a cactus.

These letters are filled with liquids. Red liquids, blue liquids, green liquids. Momentum jolts them into prose. The skeleton of a fairy dancing on a linoleum floor.

Anything automatic is ugly because it shakes, not because it is automatic. Eyes are beautiful because they are balls of jelly. Delirium comes natural to them. Talk haunts the table. Eyes penetrate eyes. Universals nucleate particulars. And vice versa. This is why I hate to go shopping. The objective is too apparent. It is preferable to stay home and put my experiences into ink. But what kind of experiences are we talking about here? The hinge on the bathroom door needs repair. The silverware is pretty intriguing. There is the essence of being to define. Not to mention the frontier between the internal and external. That is a very huge space.

The head is where it all happens. Chewing and thinking. Talking and tasting. My tongue and the light that is on it suggest a certain backyard tension between plywood and argyle. The sound of leaves wake the dog. A bizarre narration of fur and fog begin to charge the approach of afternoon with torrents of ill-defined feeling, the thump of chestnuts on the street, laughter reverberating over the stillness of the lake.

I love the word "globule." There is a viscosity in its vowels sweet and light as the juice in a cherry cordial.

Aristotle suggests that the ideal is found "inside" the phenomenon. The ear has to be quick to unzip the sound of rain. The principles of statistical mechanics tell us that the typical photon energy is proportional to the temperature, while Einstein's rule tells us that any photon's wavelength is inversely proportional to the photon energy.

The dashboard, for instance, is an environment unto itself. All the little lights and dials startle the mind with its magnetism and odor. An ohm is a form of imbroglio. A multi-layered union of crinkly tissue like an onion. Matter is without shape or purpose until we give it direction. Think of it as a taxi in Manhattan. The financial institutions collapsing everywhere around us. This happened because things lost their value. When I say things I mean X-rays, thread, lace, umbrellas, pathos. Redemption in evergreen. Whatever information we might draw from a wisp of incense.

If you can't trust a bank what can you trust? What can you invest in? Trust bricks. Trust stones. Invest in the light of the afternoon sun highlighting bricks and stones. Trust opposition. Trust evaporation. Trust muons and gluons and dense delirious dots. Trust appetite. Trust salt. Trust geometry and nerves. Trust skin. Trust your fingers and hair.

It is essence that makes matter matter. That makes quilts quilts and watermelons watermelons. Write a sequence of words and watch it rise into thought. You will see molecules become furious pieces of Tuesday. You will see the energy that changes matter become a comedy of undulation, lovely waffles, shovels in the cold. A plywood grin rolling down the sidewalk. A scientist in a white lab coat putting a vase of flowers in a laboratory. Totems in the fog. Verbs trumpeting ferns into the static of predication.

My understanding of eggs is fairly limited, but if I comb through this moment I might find Walt Whitman tasting a lump of sugar. The biochemistry of a word causes the lips to move. There is more to life than wearing a kimono in a dirigible. There is a glimmer of truth revealed among the blackberries, a silent music hatching into words, the space around a slice of cheddar imbued with its odor, a vocabulary catching fire in a thesis of liberation and air.

Taste your estrangement. Enjoy it. Not everyone can learn to play the guitar. There is also sculpture. Crickets tender as milk. Questions to inhabit. Saw the sky in half. Put a cloud on your head. The stars are cold and indifferent but there is stoicism in prose, anachronisms of melody in the shelves of the pharmacy.

Take a walk.

Invent a name.

Nail the breath of a poem to the light of a soft blue flame.

I feel a wisdom in my bones dry as oblivion and decide to go for a walk. I love to give flowers to people. Invisible flowers, like unspoken words. Things that go on in my head when I walk.

There is a huge cloud darkening to the west. It hangs there, like a postulate of mud.

Elsewhere, the sky is totally impromptu. Doesn't know what it wants to do.

I walk faster. I think about life on other planets. Sentient life. Bizarre shapes and forms, speckled sacks and tentacles. A skull in a caul of jellyfish goo.

Do you eat meat? I try not to, but sometimes the urge to chew meat is overwhelming. And sometimes I can taste the intestines of a lost sound.

Rain begins to speckle the sidewalk. I quicken my pace. How strange to have consciousness of oneself. Thoughts and desires. Intuitions. Impairments. Lobster quadrilles.

The world is more than its nouns. It is also movement.

Take Blackfoot. Many concepts that in English are expressed by separate words are incorporated into the verb in Blackfoot. The white rock is *ksikksinaattsiwa*, and the white bird is *ksikksináámma*. That's because there is a distinction in Blackfoot between animate and inanimate nouns, which sometimes have the character of verbs.

There is a mind floating in this paragraph. It may not seem that way, but there it is, bobbing up and down amid these words, ghosts and memories, a paradox warming the holes of a harmonica.

The mind is a paradox because it is nothing, and yet combines profligacy with handsprings to arrive at pink. Which is a color. Like bananas or ties.

The harmonica is a symbol. It means meanings are fingers. They press and squeeze. They caress and hold. They have muscle. They impart melioration. They make music. They peel potatoes. They get sticky. They scratch. They play the harmonica.

When I walk down the street I fall out of my eyes. Things grab my attention. A woman kneeling on the sidewalk vigorously rubbing a Yamaha Road Star with a rag soaked in turpentine. Fat people with cameras. Tin tree. People gazing at the city from the decks of a cruise ship. Tops of buildings lost in mist. Revolving door of a department store. A girl laughing at a dog.

Are there languages that nudge us a little closer to the frontier of experience, the border between the phenomenal and the mundane?

Yes, there are.

Icelandic. Tagalog. Panjabi.

The chatter of rain in the street.

The use of verbs among Blackfeet.

I don't think much of diamonds. They're hard and cold. Light seems imprisoned in them. I prefer birds. The birds I generally see are crows. Crows are great. They enrich the afternoon with their racket, their continuous hopping around pecking at somebody's discarded French fries. This is why I wear binoculars, and enjoy riding in elevators.

I also like parentheses. They're such tender little detours. Is there anything in life as sweet as a digression, as amiable as a superfluous aside, as invigorating as a deviation?

The symmetry of the diamond argues order.

The detour argues surprise.

There is a parenthesis in Montmarte in which a herd of buffalo sing the National Anthem. But the National Anthem of what country? That I do not know. But one day I would like to learn to fence. I believe it would enhance my ability to understand the art of diversion.

Over there, a face bounces across a nipple so huge it has suburbs. The nipple belongs to a giant butterfly lactating under a willow tree. This is another reason I don't like diamonds. It is not an effective anodyne for despair.

Here is my house. I was lucky to come of age in the '60s. As you can see, it is quicker to strum a guitar than harness a color with duct tape.

The really enduring things in life have a capacity to bend.

Suppleness is the kerosene of philosophy.

Name me one diamond that is supple.

Diamonds are not supple. The word "diamond" comes from ancient Greek adámas, meaning proper, or unalterable. It is an allotrope of carbon, and has the highest hardness and thermal conductivity of any bulk material synthesized so far.

All things speak to us with their qualities. The paisley on my cat's pillow reminds me of cells, mitochondria and cytoplasm. Imagine life without a body. I cannot imagine life without a body. But I can imagine life without diamonds.

Diamonds can be replaced by the look of snow melting on a mirror, or wisps of incense curling upward like the sleeves of a ghost.

Why do people write poetry, asks a man from Australia with prominent sideburns. He has a diamond stud in his ear.

Because friction is the engine of the violin, someone yells.

It is the cook. He is always yelling. He has to. The kitchen is noisy. And his brow is covered with diamonds of sweat.

There is a philosophy of space in Shakespeare's trumpets, something
like the disembodiment of pain. Something brash and quick, like
Robert Preston in *The Music Man*, or the wind, which is so foreign to
the physics of intimacy, yet so familiar with trees and streamers and
sunrise. Light up your legs with a walk. That's the best way to discover
space. Bullets of blood shoot through your brain bringing visions of
liberality, sidewalks whose cement is conjectured in squares and curbs,
where all the machinery of walking and talking finds that its enzymes
are related to the metaphysics of moss. The peel of a banana blackens
on the balustrade as it rots, blending in with the dark green patches of
moss disheveled and eccentric as a leopard at midnight. It is here that
we find that language is truly a language, a luscious daydream puck-
ered in a delinquent star of palpable calligraphy. Imagine, for instance,
that you are the poet John Keats, and that you sit on the edge of an
intensity poised to write an enchantment acute as electricity, juicy as a
nectarine. You are so absorbed in the tantalizing nuances of the after-
noon you do not notice how much the human vertebrae resembles a
clarinet until a column of air moves up and down vibrating and thrill-
ing the nerves with little holes and grit, adding a variety of striking
timbres to the orchestral palette, creating atmosphere and novel ideas
as the day evolves into a heavy abstraction crackling with transposi-
tions. And suddenly there you are, lost in the algebra of the local
shrubbery, looking for the right intonation to flesh out the neck and
necklace of a divine valentine of air artlessly represented as Thursday.
Meanwhile, the darkness of time moves toward us like a tongue of
shadow curling around a hallway door. The density of scale is a mira-
cle. Octaves are miracles. This is how sounds are shattered into apples,
and wax, while the cottonwoods reflected in the stiller parts of the
river tremble a little with a breeze announcing the nearness of noon.
Thistles insinuate themselves into the truth of nests. The truth is that
emotions arise from conflicts, boldly acclaimed fables and conjurations
of string lengthening with the paradox of rags. Nerves generate im-
pressions of bronze. The sheen of a jackknife percolating in the blood.
Comb your hair. There is singing in the streets. Mobility and migra-
tion. Each wound of our lives is a star in the heart, intricate and expo-

nential, so that all these threads you've been sewing eventually cohere into fur and bone, something wild and supple like a temperature, a predication existing in air precise as a hand, curious as fingers, an arm reaching for a cushion of bustling embroidery.

Semantic conundrums tend to make the bank nervous. When I go to the bank I try to be as clear as I can. I want money. Please give some money. The trouble begins when I am asked if I have an account. Here is where the semantic confusion begins. There is nothing that does not, in some way, depend upon a wheelbarrow glazed with rainwater, but the alphabet is not one of them. Letters have a reality all their own. A closet door that slides back and forth, a guitar leaning against a wall, none of these items are things the bank is interested in. They want numbers. I give them dimples. I give them sunsets and water pumps. I give them engines of meaning called popcorn. I slide whispers under the glass. I stand beside myself with amazement and dip into daylight for dollops of ice. There is a symmetry to my behavior, but the tellers pretend not to understand. So I try asymmetry. I try handstands and Christmas. I make words come out of my mouth. The words fall to the floor and I scoop them up and shuck them like oysters. I say salmon and salmon appear. I say hot dogs and hot dogs appear. I reveal the secret violas in everyone's heart. I demand payment. I demand money. I need an excursion. Excursions cost money. I need a house in France and a garden full of colors and wheels. I need fizzy liquids and tattoos and drapery. I need terracotta commas for my paragraph glazed with wildness. All these things require a landscape. And landscapes cost money. Military power. Orchestras and scabs. How do you feel inside? Right now, right this minute, what is going on inside your body? Because the road of life is slippery. You need to watch your step. What does money mean to you? Never shuck oysters for the rich. They'll tip you five dollars and leave you feeling like shit. Just shrug. Shrug and walk away. Go home and build a metaphor. You can do anything with a metaphor. The bank doesn't want metaphors the bank wants money. But with the right metaphor, the right caliber and the right number of bullets in the chamber, you can get away with murder. You won't lack for anything. Buttons, bullfrogs, longitude. Because ideas don't come from yarn. Ideas come from shadows. Crickets and flickers and dirt. Everything folded sweetly, so that it articulates the linen of the everyday. The murmur of trees, the enchantment of a shirt.

There are three kinds of ecstasy. One is motion, one is tone, and the third is Pennsylvania.

Why Pennsylvania? Why not Minot?

It is an arbitrary decision. Pennsylvania is rife with this kind of sediment. Wispy contours of perpetual strudel, asparagus and roses and flickers of red in a deep blue rocking chair, beards of rain dripping from chestnuts and poplars, consonants hatching vowels, vowels hatching aortas and awnings, blacksmiths hammering ecstatic horse-shoes on ecstatic anvils, a larynx dilating to let a song out, a bouquet of hours painted by hand, being and nothingness in a single lapidarian hoopoe, a lavish emotion disgorging an extrajudicial refrigerator, husky flashlights and rolls of linoleum, the occasional gurgling of the Susquehanna, the authority of words diverted into bells, cranberry bogs and Rayleigh scattering, and the interior of a pronoun with an uncanny resemblance to the keys of the rental car that has brought you here.

There is more. But I hesitate to detach it from its surrounding ply-wood. Or ironing or rain.

There is more to a pond than water. A principle of unity within duration is needed if the continual flux of consciousness is to be capa-ble of positing transcendent objects outside the flux. Consciousnesses must be perpetual syntheses of past consciousnesses and present con-sciousness. Why else do arms seek the ablution of movement?

Imagine entering another dimension. Use everything you've got. Spoons and ice cream. Metaphors and gears. Similes and tears.

Go ahead. Abuse the sun. Stay out all day.

The sun is an old man with a heart of gold.

The sun is a Laundromat on Neptune.

The sun is a herd of reindeer pulling a sled of morphine through a Yukon of motley cuticles. A ball of cellophane punctuates the cruet. Realism buckles under the weight of its own callosity. The personality of the sidewalk hangs by a description of cracks. I scratch whatever feels critical and leave the rest to sugar.

The ego is spellbound by this action, and participates with it.

The concision of the comb enlists tinctures of inscrutable pink.

All is therefore clear and lucid in consciousness: the object with its characteristic opacity is before consciousness, but consciousness is purely and simply consciousness of being consciousness of that object. This is the law of its existence.

Like sewing a button.

Or pushing the idea of silk in Philadelphia through the eye of a reader.

How can I mimic the roar of a jet when all I have are words? This is a murky area. Once this sentence achieves the thrust of an oak I will fill it with squirrels. Lather it, splash it, shave it. Make it walk. Make it talk. Conjecture bricks. Annoy people. Bump into furniture. Crash through walls. Hurl large objects. It will resemble a hat. I will name it Frankenstein. Frankenstein the Poem. Frankenstein the Fedora.

Notice I'm not wearing a hat.

The last time I wore a hat I fell asleep and awoke to find myself floating, weightless, in an elevator, surrounded by mathematical debris. It was then that the vision of a giant fedora came to me. But it would require a narrative. At the very least, a four-dimensional space-time continuum. Angular calligraphic strokes in constant tension with a rough and awkward semigeometrical stubbornness.

One day Frankenstein the Fedora went to the library in quest of answers. Answers to existence. Answers to death. Answers to the mystery of lemon meringue and metallurgy and birdcalls.

He left the library crowned in non-Euclidian glamour. He tasted a wall by selecting pink. He churned the daylight to flannel. He frightened people. For they were unused to seeing a giant fedora move around animated by nothing but words.

Words absorb everything except pain, which grows into tigers. Words are the nerves that make the river turn mohair. That maintain the microphone with reveries of gauze and gearshift, doctrine and dials.

At night, the music of instinct gets itself tangled in cabbage. Poles and thistles turn comical and brown. An abstraction buckled in gas poses ideas of azimuth and fruit.

The best way to mimic a government is to dissolve into equity and free will. Pull yourself out of a diamond and smash your feet in the sand. Twist sorrows into crystals and tendencies into birch.

When Frankenstein arrives we will brim with derbies.

When Frankenstein the Fedora arrives we will imitate grease.

If you do not have the key to the barrier of going beyond, one will be provided. It will look like a booth. It will glide like a cloth. It will lurch like a monster and read like a book. It will howl like a fish and dig like a throat. It will fiddle like a blueprint and sound like a pulse. There it is. There it is over there flowering into Saturday. Steaming in its meat. Absolved from rags. Snatched from the air and carried by sugar to a crystal of heat.

Because the work was rattling at the bars of its own creation, we did not know what it was. Some said it was pure energy, and therefore invisible. Others implied a kind of scruple, caught in the eyebrow of a sausage, too raw to gilt with erudition. Later, we administered some watercolors, and saw that it was hungry, and full of bones.

No narrative on earth could handle such wanton abandon. We needed divine intervention. We needed physics and fable. We needed fire and water. We needed faucets. We needed hoses. Horses and roses.

The work strode back and forth in its cage showing glimmers of beatitude in its eyes. I have a lot of respect for iron. But this was different. This was tinfoil. This was a language on the loose, laughing its head off and twisting descriptions of its own skin into magnets and leather.

Do you like taking pictures? Then snap this: a work of art eating the Blue Angels and spitting out testicles.

A bug in a greenhouse.

A broken radio.

Pablo Picasso in a rocking chair tickling the rain.

This is a sentence getting to the end of itself by describing a world of sweetness gone wrong in yucca. Which is why everything is various, and yellow. As if screws were involved. And cambric and silk embroidered into letters. Letters with truth in them, and feathers and wings, and details open to the idea of asteroids.

All this proves is that redemption through illusion is itself illusory. Meaning ham and cheese, or the veins on a hand, or a wildcat lapping water all have one thing in common: they are crammed with thought. It is the radius of the zipper that matters not the savor of the stairs. The stairs will take care of themselves. It is these bars that cause so much consternation. Because they aren't real. Which makes them more real. More real because less real. What does that mean?

It means everything is a mass of nerves. Pure energy so heavy it verges on blood.

Because the head is a sphere, the moon is a cup of lard in Montana. The long sugar of dawn sprinkles itself over the hills. The skeleton of a metaphor dances on the head of a pin. The door can open at any moment. There is no difficulty in melting. Everything is easy, like a peach.

What is it that fulfills you? What color is thought? How does one pierce the surface of things?

The ocean does not exclude water. Water does not exclude the ocean.

Because the head is a sphere, it is natural to think of it as a balloon full of thought instead of helium. As if thought were fine and invisible, like gas. Thought, like helium, has no odor. But if we imagine an odor, would it be correct to say that thought has an odor? Wouldn't the thought of a thought having an odor have an odor?

Accordingly, all mountains ride on clouds and walk in the sky.

The sky walked into the room dressed in doorknobs and said this is true.

These words do not lie.

I walk the line. But what the heck does that mean? It means neon is the skeleton of winter, a blue light rippling over a fold of silk.

Worry murders joy. Try to avoid worrying. Squeeze a river.

When I sleep, my worries are dragonflies. But when I awake, my worries are drunken elephants, smashing into the patio furniture on display on a mezzanine in Miami.

How did a mezzanine in Miami get into my head?

Yesterday it was two men drinking tea in Afghanistan. What happened to them?

Do you feel the light trying to get out of the metal?

What metal? The fetus of a vowel. The galaxy of words hanging from my finger. The dream of a rattlesnake. The nervous geometry of glaciers. A thought held together by breath and sensation.

Because the head is a sphere, a skull enveloped in skin and hair, there are heavy bells in the clouds and poetry bursting out of a cube of prose. This disturbs me. But I like it.

Because the head is a sphere. Because the head is a balloon, emotions are rags of steam. Because the head is round, and full of thought, my hat is a traffic light, and my thoughts are epochal and temporary and zippy. Zygotes. Zip codes. Straps.

Forests and metaphors. Abstractions in a paper sack.

CROSSWALK

Crosswalks are ambiguous, like croutons. Are croutons food, or a fac-
simile of food? Do croutons belong to the realm of parsley, or bread?
They are the italics of food. Subtleties of salad in a Harley-Davidson
world. Crosswalks have more in common with clouds than curbs. Is it
possible a crosswalk can mean something more than a membrane?
There is nothing there. Nothing but lines painted on a street. It is not
a bridge. It is not even a pontoon. Is it truly something we can entrust
our lives with? Certainly, when one is in a crosswalk, one hopes to be
recognized, ratified and respected by the oncoming traffic. We live in
an age of helmets. Dizzying velocities. Emotions dense as cherries
chirp in our minds and hearts as soon our feet hit the asphalt. Camel-
lias mean the world to us. It is how knees become knees, and necklaces
swoon and sway from our necks thrilling the light with the glitter of
their skeletons. We are more than claws, less than wings. We occupy a
space in between time and eternity. This is the crosswalk in its essence.
It is a bridge between two sides of a street. But its domain is imagi-
nary. Conceptual. Geometrical. Whether the driver chooses to respect
this domain is often a matter of personal judgment. New Mexico is
the only state I have been in where the crosswalk is a serious matter.
Stick your big toe in a crosswalk in Las Cruces or Tucumcari and cars
and trucks come to an immediate halt. But don't try experimenting or
abusing that privilege. Such octaves as these are fulfilled by language,
not lard. These are buds that bloom in the imagination. They are
drapery and birds. They are salient. They are quick. They are golden
convictions petitioned by all the metal in mayonnaise. All the distor-
tions of chrome. Nudity teaches presence. The sincerity of winter. The
reveries of summer. The delicacy of rain. What is the great truth of
the traffic light? That it makes us stop? That it makes us go? That is
not it. Experience declares that man is the only animal which devours
his own kind. For I can apply no milder term to the general prey of
the rich on the poor. But why do I stop to write this? I must hurry. A
crocodile has eaten this sentence before it had time to cross the river
and become a mist. When a mind, thoroughly understanding the
emptiness of all things, faces forms, it at once realizes their emptiness.
Nevertheless, when the body turns public it is best to be fully clothed.

Best to be in a crosswalk when crossing the street. Rapid in body rapid in stride. Rapid in the certainty of being. Of being in a body. A body crossing a street. A body crossing a street with determination across a depiction of space. A zone. A proposal. A space painted in crisp white lines. A space so charged it welcomes the calculus of walking, the refinements of risk.

Here is today's report: no condensation, as yet, in the newly repaired kitchen window. Though a chill remains near the glass, which would be spring, which is very cool this year, fashionably late, as usual.

There are gleams of light here and there penetrating the foliage which is heavy and green and punctuated by pink and white blossom.

Gas is $4.09 per gallon. Aromatic cedar mulch is $3.49 per two cubic foot bag. A flight to Paris is beyond my means.

Baghdad is full of anomalies, death, men in fatigues and concertina wire, Somalia is on the brink of famine, rice is gold, gold is climbing, the dollar is collapsing, and two men in Hawaii are pursuing a lawsuit to stop a giant particle accelerator in Switzerland from smashing protons together and creating a tiny black hole which could eat the Earth.

Starbucks' profits are off, Boeing is taking a different tack, and Miley Cyrus is in an awkward position.

In the Arabian sea, American warplanes scream off the decks of aircraft carriers while wholesalers haggle and gossip under woolen astrakhan caps at Tehran's grand bazaar.

Once there was a poet named Paul Valéry who said "Poetry is simply literature reduced to the essence of its active principle. It is purged of idols of every kind, of realistic illusions, of any conceivable equivocation between the language of 'truth' and the language of 'creation.'"

I worry about telling you the truth. The truth of existence. But I cannot. I do not know what the truth of existence is. Does it need a truth?

I work hard at telling the truth. I work equally hard at avoiding the truth.

Are birds spies? Should they be reported? Are crows terrorists? Are robins seditionists? Are blue jays anarchists? Are sparrows saboteurs?

If you are out there, somewhere far into the future, and you are reading this, that means everything implicated here is happily and blissfully false. The world did not collapse into plague, famine, and endless war. People read. There are books. There are libraries and bookstores. All of this is wrong. Maybe not all of it but most of it is wrong. Happily, rapturously wrong. My report is false. A false report. And trees continue to sway. And the wind continues to blow. And shadows continue to slide. And lovers continue to moan. And jalapeños continue to have that little squiggle over the "ñ." Because they are hot and the squiggle is pivotal. Pivotal to hot. Pivotal to punctuation. Pivotal to the truth of the jalapeño, which is infinite, and burns in the mouth like a stubborn idea.

I'd like to go on a safari tasting of eternity and write a long letter from Iceland on a mahogany desk in Madagascar. Then mail it from Egypt.

My nerves are full of coffee. My head feels like a sack full of lurid metaphors.

I am an amalgam of glands, all of them distributed in hysterical nuances of orange. Which is why I am wearing a black silk shirt dotted with skulls. Hiccups, tongues, and chaos.

I have assembled a tinfoil moon with black pearls and turbulent hymns. I jingle the bells of a hideous comb whenever I am feeling intermediary. A song rests silently on a piece of paper. It is completely intermediary.

My autobiography has been written by large green chemicals. It has resulted in a life so mobile it agrees with everything, even museum docents. It goes wherever I go. A music so sad it oozes zinnias. And controls the temperament of a polished debris I call Blob.

My heart is radiant with the nectar of repetition.

I am wild, like a washing machine.

A washing machine out of balance. Going wacko in the laundry room. Bong-a bong-a bong-a bong-a.

Can an inflammation of words cause asparagus? I believe so. Here, for instance, is an eyeball boiling with vision. You can look through it. What do you see?

I live in a black garage with a blue DeSoto. I don't know what year it is. I sleep on the seat and gaze at the keys dangling from the ignition.

Last night I leaned over the sink with a bloody nose. This happens a lot. I was raised by tigers. My childhood was filled with jewels and energy. A strange algebra of crow's nests and Ferris wheels simmered in me like a daydream. I waited patiently for the right elevator and when the doors slid open I escaped.

Now I am lost in an art museum. Don't give me typhoid. I don't need a disease I need gerunds and musk. I live in a realm of crust and tar. It is simultaneously in this world and out of this world. Let me describe it to you: it is warm. Warm like an engine. Warm like a leg.

The color of a hairdryer. The interior of an egg.

Perfume in the nostrils of a king.

Sometimes I make up stories. And sometimes the stories make up me. Who can tell the difference? A tint of black agitates a patch of green. An amethyst attracts Peru. And here it is. Actual as skin. Explicit as a pin.

What can a photograph tell us?

Tell us about light.

About life.

About ends and beginnings.

About time and beauty and shadows and quartz.

It can tell us that the canvas of time is infiltrated by detail. By image. By violet and prairie, sycamore and crow.

It can harangue the eyes with Monday, pinch the mind with glee.

There are cameras that click, cameras that whirr. Digital cameras that usurp attention. Cameras that capture antiquity.

Baudelaire warms his hands by the fire, a cat rubs his head against "Mesmeric Revelations."

But what about ocher? What can a photograph tell us about ocher? It can tell us that ocher is large and lenient as a landscape. That it is glorious with dirt. That it is soft and hard. That it is native to a hill. That it is scattered and epidemic.

Ocher is obdurate.

Ocher is the pentameter of earth.

What can a photograph say about mosques and planetariums, or a democracy drowned in money?

A photograph has its limits. An image has its limits. Even speed has its limits.

The imagination has no limits.

The imagination can pull a proverb out of a hat, or lounge in the shadows of a huckleberry.

Time convulses with huckleberry.

A galaxy still steaming with birth.

The blisters of Lisbon are fecund and white. The blisters of Lisbon are operas of chafing.

I miss my youth. But this has nothing to do with the blisters of Lisbon. Missing one's youth is a personal matter. The blisters of Lisbon are hard as gerunds. The constant applause of rain. A globule of shampoo. The gracious abstraction of the moon in the afternoon.

The anatomy of Wednesday is blue. The vinyl of Tuesday is green. The personality of an anvil is tender, whereas the anvil itself is not. All this is irrelevant. Yet part of the overall equation. The equation of quiet. Of quiet in the curtains. The curtains of a house. The curtains of a house on a hill in Lisbon.

In Lisbon where there are blisters. Blisters distributed unevenly throughout the population. Because some people chafe while some people lean into a wall full of repose.

And over there, there is a misfit thumping his leg with laughter. Everything is funny to him because he does not fit in. Does not fit in to the life of Lisbon. And yet he is the essence of Lisbon.

He has written a book. A book overflowing with the milk of paradise. And it is all about Lisbon. Lisbon ladled from the sea. Lisbon flipped over exposing what is underneath. Lisbon with a tint of black and a sliver of red which is apparent in a kiln.

Have you learned the lessons of the fog? The lessons of the fog in Lisbon?

There is no yardstick to measure the magnitude of Lisbon. Nothing there can be quantified. Not even the breath in the weather of an obdurate scallop clinging to a rock in the bay of Lisbon. The Castle of Almourol on Rio Tejo. Or the tenacity of a woman listening to classical music as she washes the windows of her car. Her arm rubbing hard and energetically above the steering wheel. Her arm rubbing diligently and earnestly above the dashboard. In circles. In ovals. In semicircles and loops. In Lisbon. In Lisbon where are there are blisters. And scrubbing and squeezing.

And rhododendrons pedaling dreams of crystal.

Because it is Lisbon.

Which is dense and alphabetic like the rhetoric of hope. The government of rope and rigging in a ship. The rattle of ladders and friction and teak. Clatter of tiles and crockery and cork. The rustle of lace. Thud of a trunk. Odor and light. Kneecap and lip. A pool of weather in a woman's cheek.

AN OFFERING

Here is a lozenge of loud denial and here is a seed containing a pluperfect flower. Here is the phantom of a jukebox nebular and ermine and here is the pathos of a lock of hair in a chest of drawers. Here is a penny of music and here is a wafer of solitude. Please. Take them. I want you to have them.

Here is an ineffability mysterious and quick. Here is the fin of a barracuda and here is a savage vowel releasing a soft pink vapor.

Here is a struggle to absorb light and here is the biography of that light written in splotches and cracks on an ancient wall.

Here is a description of land and here is a beach of dead batteries and tossed soliloquies. Go ahead. Paint it. Dip your brush in a pot of enchanted color. There is a tangle of fishing gear on the table and a pot of forsythia. Paint that. Paint it with the bristles of oblivion. The smooth silk bristles of oblivion.

Here is a morning crawling over the darkness and here is a tendril of relativity attacked by a brittle entity of punctuation.

Take it.

Take everything.

There is more where these things came from. It is all a beatitude a conviviality whose pulse is endless and whose aspirations are various as grain.

How big is your trunk? How much can you fit in your car? Do you have room for a dusk, a place for a tusk, an attic where you can squeeze a mountain, a closet where you can hang a fountain, a basement where you can install a summer, or a winter, or a spring in Montana? Can you adopt a snake pregnant with mythology? Do you have any room for an aqueduct, or a distance modeled on the squeak of time?

Here. Hold out your hand. Take this. It is warm and hypothetical. It is a riddle. It has headlights and attitude. It is sleek as a trout and chuckles like a sawhorse. It is bandaged and three-dimensional. I don't know what it is. Haven't the faintest idea. I just found it at the bottom of this paragraph. And I want you to have it.

Laboratory facts are personal facts as much as honeycombs. Turbulence is the salt of life. Any word will do. It is imperative to perpetuate turquoise. Our interpretation of the crude data obtained by our senses is apt to be a very opaque one if it is encrusted in lichen. An appliance like thumping is congenital as a ticket when it alleviates the color of a banana. There is amplitude enough to dollop rhyme on a sonnet. The pocketknife whose blades flicker utility jaw the leather of pounding. Let it, however, be remarked that the climate of personality gets beatific in zeppelins.

It's all a matter of molecules, tendencies toward mass, bedclothes hurled at a bed. Brand names are easy. Onions are difficult. The more we say the less we hear. And the more we hear the less we say. We are soaked and legislated on a long voyage toward scruple. Retaliate by cheering the tempest. Pose in the sand. Lean against the canoe. Feel that you are completely dimpled and broadcast like paint.

It makes sense to combine words in tufts of thought. Our hair veers west. But our queries blow east. The idea of medicine is tacit in a cowboy bursting in jewels. Lungs and arteries are survived by sheer affirmation. Four a.m. is holy and pure. Such neutrons hang in the air and turn quick and deliberate like the town scarecrow clattering in the wind.

It is true. We have enough money to grow yams. But that doesn't quell the need for almonds and pasta. One afternoon I found someone else's load of wash in the washer and it was total chaos. Slowly and boldly I began to remove the items and put them on the surface of the dryer. This is how the zone of the unseen becomes a wedding dress. How mirrors turn black with oblivion and dramas exist in quills. Even the funnies on Sunday slant toward something ineffable and jade. A wasp clenching the beatitude of existence in an exoskeleton. A chair churning with astronomical patterns. Rhododendrons arranged by the highway.

This is why everyone likes goldfish. The idleness of indirection in a scintillating biology. Albeit the bowl is a limit. A packet of time in a slosh of water. A language infatuated with its own scraps.

Writing is fish. And fishy. Retinas torn apart by life. By vision. By autumns eaten by winter and winters raining on bones. Look how we cringe at democracy! The ingenious restrictions we like to impose on ourselves. Like a bowl of glass. Monkeys on a dashboard. The triumph of dirt and the antithesis of grass.

Grammar is a product of the mind. A wax fused together in a reverie of vowels. The flicker and flame of a consonant at the tip of a wick. The ghost of a horse trotting toward the end of a dock. A pink infection on a black leg. The smell of Wednesday the velocity of any emotion. It is all grammar. Gastronomy and dots.

Go. Stitch the air with needles of sound. See that saddle hanging at the blacksmith's? Engage it in talk. How does it answer? If it answers with silence it is leather. But if it answers with jingles it is fate.

The dawn is dazzling in scarves. So tangible it kills. Stabs the dark with a sun and lets its great sharp light loose upon the roads.

Yellow lines floating on a highway.

Adversity sparkles like hardware. Reveille on the tongues of birds. A galaxy of chaos balanced on a nerve.

Ever see roots grow out of a sack of potatoes? Ever smell the dark in a cellar? Ever hear a zither in vapor at the top of a mountain?

History is bitter and blind. Grip felicity. Grip it with your mind.

Thursday inclines toward Friday and that is the grammar of time. Conversations about the moon tend toward alternation and that is the grammar of tides.

Everything else is air. Simple impartial and bare.

Language is a machine that runs on curiosity, a spider with eight testi-cles creating a web of bulbs and iron. What will these words do next? Shots pour out of a rifle. A parenthesis falls dead.

Money! Sure wish I had some.

I like money because it is ugly and incoherent, like poetry. Olives are more purely thermodynamic, but even they sometimes grip the sunlight like cheesecloth and stuff it with reverie and shape.

There are differences between the tablespoon and teaspoon, but how many people pay attention to that? Maybe during a special occa-sion, when the cutlery is laid out on the table in patterns of geological certainty. Structure is always solemn. It is a sanctuary for chaos.

How do you come into contact with words? With me, it is never simple. I sneak up on them. I try to catch a few. Then I begin to tame them and feed them and teach them tricks. Eventually, they get the drift of whatever it is I am trying to say, and they say it, though it comes out a little different than I had imagined. Thought travels by ear and utterance, but between those two entities is space, and space is full of tricks. Ask any astronaut. Twenty-three heads and 500 gallons of water are required to say amperage. But what does amperage mean? I mean, compared to watt, or ohm, or copper, or note.

Infinity smells like iodine. Growth requires a little dying some-times. It is dirt, after all, that initially introduces us to mysteries of life and death. Things compose and decompose. Rope or clarinets, makes little difference. This is why the word addendum has always sounded to me like a piece of anatomy. Miscellaneous paragraphs all bellowing like cows.

When language breaks it is evacuated by helicopter. But everything else just floats. The sky is inscribed with perversities of mist. Four o'clock arrives soaked in opals. Eight o'clock arrives soaked in opinion. Both are linked by the glitter of silver, the lips of a hectic attention painted on the idea of anonymity. When a washcloth is used, it all brightens, brightens into a darkness so black it is radiant, resplendent with murk.

The philodendron is a mass of ramification. Yet the velocity is naked, like month of November, in which the leaves fall, and the frost comes, and colonnades of ice and rhetoric. The rhetoric of snow, which is delicate, and soft, and blows over the highway in swirls of nuance, entities without name.

The universe is expanding. Evidence keeps turning up. Nirvana, for instance, and escalators and music. Oysters filtering seawater. A pile of rags in a Minnesota garage. Nebulous, purposeless space hung from the sad necessity of time. The weighty bones of the Irish elk as it moves through a forest converting itself into the purest energy of all which is heat. The rest is mere hydrogen, and fur and eyes.

Near the window, its dials bursting with silver, a radio gurgles the biography of pink. The astronomy of lips rattle the camellias of a rogue sentence writhing in its syntax like the pantomime of a screwdriver. We are in the realm of the empirical wondering how it all happened. This place. This world. This teaspoon. This border between the visible and the invisible postmarked with crickets.

If memory is the benediction of experience, then barnacles are the barometer of exchange.

Beauty exists abundantly in all matter but is particularly noticeable in squid.

Personalities are the candy of ingratitude. When they are flung about at high velocities they tend to release a curious behavior called dance. This cupidity for space scolds the honorable bed of matter and personalizes the naked glitter of a scorched anxiety. The entire question of existence rests on a feeling of mathematical beauty. On the imagery of the city. The towns. The ports and wharfs and tambourines and docks. Over here, quantum numbers and airy abstractions heave and bubble on a blackboard, and over there an old seaman's knife shines in a store window like an X-ray of eternity. Which is dust, which is waves? Which is real, which is dream?

Each thought is phantom of another. Another thought, another tender moment slobbering jukebox ghosts on a queasy paradigm.

How could stars fuse so much iron and still shine? There are many symmetries in music but only one colossal trombone ejecting its music into the outer atmosphere. Only one hairline bigger than chewing. Saddle that odor and ride, ride boy, ride. Ride to the end and tell us what is there. Does it shine? Does it speak? Is it confused like a salad or native like a bone? Does it glisten with mitigation or deepen in music like a flowing, forlorn tone?

It takes time to develop a thought, an abstraction dragged across the page like a Louisiana delta. Life is full of strange and hidden currents, a moth flickering through a neighbor's garden, a horse rippling with muscle, a scooter parked like a scarab next to a drugstore. If thoughts are waves then smudges haunt the glue of return. A slap against the oblique creates a more immediate awareness of someone eating a snack in the hospital cafeteria. Upstairs, there are people dying, people healing, and people answering the telephone. How lavish are your feelings? My feelings go all over the place. I can't keep track of them. Sometimes I just want to take the jack and smash it against the wheel. Nudes get cold. Obedience is inexplicable. Electrons do not mince words. Sometimes it takes a shirt churning with embroidery to reveal the beck of a beak and the tangle of blackberries. A freshly tarred road in the middle of summer ameliorates the jolts to the shocks and the body. The eyes grow tired as the twilight wrestles the sky to the ground and drags it into the night. Night is a noble ultimatum. Nothing comes from nothing and the stars make this all too apparent. It is a mystery, like the beautiful anarchy of a waterfall, or the fizz of enzymes in a laboratory jar. A greenish-black gargoyle sits on his haunches grinding away like gouache in a blue kazoo. Yet what does this image serve? I have whittled it out of air. Therefore it is vain, and useless, because we're not in school anymore, and attentiveness has become a habit. But a good habit. Because inattention destroys the world. I am trying to reach for a little objectivity here, and yet I continually fail. Even the taxi looks like an allegory. I can't stop interpreting things. Surely we're moving forward into some marvelous condition where death comes easy and life is as simple and beautiful as the rain dimpling the surface of the sea. Each wave is a narration arranged queasily on the page of a book over which leans a crabby bookstore owner, angry at Amazon. What can we do to change these things? Change them into what? Change them into duvetyn. Change them into milk and filigree. A treatise in the form of a dialogue. A frequency in the form of a monologue. The sun pushing its light through a cloud. A museum of strange emotions. A distillation of shadows folded and placed in the wallet like money. Like old dollars. Miscreant enfoldments crackling with opacity and ink. Consider the screwdriver. It is a step toward the riddle of steam. It will never be solved. But the apricots are delicious, the blisters are soothed by the balm of fiction, and the highway rises over the hill in a gentle arc of speculation hugged by the mist.

LISTEN

Hear the quiet of late August. There. In the quiescence of the trees. Here. In the ferns by the window. Rocks and bumpers repeat it in the papyrus of the afternoon. With October in the margins. When the air moves it is consonant with its vowels. Leaf and loom and loam and weed. Air tasting of hardwood and harbor, being and nothingness.

The mind is equal to what it thinks. The world is on perpetual loan. No membrane quibbles with osmosis, but swimming will get you wet.

Deep as the kingdom in a walnut is the marrow in a bone.

August is the most regal of months. August is august. The mirth of summer is tinged with the heaviness of autumn. The fall. The fall of things. The harvest and variability of things. The mystique of the philodendron and the quotient of a blackened marshmallow at the end of a stick dribble the sugar of an unreachable past.

The past is paste to the gaze of the present.

The sky to the west strides over the mountains and disappears in a blaze of gold. Thoughts mix with thoughts. The hand is exponent to the fingers. A flashlight discovers bits of peach in the sand. There is an acute sense of passage, a voice sailing through the words of a song, a ship rolling from side to side. The black shin of a rising moon permits the barter of urge and desire.

Jellyfish never give advice. They just hang in the water like music from a broken zither.

There should be a calendar of songs instead of days, out and out nirvana aglow like the light in a swimming pool.

Because at the end of summer there is always this strange quiet. This hole poked in the noisiest of places. This inkling of eternity. The fat warm narration of verdure on a trail of apparitions. Because it is August. The time of passage. The time of transition. Plates and glasses on a table after dinner. A suture of noise for a subtle incision, assassination in the leaves.

Necessity is the miracle the camaraderie of the blacktop scars. Heave your feet to the highway. Kindle your talk in metal. Humor the verdure the keen began. It is to plug the opacity of opium as it is to applaud a handshake with postcards. At that inception the objective lacks sand. Calcium does the logic of jolts. The cricket nexus crunches by. The yam is hot to the newsprint and the jet exhausts its jangle. Fluidity is available to peruse my belt. The lachrymose beak beckons its lurid appearance and the variegated scold zigzags on like another incessant humidity on the verge of majesty. The knack of appetite hungers for iron. Eyes mill the vision of a quiet identity, an aorta soaked in glee. The azalea has power. It is rather like milk. The finesse of haunting an economy with anarchic blades below the jackknife echoes wrestled out of a hectic kazoo. That, and the fringe of pathos floating around the clock. I am intrigued with anything baroque, as must be obvious by now, or I would bring this discussion to the bank and deposit it on another highway of parquet faucets. As one's soreness bangs against the fluid of one's life the sword tongue produces a bright light, not so much purple as pecan, which is how the caulk presents and seals it. Bite the cologne between its jewelry. Enforce the act of your fingers if you are holding an octopus marinated in thumps by the dangerous escalator lake. What stretches it takes to comb the bottle of holy equation. The ukulele loaf lengthens the expulsion of morning moss as a blood school accordion squeezes its chromosomal lama into beans and hectic infraction. A jaguar in one's wallet makes the lighthouse seem personal. The lily-like velour of black as it comes in the embassy of night begs the penetration of light. It is all a matter of immersion. The churning, the boiling, the logic of a letter as it lies on a desk. We all have a niche. A corner for the democracy of sight.

Letter to letter creates a fist of black, a furious ogre fiddling a fairytale, calamities of light on a folded napkin. Imagine, for instance, a waterfall folded neatly as a dollar and inserted into your wallet. Memphis sensations. An elevator that moves sideways. It is that kind of world, the world of the poem, an octave boiling in a jewel of sound. Christmas lights on a dirigible. Jewelry and gasoline. A beard of fire. Dragons sprouting from a turquoise nipple. Quakers in Montreal.

We find, everywhere, the grace of the gratuitous. Everything, in a word, is limestone. Neutrons unbind kennels of string and shave us with zeitgeist razors, which is a cause of squid. There is no reason to think experience should be separate from art. Lights flash in the swamp and the mind begins to absorb its meaning, which is small like a suitcase, but full of immeasure, and immeasurable things. Frogs. The softness of evergreen against the lips. Energy triumphs by entanglement and meringue. Thesis soothes the night, which is intermingled with day. Day and night are interrelated by hardware. Soldering iron, switch plate, and vise.

Dimmer switch, hammer, and drill.

Peruvian X-rays. A brittle Sunday caught in the whirl of delirium. Glenn Ford in *Blackboard Jungle*.

The eye cannot take in everything at once. Hence, the unity of plot is gyratory, like the naked glitter of trigonometry. This is why it has always been such a great pleasure to swim underwater and ponder the things lying in the sand: Cyrano's belt buckle, the voice of Jackson Pollock.

Bones in argument with one another.

All these instances involve a perception of meanings in which the instrumental and consummatory peculiarly intersect. In the aesthetic object tendencies are sensed as brought to fruition. Perception goes out to tendencies which have been brought to happy fruition in such a way as to release and arouse a bouncing gland of miscellaneous secretions. The acute superfluity of a light bulb in the snow, or a loose tattoo dripping tongues.

Such tapestries of sensation find their way to the mind where they become colors and udders and ghosts of intricate money. Autumn is but a jigsaw in our chemical cage. Anything moss confesses a certain flounce. Existence hugs our darkness and bites it with headlights. Bugs are little people with exoskeletons. They hop and fly around like words. Like a warm eye on a cold beauty.

Then come boxes. Gift wrapped books. The calculus of charm, which is no calculus at all, but a kind of immersion, a zeal, a zeal in oblivion. Letter to letter is a raft of light. A red hand on a blue night. The glow of a blowtorch in someone's garage. The white hot core, which is piercing. Which is thrilling. Which is the bride of vermilion.

Money does nothing. So I packed my suitcase with a little blue drop of frozen light and left for Moscow.

Moscow smelled of borscht and capitalism so I left for Katmandu. Katmandu showed me divinity in a bone so I left for places unknown.

I arrived in places unknown and got to know it better. Or perhaps I should say un-know it better.

I got to un-know it so well I could hear shovels grow lyrical with abstraction. I felt the air congeal into language. The language turned scrupulous with Gothic machinery and imposesd itself in the mind like a morning tangled in blackberries.

Is the sky a form of mind?

I believe it is. It congregates in vapors and its horsepower is olive. Horsepower is always olive. Alive with olive. First because I like the word olive and secondly because the bald reticence of pasta mimics the ramification of reverie. Which is why I wear a hat of milkweed fringed with earthquakes and purple beverages.

You could call it a handshake rippling with talk.

You could call it the fast adhesion of postage.

You could call it the meaning inside a word, any word, which is a reverie smelling of parallels.

Reality, after all, isn't a sandwich. It's a Colt 45.

That's right. I don't own a jaguar. I drive a skeleton of hope.

You must pull the meaning of these words along with your eyes. Otherwise they won't go anywhere. They will just turn vague, like the cold stone of addiction. You feel a constant hunger for something but you don't know what it is, do you, Mr. Jones.

If my hormones were dreaming this could be a retina knitting a vision of aluminum. This could be a nebula. This could be a toad.

Or a smear of toothpaste in the bathroom sink.

Or a sensation of form fringed with adjectives.

This could be a tendril of meaning spreading itself across a sheet of paper.

Like human consciousness. Like delinquent examples of ink.

Like a dragonfly darting back and forth over a dirt road.

IN SUM

If a sound is made by backbone, then the soul of it will weigh itself in glitter, and frontier aphorisms will be consummated in sympathy and stone. This is true of chins, and the anomalous bones of goldfish.

Why do we write?

We write to explain ourselves to one another. We create pills. We fix our associations to the misconceptions of dogs. We walk sidewalks in winter. There is a radio under the word "romance" and the taste of oysters under the word "declaim."

Not everything is lumber. Some things are also appliances.

The word "ultimate" is based on a private feeling.

The word "intimate" is based on an aching muscle.

This is why Spanish is always naked and German is always lumpy.

The Florida in you is a hairdo. I can see that. I can also see that the prevailing fashion of thought these days is antithetical to varnish. Everything is pixels and digits. Everything is binary. Everything is phantasmal. Everything is fictional and immersed in fog. Like the city. The city is immersed in fog. Like all things gray and ambiguous, it is a weird blend of pain and pleasure. Adversities turned to advantage. Gestures enlarged by irony. Irresolutions set adrift forever, like one of those haunting songs from the '60s, "Walk Away Renée" or "She's Not There."

All cities have ambiguities, certain quizzical features, certain energies that express themselves in velour and breastbones and breath.

The warts of Chicago.

The rafters of Boston.

The bedsprings of Zurich the hoes of Paris the engines of Guadalajara the enigmas of Rangoon.

The scratches of New Orleans the camels of Timbuktu the trigonometry of Budapest the orchids of Cincinnati.

And what is the sum of all these parts?

Blue neon on a cold winter night.

A friend appearing out of the fog.

A slight misapprehension.

An absorbed and curious dog.

I am fascinated by the interaction of chemicals. Wednesday's cartilage, for instance, drips yardsticks and marriage into the bowl of evening. The little light that is left reconciles the snow to the hills on which it rests. Our skin enters the picture and feels warm under Mongolian wool. Capitalism bounces down the street. Merchandise quivers on the shelves.

Is anything of this real? No. Well, yes and no. It is real in the sense that letters and words are real. It is not real in the sense that letters and words are not real.

Words and letters are enfranchised to cut the air into little pieces. Newspapers in a wastebasket. A glass dragon dribbling water in the shower.

Chemicals bubbling in an alembic.

Chemicals going completely drums and thunder.

Chemicals in ferns chemicals dawdling around in legumes.

Obelisks elbows remedies quarks.

It is shocking how all the complications and convolutions and circumstances and revelations that make a person into a person can disappear so quickly and so permanently. Unless that person enters into history. But even history is no guarantee that at some point that person might not mutate into a rhinoceros or footnote.

If there is a luminosity in the mustard I will wear a mask of headlights and fog. And if not, I will not wear a mask at all. I will evade mirrors and maintain the equilibrium of bile.

A pound of brain equals thirty-two pounds of thought.

A tiny denial, a giant veil, a red hand on a blue night, a colorful ballad and a moist hole.

Then come boxes. Boxes are wonderful because they bristle with edifice.

You cannot imprison a mind. What we call reality is haunted by many beautiful chemicals. The sugar of mythology, the umbrellas of Berkeley.

Writing, like chemistry, amplifies the borders of experience. When one thing combines with another thing they produce a third thing. And that third thing will one day produce a fourth thing. And a fifth and sixth and seventh thing. And an alphabet will arrive lopsided and inexplicably cloth and provide many applications, one of which will be coffee, and another of which will radiate the splendid blue light of a tense in a wad of grammar.

Perspective is everything. A single pharmaceutical can turn a misconception into a breech delivery. How do sensations become thoughts? I don't know, but you might want to keep your receipt.

I am always opening a feeling to see what is inside. A feeling inside a feeling means a solitude laminated with spectral inflammations. Means tug boats emitting red smoke on a river of gold.

The impulse to write has ceased to make sense. But did it ever make sense? You can take the breath of a poem and nail it to the light. You can oppose the banality of consumption. You can make a mask of headlights and fog. You can untangle cords, pick blackberries, discover a reality haunted by beautiful chemicals, or create fat blue sparks of unbelievable bombast. But what can poetry do to oppose a police state?

The giraffe resolves the problem of eating by growing a longer neck. This is why I have grown a pair of hydraulic eyebrows. Hegel's Sittlichkeit meant something to me. But why not grow wings?

The floorboards groan with the tariffs of youth. A network lily sparkles like a cafeteria. The true pornography of our age isn't dentifrice but tar.

Philodendrons are nice. Philodendrons lift the sky out of the tyranny and toxicity of the world and make it wide and noble and myriad with fluff. My inclination here is not so much to drool electric plugs and jaguars as to maintain an attitude of calm. Take a walk. Notice things. Imagine what it might be like to be someone else. Someone, say, like Hilary Swank or Sergei Rachmaninoff.

A felon sits on a park bench distilling his life into a yo-yo. He is fascinated by blood. When the skin breaks, blood spurts out. It coagulates almost immediately. How does it do that?

Across the street, the bank sweats commerce. The price of gold has gone through the roof.

Sometimes you need a revolution to keep your pickles fresh. It's time for some new shoes. New ideas. New seals and disquisitions.

The human body is filled with rivers. Veins and arteries. The flotsam on the beach is just another apology for the magnitude of the ocean. Don't take it so seriously. Render it in watercolor. Watercolor is less meretricious than oil.

Or just breathe. Breathing is good. Breath ignites images of locomotion. Linoleum and lemonade. All those consonants in the jukebox would be nothing without breath.

I told Gary I felt alienated and petted his dog. He said "desire weaves the violence of fire into the folly of hope." His dog said nothing. He simply wagged his tail.

How does one seize the world through writing? The sand blows over an ancient civilization in the Gobi desert. This describes writing as a brilliant lost cause, the refuge of losers, the bane of kings. Dyspeptic gerunds. Blackboard crickets create equations of leniency and delirium. Thoughts in a head an immensity of space pinned to a skull in a hall of mirrors.

The day begins with cherubim and ends with a woman licking honey from a sheet of glass. Her tongue moves round and round, a large fleshy thing muscular and hungry. The sensuality is ambiguous, like an octopus squiggling under a rock.

My hands yearn to carry the moon. Evergreens and bamboo scissor space into rags and butter.

The harmonica is a miracle of chrome.

Hope is an animal to bring up from the heart, tender and biological. It feels like a warm gun.

I spend each day in a mood of repugnance, hostility, and alienation. The glimmer of a higher truth jars the surrounding air like a mastodon howling in a book of rain. The window taunts me with its view. Anxieties harden into feathers. I have a tendency to sweat a lot. As soon as I put the bread in the toaster the washer eats my tattoos. I hope tonight we have a huge dinner.

Nothing exists that doesn't consist of other things. The tangle of cords behind the computer, the talk show host on the radio, an astronaut wandering the surface of Mars like a phantom of time, a doctor explaining how cholesterol turns to plaque on the walls of the arteries, everything writes itself into our existence in furious expositions of bud and flower.

The heart crawls toward a warm emotion. The eyes fill with the world. A blue silk blouse hanging in front of the window trembles slightly with a barely perceptible stirring of air.

Reflection leads us to truth, but truth is an horizon, not a border. It is never there when we arrive. It is elsewhere. A white moth battering itself against the walls in the hallway. A gardener's glove soaked in the rain. A blind man working his way around the grill of a truck. Estuaries and texture and slime.

And then we sometimes say to ourselves: it must be this. This light suspended above the water, this effacement effervescing out of time.

A quartz ukulele is not a thought so much as the embodiment of a thought, a thought about the ukulele, the possibility of a ukulele, a quartz ukulele, which would be a marvelous example of the ukulele, a lunar description embarrassed by ink.

Why embarrassed? Because ink is like hope: it spreads, it rolls, it swims in gardenias and scenery, tinkles in the intestine and is a balm to the eyeballs of Norway, intellectual horsepower churning in the minds of Greece, where Socrates warned against reading, it's a drug, it is full of hallucination, and guess what? He's right.

Writing is a drug and it's addictive.

This means the passions are not made of charcoal as originally conceived but are a different kind of fire, the kind that crackles among letters in equations forged in a judgment annihilated by garters. The music of the present tense, which is a fine discrimination, a membrane between the past and the future, which is not the equal of a taxi, but is clearly a way to reconcile an ankle with the femur upon which it moves, depends for movement, the way a certain species of introspection will sway in the mind, back and forth, dropping hints of watermelon.

There is a river in each of us, a momentum, a current that will not be denied, it is too strong, too willful, too full of opinion to stop and wait for a tattoo. A sequence of vowels zippered into a consonant holds a world of mist between the appearances of fish and elbows.

Fireworks interpret things differently. They explode in radiant colors, scabbards of air sharp and bright and full of inflammation, the heat of celebration, the significance of ash hissing in a downward spiral.

I am alone in my enzymes, but my enzymes are yours as well as mine, limpid hammers of protein, sequencing each of us into vengeance and boots. We are idioms of electricity. Pantomimes mirrored on paper. Daydreams vivid as jewelry, Clark Gable in Nevada, a mustang going crazy at the end of a rope.

There is more to an assumption than a mere kiss. Sometimes we have to scrounge for a reason to thrust our thoughts forward. We tell people here, look, see what I have done, I have wrought havoc in ink. I have invented a ukulele, a quartz ukulele, that cannot be played, cannot be played because it is quartz. And so it is silent. Silent as these walls. These logos. These heads in the cafeteria. These rhythms and inconsistencies so warm and meaty in the trigonometry of choice. The revelation awakened in the exercise of a judgment, the jolly ineffability of an impulse, the silly kerosene of sorrow, the felicity of distillation in the epitome of a lip.

A wedge with a bureau and a lung was applicable to tapping on a road. It is somewhat kitchen that an October alphabet rides a mnemonic flavor called tendril. It is quiet when someone crunches moss.

I thought the elephant was furthered by lamp and minuet. I revere it for the trunk and ears and the camel in the mirror.

I revere the mirror because revere and mirror sound good together.

If I had a chin like that I could be kindred to your clothes. The steep jabber of fungus is an indication that we occupy a stranger forest than Bohemia. Once the watermelon has been split open, you cannot stuff oblivion back into it. There never has been an oblivion as sweet as quince. But is that truly a species of oblivion, or just another set of molecules collecting around a spine of redemption?

Let us permit the rain the same level of reconciliation that a ladder enjoys when it leans against a wall. The ideal calamity is one that is pertinent to a hairline. The lever activates the salt. The radar is only used when there are puddles of blood in the elevator.

The trumpet that waved antiseptically next to the dog was a shovel after all. The clouds may be incised with personality but it takes a lot of luggage to bang against the woodwinds of life.

Is thinking a form of labor? Are memories coagulations of time? Why is the heart considered the seat of emotion? Why not the liver? Why not the pancreas, or kidneys?

Dawdling is similar to jetsam. That's why driftwood always looks like bones. The fat clouds that occupy the horizon will be gone in an hour from now. These beans will be cooked and the washing will be hung. Hung out to dry. And flap in the wind. Which is everpresent. And goes gliding over our feet.

The dunes are nakedly arbitrary. I've been dragging a bed around all day. I'm on my way to a colony of sleep. It is raining on the tanks. The sun is more grin than broth. The mind is more flash than breath. Merchandise seems the same wherever you go. Shirts, rugs, candles, bulbs. Melons, pedals, handshakes, oil. Elevators and halitosis.

May a sugar emerge to deliver us from nervousness. May a daydream float us through Wednesday. May a giant introspection carry us into the pharmacy free of gregariousness and malarkey.

This same wax I am singing talks of melting. Everything else is a form of emulsion. I cannot speak for the fireballs. They go screaming out of the mouth of the scarecrow more scrotum than rug, more thunder than drug.

The drummer's hands are an idiom of rhythm, a knock knock knock at the timber of time, which is a forest of life and death and daydreams.

Various emotions walk around in my skin. I'd like to think these things are incidental. But they're not. They're furiously purple.

The mouth is a hole. This is why I go outside to hug the air and burn incense in the afternoon. A zither delivers itself in mirth. There is beauty in the blood of a reptile. There is also a reptile in the blood of a reptile.

How can anyone describe the logic of color?

I'm not one of those people who adapt well to the unpleasantness of life. I wish it were smooth and simple as a gerund but it's not it's complicated and tough like meat. This is why I rely on the arrogance of juxtaposition. Black validates the absence of white. White validates the absence of black. Everything else is full of helicopters and crickets.

Have you seen Joan Jett singing "Crimson and Clover" on YouTube?

That's what I mean. The South Pacific is automatically romantic but everything else is turbulent and urgent, like dirt.

It's obvious my objective here is not to get rich. My thesis is bronze. But my breath is gouache, legion with fog. You know that moment when you knock on someone's door and wait for them to come and you can hear their footsteps and you quietly rehearse what you are going to say? That's it. That's what it's like to discover the day begins like a warrior and ends like a calliope.

Here is the X-ray of a ghost. What do you see? Do you see bones? Remember, it is a ghost. Ghosts don't have bones. They are held together by a soft blue light. The kind of neon and the kind of blue you are apt to see late at night on a motel sign somewhere in the vast solitude that is the American Midwest.

Ultraviolet is the key to understanding quartz. The smell of a mitten requires a more eclectic approach. A tinkling wart and a packet of sugar.

How did those cowboys manage to get their saddles on their horses if their horse happened to be in an ornery mood? You can just imagine the embarrassment as the herd begins to move away and you're still there at the campground trying to get a saddle on a horse that keeps moving around. That's what it's like trying to write something down that doesn't want to get written down. Can't get written down. Because it won't stay still. Because little by little the words turn into cattle and lunge and jostle over the rails of Abilene while John Wayne and Montgomery Cliff duke it out in the dust.

When was the last time you immersed yourself in a plum? It takes a cow to describe a cow, but it takes a naked variability to bend time into a stick. A good hard stick. Two sticks. Two good hard sticks. With which to click together. And pound a rhythm on a drum.

Deliriously anthological, we attack the pecans and the sand goes walnuts. The chemistry of this is intended to hold that emerging cook in you. Being honey was once silver. Now it is wax, a dent in the syntax.

I sit here writing these things with a beard of fire, a groan of variegated silver, and an apparition of mind wrestling an analysis of eggs. The main idea was to get started as a mastodon, then finish later as a misanthropic comma.

My friends continually ask why I write surrealism. Why not jars of algebra in which the brain can actually think and the jaws can actually twist bits of time into January?

I simply tell them to get into this poem and don't come out until the darkness of life begins to churn into parables we can push around with our emotions.

A reverie which nails itself to a camellia is precisely the sort of thing I'm looking for. The glitter in my elbow clicks like drapery. I need something to enhance the summer light. Perhaps some dirt will do, and some Peruvian X-rays humming with vertebrae.

California gets liquid in me like a query. The waterfront does a rhapsody and the vast ankles of twilight bounce from cheek to cheek more fire than pea, more pea than pod. The hummingbirds growl. It is an unexpected development. Even the orchids begin to get heavy. We wade across Thursday raising our arms to catch the bubbles that drift overhead appareled in soap and gravity.

I feel less democratic now than I did at the beginning. Sometimes worries about calculus prevent us from sleeping, then we realize that calculus was invented to deal with problems concerning rate of change, which is a mirthful situation to consider, and weigh in the mind like a naked pulse of watermelon dust.

Hilary has stepped down, Obama moves forward, and by the time this poem figures out just what it wants to accomplish maybe life will be discovered on Mars and we can all begin to reconcile ourselves to the doors of perception that parachute through the head, all tangled in eternity and squirming around in a gooey mess of sugar and protein.

I expect very little from politicians, but even less from poetry. I love this kind of introspection and fully endorse it, expecting the world to change when I write about it and then, when it doesn't, feel completely at liberty to go flapping around like an albatross on the deck of a ship squawking about ampersands and enzymes. Why is life so full of waffles? Why are shovels so mysterious? Why is the personality so hard to operate with scarves and groceries? The last time I put money in a jukebox I didn't get the song I wanted. I got molecules and clocks. I got kisses that didn't fit the situation. And a laboratory that did.

I have been around the sun sixty-one times. I have been to Paris and London. I have walked the streets of San Francisco in quest of drugs and nudity and books. Naked books and alphabetic drugs.

I have four names, one of which is a misdemeanor, one of which is a flashlight, one of which is still under construction, and one of which cannot be pronounced or spelled but comes in handy whenever I shake hands with a politician.

My skeleton jingles when I walk. It sounds like Christmas in a brittle oboe. It sounds like a pot of boiling trumpets. It sounds like a flock of flamingos annihilating a bathroom towel.

My eyebrows are xylophones and my ears are noises folded into skin. I am full of vanity and toothpicks. My favorite tool is an antithesis and my favorite zip code is a lip operated by a mechanical salad.

I like to get bubbly when I am feeling blue and declarative when I am feeling puce. My favorite personality is a misanthropic mustard called life and my favorite opposition is gasoline. I have the mind of a tiger and the warmth of a frontier.

I like to rub my hands with Corn Huskers Lotion when they are dry and take my feet for a walk when they are feeling inalienable and oblong.

I don't like banks. They make me feel self-conscious and never give me enough money.

Money is ambiguous, like sex and poetry. It is instinct with necessity but never quite suits the cuticles of delirium. There is no equation that can properly reduce it to groceries, or massage it until it is quiet.

Never try to cash a haiku the teller will think you're being blatantly rural and suggest you go home and smoke some opium.

I love jukeboxes. They are libraries of incentive.

It all comes down to paprika. You either love it you don't. I love paprika because it is ubiquitous and oblique. I am sending you some in the mail. It will arrive in a limestone toboggan and resemble an empire of bark.

I don't understand infinity, why it is so big and endless, but I am glad for it, glad it exists, however it exists, and sings and sings in a lather of light and silliness and rain, making midnight wonderful with cleavage and perceptions thrill with investigation. Investigations that are never resolved. Investigations invested with chemistry and ghosts. Investigations that are always ongoing and going on. Beautiful investigations and ugly investigations. This is my life. I am under investigation. But I am the investigator, so the process is lurid, and the scale is indeterminate.

This may be the most narcissistic thing I have written. I will further individualize it with a beet. Three verdant feelings and a misinterpreted irk.

It is not often that they harden, that emotions harden, that they harden into wheels. Biophysics is needed to explain crinkling. Crinkling occurs in sacks and cellophane. The emotion of this is toast. Daubs of Friday smeared on a handstand. Very current and roaring palmistry.

Palmistry is reading destiny in the lines of the hand. This is to assume that there is such a thing as destiny, and that it accommodates neon. Neon has little to do with pumice and everything to do with unction. Unction is persuasive and blue. Here the emotion gets allegorical. Dangled and wet. Like a waterfall.

Watch.

Watch an emotion wax into discourse. Discourse is a form of conversation. It can be three to four men and a woman or three to four chairs and a table or a crowd of champions and cheapskates or champion cheapskates or skates and ice or ice and hypochondriacs hypochondriacs on ice or ambassadors of horn or giraffes and creditors or watercolors and nails.

Here the emotion gets inflated. We hear a baritone. A violin and violins and the sounds of violins. Each is likely to be placed within reach or crooked under the chin.

Here the emotion gets transparent. You can see a language through it. You can see into the language. You can see into the anatomy of the language. Remember palmistry. Remember the hand. Rapidly as a calliope it tokens the camaraderie of digits. Then cups are available and organs.

Open your mouth. Open your mouth and let something out. Introducing us to you. Introducing us to brocade. Bazaars bizarreries bifocals bistros bystanders canopies and inflammation.

Language is the inflammation of air with an emotion in it. And this is called alkali. And this is called pell-mell. A red wheelbarrow beside the green calliope. Everything still as candy. And so we have before us Canada. And all its trees and rills and rivers and daffodils and hills. The many hills of Canada. Of which this is an example. Open your mouth and let us see the hill. Introducing us to wood. Introducing us to turpentine. The meaning of baggage as it stiffens the spine.

The meaning of headlights and conviction and need. Gravity broken on a fish. Cheddar on a thwart. A keen sense of navigation. Syllables annealed in meaning like a drop within a bead.

How do you market poetry you do it with shattered nights and guns shooting adhesive predications whatever exists that can exist in air the lips of Jackson Pollock the chin of Samuel Taylor Coleridge the eyes of Emily Dickinson the throat of Edgar Allan Poe the electricity of Christopher Smart. You must eat a pork chop in a department store window to have a slap worry you into writing an ode to an American totem a pinch hinged to an iron lung must germinate in mulch and broken shells precise as a hand. The coolness of a lower room ebbing into heat black hills full of sage happiness, time, truth, causality the ability to create a dukedom by ceaseless morbidity. Smack that pickle against the ribs it is likely a larynx fountaining clouds throbbing with cures noses hoses roses poses butter on a butte terracotta chickens maintaining a savage idea of laptops. You have to ask yourself what am I repeatedly across a range of temperatures dribbling black paint as much as idealism can foster fur flapping and arithmetic insisting on symmetry. Semantic conundrums tend to make the bank nervous so always institute a sense of broomweed a place for words spitting out of a baroque wreckage mirroring the backbone of a clarinet. Ask yourself what is describing this to me the behavior of water or the bump on the bathtub go ahead mow the lawn do it in return for tin the temperament of a waterfall. Provide an area for an aria wool in the well a knapsack stuffed with willow cogito ergo sum. Nothing that does not depend on the presence of air the nuance of asparagus is made perfectly for the goo of it and when it is snapped and blowing shuffle an awful waffle wispy bolts of cloud garner evidence of ablution which was always so unsatisfactory in the twentieth century. The formation of dew is a wonderful topic age is a reflection of currents which is how gas becomes green by accommodating gray. Difficulties serve as metaphors for the physics of sailing grass high behind a fence the philosophy of mathematics which is sometimes erroneously associated with the relative humidity of bohemian dirt. When it matters most to say what is urgent and bells in you a tornado will turn the brown glaze on a fervid hat to a madcap representation of nipples chafed by cotton. You need to wear a maple helmet brawling with silk to twist this gestation to a better understanding of particle physics. The study of being or existence is often ornamented by such watercolor. If there is a raft stuck in the sand the cause of writing poetry is served by phantasmal furniture which is why a knoll appears to cushion a realm of palpable air. A serial cereal or cereal serial will crash into gravel if these veins are full of Cytherea. The imaginary audience that individuals use to flatter being or existence comprise a few of the gears meshing to move a bulldozer in which it is the wild intonation of pistons popping that enters the book of wonky tonky outskirts. An orange finger of critical mass points to the sunlight realized in denim as well as the incisions made on a piece of rawhide. When thinking about the self it is useful to define entities of reef and reference as a milieu of asterisks. Eternity sneezing breasts because the intensity of it demands to be ogled by a rogue contour in search of a shape. A temperament arraigned by lilacs. A lung ascending the cottonwood by the river of blue currents. Raisons reasons visions Italian glistens when it teems with metabolism which is taken to be conflicts obstacles neon lights fast women golf at midnight a burning desire thinking with sticks wrap it in linguistic machinery crackle like a cake notably of the Platonic school. Feeling espoused as a membrane nosegay of a given parcel of air proximity to a marquee inclined for the pleasure of broadcast lilacs are an event it is evident that a consonant contains a suite of angular thumbs buzzing humming groaning moaning all nouns refer to entities the blister is the temperature names in glittering lights presented in a Vermeer still life diameter lavish with pi. Emotions wrestle with consequence noon is a magnet pulling chaos wrapped in cellophane cat litter underfoot in the bathroom to which the parcel of meaning must be cooled. If there is a lasagna in the oven the feeling knocks against the snow just as when the coal smolders. A doctrine of beauty harbors itself in a solo purple as a yellow diesel. English is a form of clay a lasso going round and round and round crowned in naked impulse. I am waiting sing the Rolling Stones at constant barometric pressure steel tools French antiques everything a tableau it is partly made of dirt long and tossed a hemorrhage of thread pain is a bridge to whiskers. You can sculpt sound so that it resembles a lasso at noon. The mind is fast when it is heated by words mental events experienced by carving consonants out of air and providing galaxies for the water vapor component a sonnet bleeding gerunds it is raw to be sautéed like that blasted into Japanese. A kimono surgically removed from a maraschino letter. Stars cackling in oblivion. Words refer to entities called dew inflation is a vehicle to surfeit depravity introduced in a particular monster pink crocodile swimming with wavy fenders of ocarina chrome. Puddle of blue on a secret canvas of the soul trowels vowels towels moments of provocation tracks in the mud cinnamon in the cupboard. Ring in a gondola raw lines of legendary breathing electrons energy Italian. When the dew turns to yellow smoke emerging from a wound it is time to bang an analogy against a diagnosis a moth flying out of a mouth means don't handle the merchandise draw the blinds for the cat acoustic snaps instead of creating frost as the tannin falls below freezing pessimism meets harmonics it is appointed with paper because icicles agree with eaves and poetry sells an emotion in blue glue it down use it to fill the viola with bees.

The problem of consciousness is glazed with language. How can meaning, design and morality arise in a universe that began as meaningless, void and without form? Philosophy sugars thought with design because design arises from the experience of nature itself. We strike gold in the dark. In the temples of the moon the tang of wisdom is fat as rain.

Our brains are syntactic engines. Their concatenations crackle with significance. Words swarming around a metaphor. Red dots and a red handprint in a cave illuminated by animal fat and Juniper wick. An ancient bone pitted with markings. Animals and symbols engraved on a reindeer antler.

Thought is reflective. Geometry is yardarms. What happens in the brain to make a mind glisten with refractive chrome? Saddle a bone with a diffusion of red, bottle a thirst in a blade of morning?

As above, so below. Each fabric of the visible is also the fabric of an invisible being. The more intensely we look and feel, the more intensely does the world communicate with us. What we believe we see is a preordained harmony. What we actually see is chaos. The fossils of imaginary worlds mingled among the bones of the real.

What is perception without language? An instinct.

What makes a concerto pink?

Ornaments of sound organized into silk.

There is something in human consciousness that needs to make a story of things. Japanese characters on a kitchen blade. A dish of apricots. "Bang a Gong (Get it On)" pouring out of a red radio.

A young woman walking slowly in late March drizzle, her look askance as she cradles a cell phone beneath her chin, absorbed and distant.

A man carrying a vase of gladiolas through a graveyard.

Purple balloon caught in a telephone wire.

Can there be consciousness without words?

What a silly question.

Cement, for example, argues cause and effect without benefit of a brain or doodlebug.

A word is a crisis of sound and mimicry. James Dean in a planetarium. Louis XIV mounting a chamber pot surrounded by mirrors. Li Po in a boat drifting along in the Yangtze River.

Do animals imagine themselves as other animals? Does a butterfly "with the daily news printed in blood on its wings" dream of being a bartender in Venezuela?

Once upon a time, Chuang Tzu dreamed that he was a butterfly, flying about enjoying itself. It did not know that it was Chuang Tzu. Suddenly he awoke, and veritably was Chuang Tzu again. He did not know whether it was Chuang Tzu dreaming that he was a butterfly, or whether it was the butterfly dreaming that it was Chuang Tzu.

The highway of the fantastic is paved with reverie. Postcard on the floor. Little red light in a computer tower. White cord under the bookcase.

Words float ideas. Little words that two can say. Commit heat until it is hot, hot and sharp, alien and nebulous, mutilated and penetrated, mathematical and squeaking. At fat bolt crow, at fat fat at, at fat at fat, fat at fat at, fat at fat crow fat bolt fat black fat black fat, crow fat, bolt fat, fat black crow, black bolt, crow bolt.

Crowbar.

That man over there getting out of his car to operate a gas pump, what is he thinking? What worries does he have that I might also have? Will he be irritated, as I am, at the reek of gasoline on his hands? Will he wish that he lived in Oregon where it is against the law to pump your own gas as I do?

If brains are syntactic engines that can mimic the competence of semantic engines, then where does a sense of communion come in? Why is the somber atmosphere of a cocktail lounge so soothing? And why, particularly, does it so persistently seem that there is more to things than what we see?

Realism is lavish with physics. Romance is closer to the neck. Both embody the kind of inflammations that enrich our spiritual hardware, elevate our sense of things. They do not answer to what consciousness is, but they do enlarge it for the tourists, transfigure it into insinuations so eloquent and penetrating they make death seem delirious with intimacy. A leopard at midnight, surgery at dawn.

The mind is a metaphor. Dusk on a desk. Wine in the spine. All things bend to the slap of gasoline. Which is unnatural and wax, like punctuation. Think gouache. This is because the universe is the first bell to further science. Imagine pudding. A lump of heat, thick jaw with a green wire and yellow wings. The mind is a metaphor because thought is made of experience, ten sanguine lawyers and a quart of Welsh. Words clinging to consciousness like belief. Words popping out of space and a long black liquid truant to its own proposition. A 30 lb. emotion in a 5 oz. bird. A fire in the eyes. A mouth crashing through a poem in a tumult of skin.

Time is a window swimming with pain. Behavior is mostly parody. Surrealists in the rain. Salve and salivation and especially tin.

Every perceived thing — color, texture, shape, compression, funeral, fugue, jingle, discharge, current, buffalo robe — is a knot in the loom of simultaneity. It is a concretion of the visible. But it is also a thread in the fabric of the invisible. Each perceived thing is a fossil drawn from the bottom of imaginary worlds. There can be no single, hard, indivisible piece of pure being, but rather a narrow passage between the horizons of the exterior and interior worlds, something that lightly touches and resonates at a distance diverse regions of the world of color and visibility, a certain differentiation, an ephemeral modulation of this world, a momentary crystallization of latency and potentiality.

Roll behind the scripture and bingo you're bearing a castle in your postulate. Position is simply gates. Push your presence into flannel. It matters a great deal that the west is renewed in the east. We stagger through the flux of day interpreting the rhetoric of things in journals and juxtapositions. Coffee is faster when it's hot, a delicacy of such pleasure it overwhelms thrift. This is because gravity is an amber grammar and a patch of khaki is instrumental to a birthmark. Protoplasm is work. Consciousness grows gooey with gouache. The lake obeys its water and the wind lifts the prairie into gold. The brook hurries through itself in outbursts of water. Space is more than feeling. It is also billows, pillows, and beaks.

Each gaze envelops, fondles, marries the visible world. It is as if there were a pre-established harmony between the organ of sight and the thing seen, between the organ of touch and the thing felt, as if our senses were somehow familiar with phenomena before feeling phenomena, and yet our perspectives are far from indiscriminate, flotsam on a sea of turmoil and chaos, but are guided from within. There is will. Volition. Ideas of heat and honey. We are just now beginning to understand the elevator. Hits from the '70s that continue to unravel in the miscellany of the future.

An attic is not the same as a tattoo.

Lay down and cut the wind into such matter that belief appears protoplasmic or toes. The sweatshirt shows its equations are wet after the mountain articulates its sage and basalt. Textures of smooth and rough, velvety and gnarled, glassy and barbed, bristly and studded. It must be that between my exploration of the world and what it can teach me, between my movements and whatever I touch, there is a rapport, a guiding principle according to which these perceptions keep from being the mere willy-nilly pseudopodia of the amoeba, ephemeral waves and distortions of space, but the initiations and overtures to the palpable world. This can only be if my hands are in some way a part of what they touch.

Motorcycles prove nothing. Use your lips. Each gaze is a four-dimensional sculpture dangling from a chemical. Perceptions sprawl about in words because it is in words that consciousness turns extra-ordinary and redwood. A scarf makes it all seem genial.

The visible is cut from the tangible. And everything tangible promises in some way to be visible. There is overlapping not only be-tween the thing touched and the one who touches but between the visible and the tactile. Touching and seeing belong to the same world. Thus, it is evident that vision is palpation by gazing, and the gazer and the gazed at are one and the same. This equation brackets dusk. Get a grip.

Water uses the idiosyncrasies of itself to present us with skin. Wings declare the sky palpable. Hair flung into art. A stately waltz. Horses thundering down a hill. A genius seething with wasps, a hun-gry ride, a wet truck, a kind of neck, a heavy pitch, a shifting rain, a blue bulb, a fluttering pain, a lousy gravity, a flexible hysteria, a flying lightning, an inclement wallop, a definitive okra, a bulbous vase and an orbit and an obligation and a radius and an intrinsic cold and a croco-dile and a quarry and a dancelike invasion and an expansion in sensa-tion, in a sensation being a sensation and sometimes a bandaged muta-tion, in being a sensation and equivalency and blazing and cracks, really violet and mostly orchestral and particularly thin and counter-clockwise, thick or thin but really gathered, and almost always thunder.

On this side hangs a forest. I did not see this coming, but here it is. Lumps and mosaics and arteries and leaves. Everything that makes a forest a forest and ears to hear what is happening there. As soon as we experience something, we see ourselves outside of ourselves, and the real wilderness continues and grows within ourselves, while outside the simultaneity of everything balloons into memory. Everything is synonymous. Outside is inside and inside is outside. The mind is a metaphor.

The mind is a metaphor of meat. Heat and noise and thermodynamic timber. Glistening amulets. Decorum in sage and logic. Kitchens immersed in haiku. Vowel engine stained into lichen.

The mind is a metaphor because there is no mind. There is supposition and music. Jelly and calculus. Mythology and time. A neural blaze in a slice of water. The quiescence of mud. Perspective brightened into the jewelry of language. That liquid in you tickling like query. Drops of thought on a ribbon of hurt.

The mind is a grip on oblivion. Death unsnaps its math and paradisiacal crickets riddle the night. Dawn rides over the mountains and creates a rhythm of steam and penetration. The bright legacy of hands unlock the door to the great green world and the weather of the mind finds its place in the sun. Space and time and pinwheels in the dirt.

There exists in writing an impulse to make things different. More intense, more inexplicable, more singular and strange. The key unlocks the prison and the King of Turquoise walks out. A kitchen chews light into a morsel of foam wrestling with itself. Ten cherubim wait in line at a cash machine. A camera could swallow these things and spit them back out on a screen, but the slow drool of time would eventually bleed them dry.

But time is not the enemy. I remember the hits of 1966 like it was yesterday. "96 Tears." "Walk Away Renee." "Wild Thing." "When a Man Loves a Woman." Shall I list them all? Believe me, it's not necessary. All around, everywhere, words create a fabric of naked black oblivion.

Go ahead. Try it on. How does it feel?

Tar and taffeta create a voice for the bicycle. The bicycle refuses to speak. A truck full of orchids lunges forward in a geometry of whimsicality and laughter. The femurs are small, but the gallantry is big.

Hamlet ponders a hacksaw. The ghost of a clam says "identity often culminates in a beard." The hawk sagely nods. The hawk wears a wig.

Is any of this making sense? Would you like some water? See my ankle? It bleeds twilight.

Somewhere in this room is a fifty-horsepower enzyme for giving this assembly a palpable reality. The jackhammer pounds Florida. The atmosphere in the candle factory goes crazy. In walks Mick Jagger singing "Ruby Tuesday" in a gold lamé jacket. Brian Jones appears in a fetus of gas. He is smiling, and plays the dulcimer.

Here is a metaphor haunted by its own yolk.

A kiss is more like a laceration. A kiss is an earthquake marinated in scarlet.

What is the difference between a description and a moon? The moon creates a tissue of silence and a description is loud like a yellow room.

I like thoughts that wander. Do you like thoughts that wander? Have you ever seen a thought wander? Where did it wander?

Teak and naphtha are triumphs of the material world.

I say this partly out of sadness and partly out of absorption.

If a sound is made of thought will it quiver with teeth?

Meanwhile, back at the candle factory, Harpo Marx is crawling on the ceiling. This is why Spanish is always naked and English is always pearl. Spanish dances and English reeks of urgency. This is why skin and bone go so well together. This is why the intestines are convoluted and blisters are not. This is natural. This is calm. This is a morning in Norway and this is a jagged ramification. This word has a village in it and this word is wrestling with a creature of ink. This is a burning desire and this is its nerve, wrapped around a sentence like a raw but beautiful emergency.

One might say that strangeness was first introduced to the world in 1954 by Murray Gell-Mann and Kazuhiko Nishijima to explain the fact that certain particles are created easily in collision yet decayed much more slowly than expected for their large masses and large potential for interaction.

One might say with equal conviction that strangeness was first introduced to the world in 1868 when *Maldoror* was first published, a book written by a young man who called himself Comte de Lautréaumont and died soon after writing it, or 1902 when *Le Voyage dans la lune* by Georges Méliès first appeared.

But strangeness, of course, has been around a long time.

What isn't strange?

Even a rubber band is strange. The rubber band is extremely strange. Rubber, in and of itself, is strange. The Indians were familiar with its properties, but when the Europeans first saw it, they thought it was alive, which made the Indians laugh, because they knew what rubber was, and how to make it.

What about staplers? Paper clips? Cameras? Suitcases? Extension cords? Cities? Nutcrackers? Plywood? Pumps? Shorelines? Tiger lilies?

All strange. Very strange.

What about fingers? Thumbs? Eyeballs? Eyelashes? Legs? Arms? Hermit thrushes? Hermit crabs? Edelweiss? Tea? T-bones? Ukuleles?

All strange. Exceedingly strange.

What about Bob Dylan selling Cadillac Escalades?

Honey, do you have to ask?

Whenever somebody says they are feeling strange my ears perk up. What a great feeling it is to feel strange. I want to hear all about it. Why is this person feeling strange? Quite often, the person feeling strange doesn't know why they are feeling strange. So they give it a name. They call it foreboding. They call it premonition. They call it clairvoyance.

Clairvoyance means clear-seeing. When someone sees things clearly things feel strange. How else could they feel? They would certainly not feel ordinary. Or familiar.

Strange what love does, goes the song. Note the word "does." That is strange. It is one thing to feel love. But something slightly different to feel love doing something to you.

Love makes people strange. People in love do strange things. They are enthralled. They are driven. They are in a spell. They are bewitched.

They become monstrous. They become sublime. They become violent and mad. They become lavish and wild. They deepen and churn. They roar and thunder. They warp. They shuffle. They change.

They become strange.

To cease working in shadow with the light against us is a circumstance devoutly to be wished. Hence, each line is a struggle, a line cast into some river, Pecos or Snake or Missouri, a stream of consciousness in which, as actual water, we find the elation we're looking for, the bright spinning lure of desire cast high and far into that sparkle against the rock, against the light, *and once the experiment has begun to make an end of it, so that no frontiers whatever be accredited* to anything other than my response to Tarn's clean lines. These beautiful abstractions. These bright tumbling words drawn into long speculative lines. I love to read this sort of thing, this questioning of the world, the word, the words, working, in open light, hard and sharp and bright. Diamond-like. *This is the discipline required of us now*, this search for clarity, for elation, for light in a world full of shadows and power-mad politicians, these maggots in a cadaver of the body politic stabbed by greed.

It is a myth you know that desire dissolves all obstacles. Yes, I do know. But what happens in a poem of this length and stately composition is teased, *au rebours*, against the grain, into burning contradictions. Doesn't desire *create* obstacles? These myths put forward by positivists, that where there is will there is a way, are cruelly disappointing. What desire ever achieved its fulfillment in a world of worms and yardsticks? *Because there is no end to the production and destruction of mountains.* Meaning nothing lasts. Nothing but nothing.

What are the laws of the world? What, in the end, are mountains, rivers, earth, human beings, animals, and houses? What is a shore? What is a wave?

The ocean does not exclude water; the water does not exclude the ocean. *This is the discipline required of us now.* To understand the one in the many and the many in the one. *The skin we wear having been designed to fit each one of us* represents a splendid opportunity for each of us to enter into the mud and study this in detail. Do not regard a pound as light or a ton as heavy. If you point your finger at a cloud, do not expect the sky to get stuck there.

The unreality of art is unreliable. Take the elevator. Choose your floor. Push a button. If you can do this in the middle of a desert, with no one around except a hummingbird or two, a rattlesnake languishing on a rock, then you may need to take a breath, sit down, and ponder the world with greater acuity.

How often do we feel for any lasting moment that we are inhabited by the exact voice of what we need to say?

Several hours ago, when I began reading these poems by Nathaniel Tarn, these lines in their ardent intent to understand the nature of reality more deeply, I was not the same as I am now, eager to go back, and begin again, what is more than a reading, more than an absorption, but a study of the bow, the bend of the bow, the tension in the bow, and how to pull the string, and hold the arrow, that arrow in its blaze of feathers, that arrow with its sharp point aimed at infinity, where there is no target, and where any trajectory will do, provided it shoots high from this world, in a voice taut with understanding. There is simply no other way to put it.

And so when my eye rides along the line, *let it be my task, my pride, to ride it out like breakers. Let me be at its mercy like a swimmer in water. A bird on the wind.* So that what happens is words, and more than words, more than thought unveiled in its gauze, more than a pill of intonation swallowed alone, in the quiet of home, more than a slap of water on a beach, the spread of its froth, the spread of its bubbles and lace, but an actuality, a franchise, an egg broken on a rock, a metabolism crawling with the slobber of life, formulations of amino acid and slime congealing to form a fin, a gill, an eye, an arm, a tentacle or mind afloat in a pool of reverie.

Who then, charged with the task of preserving language, in this babel of dialects where none has the desire to legislate anymore, but only blindly and efficiently follow the conventions of his task, shall discriminate, select, unite the corpus of law, if not the poet. Now we're talking. Because that role has been so diminished and trivialized by our society as to become virtually meaningless. We need a Tarn to untarnish it. To give that commitment true devotion. To stand by the abyss in a lather of novelty. To decipher the froth. To X-ray the clouds and study their bones. Their lightning and ermine. Their butter and amplitude. Their curves and anacondas. The mind is an apparatus for mapping chaos. Hoist a ladder to the moon. Oil a blue star with words soaked in aberration.

The poet is a modern contrarian. A Sacred Clown. Anyone with time to spare *for the most beautiful revolution of all,* which is living. Being alive.

Where can I speak to you face to face if not here, could have been written by Whitman, because he, too, was that intent on bringing the actuality of life to these words. Dead in their ink until a pair of eyes brings them alive. Provokes them into life. Causes this black distillation to grow into light, crackle with significance, swords of exuberant metal, *some of which are of spirit.*

Or mettle. As if they hung *from the bosom of the sky.* A veil of mauve and thunder in the distance, a curtain of rain, the smell of it heavy in the desert air, mingled with odors of sage and yucca, *lamparas de dios,* "Lamps of the Lord."

The pantomime was miserable in the jalopy. There was less of a beat to keep the flow going. The philodendron aorta blazed a blackball sonata. So we walked past the steep hill because reality felt dated and beaked. And the umbrella we carried had a queasy wavelength. There was more kilowatt thunder in the walnut. We could see the details through the eyes of a tarantula flexing its muscles in the flux anthology. Here is where we began to engineer boots for our ankles, which were felonies of bone. Now think about bone a minute. The skeleton is a form of architecture. This is important to keep in mind. The mind is not an architecture. The mind is a phantom dancing on a yardarm. The mind is a mood, like September. Sometimes we joke about it. The mud is oblivious to our deciphering. We soak it in buckets then drag it around with chains. A combination of firearms keeps our passions lifted and intrepid. The nasty Bahamas tinfoil was enough to handle, but the ornament tissues were added for their luster. Never go through life without a membrane. There are levers for this. Buttons and parachutes. A jar for whatever blemishes you may choose to preserve. And sometimes we leave a trail of scarves behind us. It is time to engineer another queen. The anaconda technician fluid has turned black and ugly. The Middle Ages is just another way to percolate your clothes. Imbue the bicycle with a paradigm. Wheels, for instance, or gears or spokes. A smooth rope snatched from the gullet of a taillight. In melting we find scintillation and pecan, epidemic narcotics like quiet. Greenery is engaging. Until the garters snap. Then everything changes. As yeast to a handkerchief, so is beauty to a queasy necessity, a tissue for the nose and everything else that goes with it, like quartz and dissolution. The mind parachuting through a big idea. Thick in bloom and thicker in drool. A legion of thoughts quivering with biochemical monuments, all of them deliriously rendered in snow. Never mind the mirror. All it does is reflect things. Pay attention to blood. The loudness of it. The redness of it. The sheer boldness and density of it. Circulating and feeding all those bones.

Every atom is a bundle of energy, Monday marinated in dirt. This is how we push the day through its kerosene. The earth stays warm because it is heated. We stay warm because we are alive and full of blood. Blood bursting with silver. Mostly in terms of probabilities. Things like spoons and music. Things like British swords. Things like introversion, which is psychological, and handstands, which are not. Handstands gather in perspective and create more handstands, like those at the edge of a black hole, feet high in the air balancing space and white dwarfs. Each moment is an atomic rapture lurid as gasoline. Some ask: what is the path? But there is no path. When space is curved and time becomes pliant as a tattoo churning with reverie the most one can expect is a zeitgeist shaving a tear. A tear is a thing of salt and water exiting the tear duct during a moment of sadness. Sadness is heavier than helium but lighter than a planet. Fire attends the nails in the blacksmith's shop. Thomas Jefferson staring at a shovel. It is an aphoristic shovel. But then, all shovels are aphoristic, particularly the ones that lean against a museum wall anticipating arms. Broken arms. Stars have a license to shine but arms do not. Arms hang around in sleeves growing hair and hands. They sometimes release themselves into space and this is good. This is a good thing. A thing like poetry. Poetry converts matter into energy. Energy is deliriously real, as are mirrors, taxis, and pennies ablaze with folklore. Sometimes a sentence will crawl across a piece of paper by way of syntax, or twitch convulsively in the sand as it seethes with life and changes into a head of lettuce, or a cloud of fairies flittering across the moors at dawn. This is what happens when protons collide. Innovative mutations assume the ideal color for the smell of labor and alter the history of matter into a pliable identity in which water defines itself as a hug and a suitcase lambent as a metaphor pops open letting out pronouns bald as catfish and white moths flickering over a layer of freshly fallen snow. What physicists call a plasma is, in fact, a waterfall banging around in a thyroid. Sometimes life becomes gigantic and overwhelms you with its marmalade and fauna. Why else would one's nerves applaud the apology that is Christmas and immerse their personal histories in ink, leaving a residue of language and a quantum indeterminacy skidding from left to right as if frantic to seize the space around it? These comparisons break down on the microscopic level. The world as perceived by the eye is just an illusion. But the world created by dirt echoes through the forests of Virginia, and visions get wedged between words like an eye.

Clang during daze evaporates in particles. The rattle of cells hung out
in bites. The brain is the anther, anxiety the mechanism. This is the
means by which the gleam metabolisms are arbitrary. Otherwise they
would have episodes of dirt that moan into solitude. A narcotic vanity
has but a short appetite. It is the antiseptic apparel of a dime that gets
you into life. Just as the toe propellers mount the skull, the movie goes
all incident and miscellaneous. A gas which the antlers have gathered
from quills. Harness the aviary to the calabash. Scowl the moccasin a
fish. Clobber the frontier into a newscast. The guide will bring us ferns
for Christmas. We will therefore explore the bedding unanimously.
The chromosomal indentations were easily replicated in coasters. Af-
ter dawn, we all felt the autonomy of firecrackers. An antique lambent
embarrassment recommended the use of forks. The gingko stomach
convinced everyone fecundity was the right form of tripod to use for
expressing the jewelry of letters. The minaret vanished from the um-
brage of the other guests. A radiance parachuted through the river
puddle creating salt and globules in waves. The liberality of our felicity
was its own calcification. We arranged it into verbal passports that al-
lowed us entry into yarn. Feathers for the meat, shoelaces for the
wafers. The horizon prowled the crest in tigers. The pounding of milk
furthered the kilohertz. Be it lipstick, be it a knife, there is always an
analogy to mount on the dashboard. Legislate the closet with boxes.
So many assets which invite the liability of pewter. Glint forms an-
other mince with the quench of thirst in the war laboratory. Some-
times by gliding the tallow of the globe turns specific as ethics and a
peep steams the glob of blackboard vegetation. The energy of a banana
provides a window for thought. Your rain in editions of engaging
chrome. There is a vein that hammers the flashes that fold and drinks
the similarity of maps to open a gate of further association. The map
is not the territory, but an antithesis open to the knees. A vast radial
bleat or dry television in which the goldfish are miserable and the tem-
peratures are ugly. A nose could incite such vengeance if the moccasin
had more delivery. Black is a philosophy. Yellow is a theory. Red in-

cludes the logic of green, but everything dangles from blue. The dapple of leaves in the street. Cracks and irregularities in all the sidewalks. Cuticles and cubicles and a consonant with velvet heat.

The tang of day the sway of night it is all a matter of rotation. Pile the documents on the desk and visit fortitude. We might pamper the gulp with olives of pungent attention. Blow the bamboo and begin to rocket the jackpot packed with everything cream on the basis of sculpture. It is startling to observe a gallop as an ornery way of walking. I warrant it will make you lambent and fast in the vector but the depiction will be worth it when the larger issues twist themselves into wings. So go ahead. Varnish the surface with seaplanes. The rug is pounding with combat. Daub Bach with pitch. Let all things visceral and bouncy intone adages of art and mustard. It doesn't matter if the sprig between revolution and grumbling goes attired in movement. A sprig is not a spree and a spree is not a spread. Spread the sprig with a spree and you will arrive at the postage of daybreak. Lick it. Stick it on your envelope. But don't forget to put the letter inside. You might want to fold it first. There is always time for heaven. All it takes is a few sporadic thumps on a tambourine to get there. If you think this is venturesome you should try to go behind your tongue to taste the real cocoa. Bulging like that takes practice. A sonata played in the old-fashioned way, with a Baroque parrot on your shoulder and a wilderness of feeling in your heart will cause the variables to open up and show you the kind of space that liberates wads of heat. You'll need that rampart. Don't drop it. Don't lose it. A henna dragon will never associate itself with a haddock on a belt buckle. This is why the electricity must be pounded into each line where it will pulse and drive the ornaments forward into spectral cackling. Chickens anyone can imitate in a bathroom. The heft of such insights attests to the very enclosure in which they disentangle themselves from worry. Worry is nowhere. Goes nowhere. Does nothing but causes more worry. Grip jasper. Be deliberate as a crowbar. Pry your life open. Open to overflowing. Ideas such as this need sweat and definition. Conceptions are like postcards. They show where we might be, not where we've been. Where we might be is always tantalizing. Where we might be is not a place. There is no address for that. Just glitter and pins.

The steak goes on and on yet I have worked a piece of it into the side of my mouth I have sipped water and tickled everyone. Is that a glimmer in your eye or a stratosphere? Scrubbing brings vibration decongestants or towels. To live is to cackle. But to scrub is to reach one's true potential as a polyphonic sarcophagus overlapping the choir. You can get rid of pain by stiffening into a melody based on morning. For instance: coral. To squat you must erupt into knowledge. The observation becomes grease. A nerve that shocks itself with robins. You is a position throughout the perception of painting, which is atropine. I smell atoms. Molecules congealing into Ecuador. The genius of orbiting one's autobiography shifts into burlap. What did you think this was all about? An earthquake is always original but ultimately horizontal. This gets slapped against the floor and heaved into variables. I am here to further the line. The jelly is a malady. Time sliced and spread on a gelatinous heat called language. Language is where everything happens including concepts and X-rays. Literal ups and downs a tumult of levels cracked into elephants. Can you feel the weight of them? This is my life I'm talking about. Thursday was sometimes involved, and so was Saturday, which was slightly more syntactical. Syllables held together by sprocket and chain moving atonement and reference and twine. Twine is wasps. Wilderness and dance-like bulges of women. Twinkles with postage. Concertos with bulbs. Vertebrae respectable as diamonds vibrating eternity. More time than anyone had in mind. A pulchritude understood as translucence, transformation jammed with veins. Statements that have something objective in them, like bolts and lakes. Amethyst pushed into bone so that it can jerk around and cry. Boil into Italian and sing the diffusion of fluid. Consciousness in a fetus of useful rotation.

Can blowing a shadow into catfish expand the meaning of catgut? The wind, scrubbing a style to pure equation, seeds the field with circumstance. The installment in it exposes color. Understanding resin approaches the smell of summer. It is a good thing. The wasp can flourish when the boulders bounce. Time is a beach whose brush-strokes move the ocean to slather its predications on sand. While the scenery of expansion flows with rapture the riddle of life turns subterranean. The candle must be monstrous with wax. The darkness sides with the light. It is as if a texture could work as a slap, or talon. The sky sounds furry as it orbits the eye. Space is like that, always rising, always risen, always risible. It is so orchestral that its very overture is uneasy with voices. The kind of plane that convinces an overlapping fish to prophesy mirrors. If there is a well plunged into feeling there will be graphs to lengthen its chronology. Electricity cleanses tone. Large movements that show the curriculum of the crowbar. Here is where the crocodile assumes its heat. It is heading back to pulchritude, more than ten pounds of beauty. Green will be called before the postage is tusked. There is a spiral to the deadness of dinosaur eggs that belies the arrival of guests at the hotel. The circle on the upright created a panic. It was when we were on the verge of tasting our food that we noticed some scrap lightning in the dog had begun manifesting itself as fur. In recent time this has begun to look suspiciously like poetry. A gun roiling with designs on the handle, a forest of vowels operating as worlds of flotation. This anchoring after the serpentine's facial crumpled hard in the rapid idea intended to express our sovereignty. The sonatas the eyebrow parched hinted at a daily understanding of oblivion, a morning striated with arteries stumbling over the mountains in order to obscure the night. This is when it occurred to me to ornament paper with chlorophyll so that it might thicken into theorems of wood at the base of the volcano. I was then shown the biggest camera I have ever seen and told that it might involve toast if the octagons turned political. I would rather assemble an emotion in a cage of gold than betray the denim of lifting such things into oratory. The complexity of the rose ratifies hospitality. But that's not what this is about. This is about striking a deal with reality. You go your way, and I'll go mine. Somewhere in between we might find our words trembling with similarities to things no one expected. Things like walnut. Things like oak.

The headland testimony holds the puff which hinges on resonance. The garret's symptoms will be dumped if our weight springs forward opulent and triangular as poetry. This is how we open the drawer and swallow its knives. To explore stickiness is to sip the painter's canvas. The butter is seen to be just right said Apollinaire to his peculiarities. It perturbs my personality to be fat like cash. I see through all the bouillon. Electricity's angels build an engine around the harpsichord and its rags. The doctrine is dusty and has a violent light. The conspicuous morning endeavors to push a root into fragrant understanding. The coffee is on attack. The harmonica should hold its secrets. I have brooked a finger to expand my description. It is a diversion, I know, but the tubes are a cause of fluidity. Examine this fold. What does it remind you of? I understand it is rough, but the mustard is sophisticated. Sleeve these knots for the alligator and its ecstasy of primordial brier. The swamp crawls through itself defining the essence of reeds. The painter skulks around his brush. He paints the scenery between calls and fiduciary armchairs set out on the lawn. There is a timeless harmonica in all of us. Can you feel your tide pools? Can you feel the aurora of time green and tilted in your bones? Be anarchic. Cut your stems into frames and hand us the audacity of a jaw, a mouth in movement making words come out, the tongue swimming in its windows like ink.

Instinctive came as a tricky cabbage. That is to say that a balloon doesn't herd iron so much as salve the punishment of life with suitcases. The wild epilogue faucet disavows consequence in smears a thick old steam stirs. This is why a compilation of trees will sometimes extend an oak to a mind of jungles. Nerves that provide a version of the world through five senses and a conceptual fidgeting with structure. He who brooks a throat in spots will one day choose the buckles of alchemy by stick, sawdust, and whale. The potato is meant to garnish our approval with a blow on its steam and its form of parable, which is a carbohydrate packaged in the fine skin of a shout at loss. Butter does everything else. Let's put autumn where it belongs, in a haiku, where it can absorb the universe and throb with hills. The frame is constrained to that ultimate ocean whose physiology lengthens its hiatus in fiddles. The latitude anthology shrewdly touches an appliance in elegy. Elemental perception stilts in your clumsy hibachi. An absorbed muscle the bacteria submits confirms this mutation. Go ahead and abstract that bangle you call a crystal. Spoon plaster some cubes to the amber French. The idea of squashing a giant photograph was turned mockingbird in such adjustment. If you enjoy this life, and like living on this planet, take pictures of it. But if you don't, gush the day in roots. A batch of intuition will one day pedal this bicycle forward pleading for broadcloth and a good canoe. Juggling can cure most any disease, including didacticism. The resource for this story is a tangible room of mosquitoes and flowers. Think Braque at a canvas. An area of spars to harness this paper to the spine of a parody pushing water into your world. A chord in naked music floating to the top of an opulent expansion. And what are the bleachers for, you might ask, and the blood and the blankets and pulleys and mist? The recruitment of a dream unravels the shape of a sanguine lip. The circumference of this is the yolk in the egg of verticality, which is always a narrative coffee, lamp black with a touch of cinnamon.

I am wearing the hat which has just now introverted my fingers. It impels my mood into a nebula of willingness that begins by greeting clappers and planets. The oasis has been created by a faucet of beautiful chrome, bald to the vision as the opulence of French to a tongue of steel. Its very sphere is a job to open. If we fold this genre of speaking into a paragraph we will become ravenous for dots. Seclusion is shattering my circle. The air is ablaze. Symptoms of independence are ambushed and farmed. The clash of powerful coffees transforms our extroversion to metaphorical ash. The asphalt has been respectably milked into handsprings red from potatoes. Grace to propellers. Their elegy is growling. We have painted the sound late at night on the glowing roots of a bloated punctuation. Rumor is a rascal, a bang in Céret. The flaming murmurs next to your table are bone. Only the texture of certain fibers can begin the wealth of denim. It is a private ghost that endeavors to ride the horses of prayer. Muscle a bruise into nails and the universe will tremble. There is a churning in your skull whose virtue will be realized once the sidewalk has been explored. Your thumb is laughing because the ovation is languorous. We anticipated a more photogenic snow. The latitude of our eyebrows has turned to cement. The spars of our ship are on a level of grandeur equal to the biology of birds. It is afloat in my novel now, the words carried into echoes on the sanguine back of a purposeless swan, intriguing and fat. Go ahead. Knock at the door. It is all a fantasy anyway, this constant reaching for things that are upside down, ships and lips and this enormous hypothetical hat whose brim is a replica of Dublin and whose crown is a proposal of auk.

Pasting blood to a compilation exalts the presence of heat. The tube is a parable. The dump is haunted with light. Nothingness is a fang in the arrival of night. Umber is a characteristic of earth and attracts oddities like crust and declivity. This is why the imponderable fireworks of spirit are sometimes fingered into a punching bag. The lingering lung of pink slithers into an empty can. Effervescence is intended for the conquest of clouds. Heat is overt. It must be propelled by steam. Meanwhile, oak and elm shade the fat pavement. Appliances are sometimes required for the theory of the hinge. The headland is exchanged for the color red. The ceiling is long and stirs with the chemistry of nothingness. The mud is an eye antithetical to time. The tongue is anchored in a soliciting that smooths. This is so seamlessness achieves the status of a sensation in the pamphlets of smell. Turpentine, for instance, is a hypothesis roughly suitable for the charm of stratification. The flower cab is late. But today I am a wild tonic respectful of creosote. The density of the sky is oak on the veins, a blue elixir as yet unmapped in existence. It is considered thick to feel meat. There is a sense of raising things to the surface, the smell of a sentence whose noise is a commentary on inflammation. There is an understanding that reading is a form of eating and that a Picasso inflates with the mingling of black. The ports buckle under the weight of the sun, enhancing the shine of collision. The history of space. Cubes between bruises. The taste of coffee on the morning of your birthday, which is round with glistening.

It is stunning to coast among myths. The mythology of dirt is adaptable to the shovels and trowels of sophistry. The map of insoluble fish has sticks. Corot is octagonal but the halibut are pure sculpture. The jaw that life pushes is more than mechanical. It is the roar of the robin, the scream of the orchid. Talking is but the pinned grace of a gardenia. Breakfast imbued with mirrors and trousers. The gantry of algebra hoists itself into subtleties of compelling logic. Propane stabs the sleeves of an elegant pain by the cemetery wall. The fish we put in the net had strength and odor, their dissonance washed by sheer physiology, the emotion of a scrumptious swelling. Elevate the cubes to water. Bouillon's concentration is impenetrable to the taste of the piano machines. A brush with the right sonata will make you go wild. Think of it as the extraverted beauty of a sound that has been folded and inserted in someone's wallet. It's hard to fathom the beauty of the sternum without sugar. Gambling is another form of beauty. The beauty of risk. The beauty of chance. The beauty of pink, which is tangible with desire. Silver figured in coins. Stew and wood occur by the oranges. It's a problem sucking energy out of them, but doable. Bugs go faster when the light comes on. It's an easy solution. Just about anything can be solved with a little ivory, ink, and gravity. But if you're hoping to find an epiphany among these metals, notice how variable the light is when it crashes through the window at four o'clock. We have a saying here, which is that laughter is the same as water, only a little meatier. See that door? It has been left open for a reason. The scalpel is so much more than a daydream. It has utility. These words, however, are better understood as yardarms. The tapestry of unfurling anything slightly aquatic. Perhaps even amazing. And what is more amazing than writing? Or cooking? Putting things together. Applying heat. Intestines. Ideas. Talking and melting. Folding the smell of an erratic plot into a zinnia, so that it holds parlors of ripped parameter, a slippery sky and a dollar of hurt.

Reality is never routine reality is wild. A yellow curb for delivery
trucks might be embodied in a single nerve, preserved like an inheri-
tance, a glimmer in the spine, then processed into a soliloquy heavy
with dream. Reflection leads to ovulation. Reality leads to grumbling.
Conversation, after all, is an art, even though the tongue is an absurd
idea. Reality is not a performance or a movie. You cannot get up and
leave. Our only real resource is to talk about it. Because it is crunchy,
we can pummel it with our fists, or paint it and hang it on a wall. We
can cauterize the light with an abstraction, or offer it a bowl of eye-
balls, each eyeball filled with a beautiful blue light, like the numinous
caul of blue stars surrounding the black hole in Andromeda's core. Re-
ality is flexible. Long halls of reverie snap into place with a single word.
We live a day, we die a day. If there is a blister on the heel of my left
foot, I have something to mull. Something to interpret. Something to
brandish and rock. I can watch as it becomes a slow yellow box or
soothe it with a fistful of doors. Reality is not a country. Reality is a
dragon shivering with soul. Music causes the backbone to grow vivid
and iron. This is a fact. A gargoyle riding a satellite might serve as an
uninhibited example of absorption, an antique spittle on a copper
shoe. It is the kind of thing the Beatles might have sung about. Which
proves my point. If there is a brain with a landscape in it all that ran-
dom geology is bound to come out sooner or later in the form of a tail
rotor. Predication is largely acrylic, though there are times chalk or
marble might better fulfill the dreams of an indigo glissando. Blood is
a cause of weight and identity, Walt Whitman in the kitchen wearing
a necklace of water boiling with language. That's reality. Flags are rags.
Clouds are groins. Winter rain on a tinfoil sun. You cannot fold a feel-
ing and put it in your wallet unless it is first implicated in some sense.
A sidewalk bathed in a thousand throats of light shows there is lettuce
in lattice and resin in reason. Beauty is a semantic bump on the road
to rapture. Reality gives it bounce. An egg broken on the edge of a cast
iron pan. Crackle and hiss. The sky crawling toward a hat. A chair
made of air. The world in a kiss.

The rain does not come from hypothetical neutrons but the beatitude of mass. It is neither wafer, hassock, or scalpel, but comes as commas and nickels of water. A keg of cloud in noble backflip. Incident light. Miscellaneous gleams. If the date is wrong, drag it to the horizon. There will be another waiting. Then by thread and thought the edge will fringe. Engines of milk and paper will drive the necessary diversions, the splendid spins and dips of desire. An embassy of stars had risen during the night and claimed the sky in deep immersion. A zigzag crashed around in a cage of geometry. The opacity of the marshmallow hinted at the humidity of the road. An armada of spoons occupied the drawer and jingled whenever it opened. This became a poem in which a certain kindred monster scowled in burlap. A fecund veil of sugar indicated being as a gateway. But a gateway to what? And why a gateway? Why not a door? Or a word? A blessing or a curse? Something that rhymes with hearse? The brain is a numenal faucet. A taxi pounding its millipede of daily impediment. You know what I mean. A romantic bowl of purple dye and a tube of lipstick in the green room of a giant apprehension. Ophelia donning her makeup. Light this candle. Tell me how it looks. Does the light bounce on the walls as if inhabited by spirits? I have a theory that December is more than just a yearning, more than just a rectangle of time hanging on the wall with the usual picturesque mountains and sleighs. It is a measure of air infiltrated by boughs of heavy snow. A filtration of light in which a certain enchantment points to the velvet of midnight. The solstice of our toils. Our comedy all propeller and cherry. Minerals and swords in a bivouac of ladled reconciliation. The scintillating snow. Breath on a window. The wide mad whirl of the universe.

Life is incurable. Hundreds of words move in and out of me. Each one is a ferocious piece of energy. My neck is a tunnel of clouds. My nose is a pastime. My ears are waterfalls. I have a Jackson Pollock belt buckle and a cricket cantata hairdo. There is a jewel of energy boiling in my leg and a fat black spider crossing a dried cracked riverbed. When I was a kid I was curious about wrinkles and now I have a few. I have given them names. Names like Alice and Henry, Philip and Sue. I sleep in a toolbox. People think I'm a wrench, but I'm actually a landscape. I can crawl into a song by Bob Dylan and come out the other side looking like a forest plunged in winter, or a jukebox holding a fistful of stars. I love being underwater and moving through it like a garden of arteries, a fluid in a fluid, though this has nothing to do with linoleum, or declension. Abstraction is a framework for deerskin. Diamonds, frogs, and blood. There are days when everything eludes definition, and days when everything reeks of realism. I believe Mahler tastes of olives and yearning, and that tinfoil is from the fourth dimension. There are things I can do and there are things I cannot do. Fear is a prison. Wind is wide. I can tie water in knots and waltz the skeleton of a cloud. I can lean the ocean against a predicate in the scrotum of a moose and nail a drop of perfume to a blister of light. All men know the utility of useful things, observed Chuang Tzu, but they do not know the utility of futility. There is nothing so sad as a gas station in the dead of night.

A bathrobe annihilated by sparks pushes bliss to a new beauty. Automatic butter all over the emergency. Borders created by jewelry, one shoulder all gold. Which is why the limousine's tarnished bumper has a hearth in it. There is a delivery about the cypress imbued with mirth. You like September since its hormones intrigue this thought. A white database to enhance the echo of pink. Analyze its glimmers that happen for omelettes. The wedge began by dripping up the industry of hope, then awakened the adrenaline of incentive. So speeds the wet rope through its television of watermelon analysis. It is as if seeds were some form of question. A calculus in colonies is hardly clappers. A kangaroo history incites by truck and scoop. Cue sticks permeate pool however there is anything variegated or chest. Ventilate had scabbards between while tarpaulins talk the mind. The bivouac that vases for open hums, the Wednesday that is incidental to the vestige of an apple. It is just a soar born from a fern and its shapely inducement to noon. Put this fire on the floor and quell it with energy. You might try dancing the washcloth without always marinating the reverie. Another thump in the arm to quarter an epicurean. Beaten by velour, the appellate court is haunted by its judgments. It is a sign that bedding the elbow has a day to become a letter. Peach to everything including the stomach of the giraffe. It is similar to churning flags with the thunder nature has given us to bleat into black. A felon studying the radius of a ticket anticipates the zenith surrounding the perfume of a ghostly cast. Heart and kneecap are engines in then. The delirium happens to an amphitheatre before spreading through the radar of a noble engraving. Goldfish lambent from mince push the amenity toward its apotheosis in beets. A quiet weave then enveloped the dawn. Scrawl a temperament on paper and score such happenings throughout the laughter of a curved jonquil. It is gastric to stomach the lemonade of zeppelins. An apricot forehead exposes the camaraderie that obliges us to shake hands. This is how the penny has blunted the bank. The jackpot is not in the hassock. The jackpot is ductile. The jackpot is in sealing the future with the salt of the past.

The steaming nexus that is my assembly had begun to percolate because that is what words do. They glimpse a higher reality. The climate is unanimous. That is their stride. If the wolf is misinterpreted the ample energy that is teak is not. The same firearm has a dashing voice. It is honest how batons yaw into calamity. A gerund once felony grows bleary with birth. The exposure waxes scarab during the bulb's moan. Yap your photograph to pathos. The kettledrum has many rhythms that danger bites into omelettes. What is life on a democratic escalator? Is it just a pond? The yarn is done with blowing and has been inveigled by language. Henna sits on the verge of nobility. The zip code bench is indulged as a forehead. During the investigation the entire paragraph turned vapid and sprawled into labyrinths of autocratic quill. There is a market for this, though perhaps not on earth. Perhaps on some other plane where sugar is more fully appreciated for what it is, and what it is not. Show it a pea and the brain begins to bleed in rice and tranquility. The hiss in that parable indicates a new revelation, a dirt canoe all curlicue and embarrassment. If you think this is metaphorical you may be right. The racket has been packed in tangerines and the pepper grows long as a limousine. Cage bronze in reconciliation. An incipient fedora on the head of a blaze. An apricot is more immersion than cane. Glaze on a goldfish. Ginseng in an English garden. The flavors in the cauldron gathered in a single tongue of unmediated speculation. Sip this dashboard. Tell me the harbor is not filled with bleach. We haggle over batteries yet turn profligate as dolphins when it comes to beans. The river is epicurean. It flows through the nerves with the liberal stealth of a renaissance tiger. Will our hysteria ever be explored? Will we one day raise millipedes on Mars? When will we grind the millennium to vermicelli? Knead this pasta to instant vegetation? A dent in the syntax twists into January. We demand talismans. We receive perspective. We demand jokes, and receive laws haunted by Christmas.

Because the tailgate has the same opacity as yearning it should occupy a place in one's hormones as an injunction to paint locution with a deeper scarlet than what appears in an omelette embarrassed by its own flamboyance. Or would you rather blacken from the umbilicus aviary? The beet is easily enough beaten by its own lack of feathers. Jiggle the lever to bone that. The bronze behavior of such ventilation is combustible by dollops of correlation. I mean, that's what this is about, n'est-ce pas? Peep at the avocado on your wedding night if you don't believe me. The vegetation of such a statement grows systematically bitter unless it is watered by the attention of someone's eyes as they travel through these sentences seeking the auxiliary lung, no doubt, of a long silver spoon. The felon has invaded his own octopus. Some of the holes are ferns. And there is at least one unassuming leg to stand on while the other leg does a jig. Whenever you are in such a rough situation you should rely on pliers, not just sit there and beep your horn. Lick the breath of some reveille, some hair-raising scallop crawling over the chain of a torpid truth. That reptile can blow scalpels. I have seen it before. Once in Bali, and once in Ohio, during an election year. You cannot quench cheese with a flagstone. The tea is operable by this incident fold you call a snout. Breathe in. Breathe out. This is how we attend the blood jamboree. We play a ukulele of moss and glide through the scenery as if it were the landscape of some long forgotten song, some scant meaningful remnant of venerable standing resurrected in someone's mouth, if only for an instant. Until we have more wealth let us continue our singing in the basement. The omelette's dent would tend to indicate such a decision as prudent, if not the onyx necessity of a chapter on minuets nailed to the coma of a deeply flawed color. A habitation, say, in a pea. The yak standing at the frontier of a kaleidoscope. Let us dart through a washcloth mingling spoon and pound as if the anthology that comprised our mutual lives were one day mince, one day tangerine. John Keats striding across the Bahamas. Note the kite he has fashioned of copper, and the velvet of his gloom. Hardware has its inclement forms but its sweeter utilities as well. Faucets, pantomime and washers. Ampersands for the pecan and yarn for the steam rising from the apostrophe of the doorknob.

That gate of glass we all recognize as feeling, if not the very emotion of a freshly peeled banana. The rhythm for this has not yet been invented, but a few of us are working on it, hanging our perceptions from gearshifts, and making ourselves available to the stars.

Chew ink. Chew ink because it is ugly not to. Chew ink because prepositions are bleak without embroidery. Chew ink because rumination calls for pen and paper. Chew ink because pixels are commas in a universe of night. Lessons of parallelism bubble from the hardware. There is a grimace in the glockenspiel. A radius that echoes everything with scenery. Each tree is an episode, a story told in limbs, a parable of leaves. Onyx crackles on the surface of a moan. Radishes begin the beauty of dirt. The perpetual beauty of letters which scorch the silence and boil in hypothesis. Pushing is combustible if it jets tapioca. Wednesday nags Thursday on its tripod of time and putty. Pathos lies in tangles. The temperature of reconciliation cajoles the rhetoric of weight. A barrel tumbles down the road. Our elbows articulate the spectacle of our arms. If the snow has an amperage, it is because each bug has a skull. The geography of the lurid indicates a return to newsprint. Reading is like walking only it is performed with the eyes instead of the legs. It is more natural to walk on the eyes when the way is paved with pennies. I prefer mustard to ketchup because mustard is a sign of vegetation and ketchup is slow as winter. We stride through the hardware store believing in purpose and labor. Our chins indulge gargantuan beards. The radio emits a species of knapsack gouache that is impossible to describe without calliopes and clover. Each word is an apparatus for the highway of imagination. We are to inhabit these things alone, but with other people, who live alone, and travel in groups, and use hemoglobin to enfranchise the use of scissors when the bureau spirals through its walls and we lift a spoon of quartz for the declamation of liquid. The ultimate grout wagon runs on the antifreeze of a sigh. Redemption begins with cleats. The tiger sleeps below our act. The scene grows blatant. We rattle quintessence from signs and knowledge from ghosts. Chew ink. Chew ink because it is wanton. Warm and reckless and quick to think.

I'm going to construct a machine which lactates tinfoil. The luggage has gotten cold and haphazard and I need a few ferns for the leopard exhibit. Pole vaulting has never been my usual practice and my perceptions are predisposed toward filigree. There is only a small vestige left of my previous kingdom. Even the heat is antique. We have to decorate our drugs with Florida. Each scratched dolphin hides a melody in his heart. The lightning is consonant with the stains of our appetite. Many of the autopsies have revealed the minerals of an antiseptic nirvana. An appellate light trickles throughout our calculus which is why our emotions radiate a deep comedy of lures and renegades. I have become smooth with savage ideals and bring medicine and hardware to the actor's guild. I'm fascinated by the femininity of zeppelins. Pintos are another matter. Language, I believe, is catastrophically portable. I have nailed some apparitions to a dead clam in order to demonstrate the imperfections of rain. I have also raised the heat. My next machine will be a sonnet for the poetry industry. I have a jar filled with highways and a barn full of rhymes. There is a wraith of mist above the fjord. It is so beautiful that the comic from the casino stands on the shore incessantly drooling. All we need now are hoes, mittens, and silverware. December is immersed in ornaments. There is a ghost standing at the end of the dock. He says he is someone's father and wants revenge. Go tell him breakfast is ready. Everywhere I go I carry a cactus and a cave. I have a suitcase packed with scraggly, misbegotten perceptions which I plan to shatter into prescient, insightful paragraphs. I will donate these to the Community for the Preservation of Wordy Epitaphs. My next invention will be a taillight so blurred with vision we will feel an overwhelming urge to paint the forklifts green. This is also why I carry a library voice close to my chest and continually comb it with a peppery curriculum of irreconcilable fedoras and Dusty Springfield songs. I have catalogued each box by size and volume and filled them with Elizabethan screwdrivers and landslides bloated with gravity. In the morning, people pour out of the nightclubs holding their bellies with laughter. All the olives can do is hang there like bells and register the arrival of noon with mute bravado. The same goes for the oboes. The flavor of trigonometry is supple as thermodynamic turquoise. Bowls of beautiful beans. It is in such manner that I arrive at the phenomenon of ignition. To begin anything is simply to begin. But to end something is never quite so simple. There has to be a sense of perpetuity, and perversity and pies and a logarithmic trampoline. This is my machine. This is what it will do. And not do. It will not kill, or appease the powerful with lies. But it will blaze like hair, and howl ineffable melodies among the evergreens.

A dawn is anything moss. We dawdle among the mechanisms on the boulevard holding peas of reality, black screwdrivers in our beams. Christmas feels like a scarf in the fog. You can engender a storm easily by holding the warm eye of a firecracker. That red rag over there is an avalanche of folds with a bug on it. I have taped a candle to the elevator so that when the veils of illusion lift we will be able to see ourselves in globules of yellow incense. We are at war with data. Handshakes bounce around on the floor limpid and tall and vast with fingers. We are in a realm of enchantment. We are taut with perpendicularity. I welcome your eyes among these words. These words will lead your eyes to the end of this sentence where an honest reticence will unfold in humidity revealing a system of misinterpretations and fjords. Molecules, habits, and straw. Names whose sounds are surrounded by ink. Imbued with the bruise of description. There is a big difference between tea and coffee. Between a commercial bank and an investment bank. Perhaps it is apparent by now that I am writing this during a time of great financial insecurity. This is why we give names to experiences. If the sound of something travels up and down the spine it could eventually weigh as much as a jade perception. A yardarm whose sail has just been unfolded, tumbling down in a cascade of incipient flaps. We're on our way now. Going where, I don't know. There are laws, and there are roads. Roads do not always follow laws and laws do not always follow roads. The music of the present tense juggles vast quilts of hectic eternity. Some ideas are too nebulous to be considered as thought. They drift among the woodwinds attenuated and sweet. A little espresso clings to the bottom of the demitasse. Reading becomes honey, a slow contemplation of light as it passes through a medium of lassitude, a latitude cathartic as foam. Skeletons honored by the truth of linoleum. Remember the way floors used to look? The many swirls? The many cracks and stains? This is how meaning builds on a sheet of paper. This is where reveries are lurid as the pulse of the wrist. Where the borders are uncertain. Where the skin itself is a revelation. Where everything is permitted. Where all is forgiven. Where mass is mass and moss is anything green in the mist.

Reality goes against the gauntlet while a parachute of water assumes the madcap shapes of a fish. I use my nose to persuade the indignation of falling that the anvil is laborious and this is how a nail gets percussion. I need salt. Quarters for the Laundromat and a grotto for my antifreeze. The clamp is ugly as it drops through the scar to get painted in lettuce by daybreak. I pounded the tart into an apple again. The gravel behind your velvet immersion heats the incisions that fringe the jukebox. Thank you. My passion is shaped like a paradigm in velvet. The zinnia is mapped with data until it becomes an octopus. The apparition of a melody shines like nickels in a mound of kelp kindred to the doors of perception bursting with paradise. Somewhere between these thoughts is a reticent sunlight cracking a calabash while the snow falls on some misbehavior no one bothers to photograph. There is a swamp rattling around in the jukebox I can hear it come singing out of the speaker in chains of lambent music and I go all demure and cheesecloth just to pinch it in theory. That light has a bandage, the one we call Jackpot. The gloom of a midnight pharmacy remains immersed in its opinions. Persistence is chemical. There is no barometer for chaos. We must veil our cleats with revival. We need to talk. The thermometers are mirrored in the water as it twists around the subject. There is an anxiety lying around on the floor but no one bothers to tell us. A metaphor hugs an oak. August is the most autonomous of months because it is not tattooed the same way as the dust. Its noise is not like fireworks. It never causes snow. It is always hot. The sugar between our glands cajoles the forks. Our calculus is naked. Our memories are supple. Our intuition gargles the anachronism of cheddar. May you carry a scraggily highway when the apocalypse comes. The library is bitter yet open to its own vapory quintessence. This is the place we should be. This place of quiet where the clouds are done raising themselves and all of our emotions glisten from rain, tall and sinewy as apocryphal combs.

I can yank the day open with a pull on the Christmas curtain. Tarpaulins may, during redemption, increase our understanding of vision. Broth is fuel. You should drink as much as possible. Or would that be eat? Does one drink broth or eat broth? Or both? Every medicine I have known bursts in the body and turns to pathos. Some things just need to be shoveled. Think about kiwi. Think about napkins. The tactics emotions require in order to bring them into alignment with your clothing. A blazer, for instance, or shirt annealed to the skin like ebony. Our ankles might begin our blood in eternity, but it is exquisite to see how the gingko cooks itself into the noon of a beckoning blackboard. Arm yourself with memories. Cherries that attend to their own cleavage. The hemoglobin of clerks. The chemistry in our haggles with the world. The chemistry turning to blister and bulb. The chemistry of digestion. A stomach full of scallops that acts handled between the melodies of a nervous anachronism. I get ephemeral from this. I get so I enjoy silver more, and avocados and hardwood. I tend to favor objects that resemble globes. I like to write such things because the fetus to say so is pink in its paroxysms like words tinkled in the arbitrary holes of an Elizabethan sonnet. This causes sauce and seething and varnish. The many things of this world that tend to rhyme in substance. The many things of this world that defy understanding. The many things of this world that attack for no reason. That turn scarlet. That perplex the engineer. That vaunt the visible world. That bracket themselves in the brain. And abide the hands. And vivify perspective. And dazzle the waves. These are the things I like to put into words. Because words defer certainty to speculation. Which is the jelly of dragons. And the essence of calm.

THE POEM SEARCHES FOR SOME ALTERNATIVES TO RABIES

> I wish to write such rhymes as shall not suggest a restraint,
> but contrariwise the wildest freedom.
> —Ralph Waldo Emerson

The decorum of the zipper is a syntax of cosmic deutzia. Pull yourself out of yourself and show the world what you are made of: blood and bone and a thousand anxieties that dazzle the mind with idioms of silver. That scream for lamé. Pretty noises of pretty chemistry strain to boil our consonants into henna, for the retina is a pool for the tinctures of variation. Energy triumphs by nasturtium. The bank is an example of strata. You need to get outside more often. There is wealth in breath. Delirium in dirt. Mimicry in squid. You must tape your throat to the air and induce it to sing. We live in an age of feeling created by glittery objects. Forget glittery objects. Emotion should be like an egg, words repudiating their meaning in order to regain their meaning, win back remnants of vernacular candor. Meaning should cohere in opposition to the perversity of mirrors. It should stroll around a little, turn, saunter, promenade, like a woman modeling a dress of white satin as Yves Saint-Laurent looks on with a look of rapt attention. It is a moment of wild beauty because there is still tension, the electric disequilibrium of creation before it has attained the balance of completion, the summation of a hem or the flourish of a pen. No one writes with quills anymore. We use crabs. Ballpoints and kerosene. Torches. Wedlock. Alphabets curious as scabs. We need to declare ourselves with the amplitude of autumn, the clarity of winter, the enigmas of spring, the sumptuous juices of summer. It is gleeful to perch on a telephone wire. Do that. Do it until you are black-and-blue. Do it in your shoes. Do it with cake. With bluster. With expulsion. With papyrus and grommets. With caissons. Do it in a lake. Everything gets wet eventually. A lamp is more than its light. It is also a leopard enhanced by the ecstasy of iron. The worst thing in the world is to feel one has to hide one's feelings. This is not warmth. This is servitude. I want a language of dispersion. Absorption, assimilation, swerve and discrepancy. Christmas should be against the law.

The question was born in an elevator, but it was too big for anyone to ask. Everyone felt tarnished by time. Sometimes we used parrots, or the color violet, to communicate our deeper needs, things with which we were too encumbered to say with chalk. Dense scarlet bleachers opened us to unspeakable possibilities. I wrapped a bulb in a flannel shirt and burned the rest of my clothes among the ferns. Feeling chemicals put reality in its place. I bicycled to the end of a jetty and felt the cold wind declare itself on my face. Are beans vegetables? Is medicine an argument with nature? Can photographs be displayed on the radio? The embarrassments of eternity are steep, like a belt of stars, and the xylophones are beaten into life with little red hammers. Vaudeville lobsters quadrille through a ballad of hair. Ecstasy invades a taxi. The earthquake tool turns blue in the water. The air is twisted into mirrors. Their reflections turn brittle and dry, like roadside curiosities. My temperament drools all over the ink. My thesis becomes a fury of outrageous similarities. Gigantic eggs hatch in an alphabet of iron. The rain becomes gritty and inconvenient. We hear a crunch crunch crunch in the kennel. Our blood retaliates by hoisting the autobiography of an X-ray through our bones. Our bad bad bones. The nobility of our backs. Our lavish strides. Our critical scores. Our gourds and crocodiles. It is all so easy. So easy to forget. So easy to remember. Yet none of us can ask. Bring ourselves to say it. Scrape it, cut it, let it all out. Out in the open. Where even the slightest sound can appear scarred with its own history.

The separate opening is a pulse realized in writing. It is a malady we can endure for a while because it modifies our spoons. Still Cézannian, those sonatas exploded out of the brook to bolt themselves to our excursion. It all aspires to be how the banana rises in hyperbola to do its style. The atoms of a harpsichord are little more than clucks until they are written as rhythms of fat lightning. Five are similar to fiber. The play shows how their analogous hammers make dishevelment glitter. Attitude shapes these bagatelles into sculptured bamboo. A face shaped like a cactus. An overlapping tone of wetness, or augmented coo. Toss you. Engage yourself on the atomic contrapuntal. Attempt being. And volume. Not the least clavier is squeezed by the derricks. Use geometry. It is larger to be a stem than a stencil. Or a section of chocolate in a mosaic of mathematical probabilities. Never pat a lyrical surface. It is a cold bag of rain. A perception of harmonies too big for culture but fine for altitude. Two fingers based on a cello. It is but a way to invent yourself as an involuntary rising, or introductory verse. A turning toward, or a turning away from. In a pinch, the pattern of a buggy. Or all of this in a corner correlating to paste. The cloud, overwhelmed by movement, stretches into a furious wraith. The irregularities in the elms are a dimension of scale. So tell me: which dimension is thin, which dimension is fat and slow? The non-Euclidean window has brought us chimerical views. But what I really want to talk about are cherries. How bright they are. How sweet. How touching on cherries brings nature into the picture. The big world wiggled in the wheeze of the weather. Charity, charm, and a cherry hung with snow.

PREPOSITIONS

for Claude Royet-Journoud

Prepositions are olives bouncing on a hardwood floor. A compass needle trembling as it points north. Of in of. The trembling of a reflection in a glass of wine. In of in. The thread of a thought in a fabric of mind. Prepositions are between themselves in pantomime. Prepositions are the mud of proverbs. Prepositions are the algebra of myth. When prepositions are spun from fiddlesticks they become discriminating and tangible and war is broken over bread. Prepositions are revelatory as a house. Language is a machine and prepositions are oil. Poise in the gaze of an animal. The glow of its eyes at night. Prepositions mirror the vanity of invention. Vowels voluminous as bowls. Consonants kinky as pine. This is why prepositions culminate in structure. They sleep in the weave of a cloth wrapped around a Montmartre jug. Prepositions baked in a mouth are tremulous with luminance and magnetic flux. Prepositions pull the delicacy of interrelation through substantive and verb. The luster of potentiality is nucleated in the leathery grip of morning. This is where prepositions hook the crackle of hope to an ancient phonograph of rosewood tones. I inhabit this mood like a soft blue glow. There is a jukebox in the room. I am sitting on a chair. This is the story of prepositions. This is the progress and reach of prepositions. The bubble and squeak of prepositions. Here is a sentence manipulating the sound of things. The silence between agates. The sky below. The ground above. Water dripping from a mimosa. Bob Dylan driving an Escalade. Sophia Coppola in a red Stetson. Bill Murray on a twilight spin in a strawberry golf cart in Stockholm. A man with a clipboard looking for grace. A preposition crackling with limitless space. A preposition welding a whirl of verbs to a web of nouns. A preposition is a pivot. Symmetry in a feather. The vagaries of weather. A book on bark. A book on song. In and on and under and within. Up and down and in between. Prepositions bend the world into being. The prosceniums of belong. The puttering of along. The quiver of with the rub of among.

The first punch sent me flying into a Christmas tree. The second put me on the floor on my hands and knees, blood dripping from my nose. I tumbled outside, caught a train to North Dakota, and went to college. I listened to Bob Dylan. I went to California. I got high on LSD. I flew apart on LSD. I reassembled myself. I went north to Seattle. I worked at Boeing. Boeing was dark and boring. I quit Boeing. I went back to California. I lived in a bus. I got called to the army induction center to go fight in Vietnam. I told them I was gay. They let me go.

I went north to Humboldt County. Everything smelled like burning wood. I watched the bottoms of clouds burn red with sawmill smoke. I consorted with Wordsworth, Keats, and Shakespeare. I inoculated myself with Blake. I lived in a trailer in back of a Mexican restaurant. I lived in a hotel. I went to San Jose one summer. I met a woman. I got married. I got divorced.

I went north again to Seattle. I got a job in a hospital. I rode up and down on an elevator. I delivered IV stands, surgical trays, anti-embolism stockings, diabetes socks, cervical pillows, catheters, exam gloves, commodes, consultation coats and spin hematocrits. I quit that job and got another job in a mailroom. I ran mail, sorted mail, weighed mail, maneuvered mail, threw mail, shuffled mail, delivered mail, collected mail, traced mail, dispersed, disposed, and processed mail. I did this for nineteen years. I began to hate mail. I got drunk a lot. I met a woman in the mailroom. I got married to the woman I met in the mailroom. I got divorced from the woman I met in the mailroom. The woman in the mailroom kicked me out of the house and began life with a Guatemalan who liked gardening.

I continued to work in the mailroom but began to live my life elsewhere. Existence is elsewhere.

I quit working in the mailroom. I met a woman who writes poetry. This made everything in life easier. Easier to be alive. We got married at the top of a hotel with all our friends. We rode pintos to the moon.

One day I noticed I was still living and so made room for another paragraph. I had room for a paragraph but nothing to put in it yet. And so the paragraph is not quite yet a separate thing from my life. It is a membranous organ. It is amorphous and void. I am free to invent whatever I want to put in it. Sometimes this fills me with panic. But then I sit down to eat a doughnut. Calm returns. I sip some coffee. I eat a banana. I eat an orange. I find a paring knife in the drawer and peel away the upper and lower poles of the orange. Then I make slices. Lacerations from pole to pole. Juice comes out. My fingers get wet. I peel the skin away. I separate the juicy chunks of orange and eat them. This could be a paragraph in the process of acquiring a text. This could be a life. The life of a man eating an orange. The life of a man finishing an orange and cleaning a plate. The life of a man staring at a plate. The life of a man wondering what to do next.

FORTY-TWO THINGS I DO DURING THE DAY (MORE OR LESS)

Make coffee. Drink coffee. Calculate the trajectory of a word through a sentence of delinquent apparitions. Get a handle on life. Buy a jack-knife. Get dressed. Get undressed. Live a little. Die a little. Lavish analysis on the power of brown and gold in Rembrandt's *Philosopher in Meditation*. Play with the cat. Tend to my wounds. Open doors. Close doors. Watch YouTube. Describe the taste of archaeology in a perverse opinion. Make things up. Lament the inherent gloom of copper. Repair something, orthopedic sole or cast iron pan. Write a letter. Take a shower. Brush my teeth. Brush my hair. Shave. Watch the news. Perform an autopsy on a dead emotion. Blow my nose. Hold the world in contempt. Draw a dwarf. Make a bubbling sound. Ponder a pomegranate. Play a trick on reality. Interrogate a table. Flow. Flounce. Flourish. Palpate a pillow. Take a nap. Map infinity. Evolve into a large, fanlike leaf. Avoid golf. Emulate grapes.

Adjust the temperature. If it is hot you may open the front window a little. It slides easily. If it is cold, there is a thermostat in the living room facing east, and a thermostat in the bedroom, facing west.

Ponder existence.

Think about forklifts. And whippoorwills and whirlpools and silk.

Rub your hands with Corn Husker Lotion. Think about corn. Think about lotion. Think about Spencer Selby in Iowa.

Play with the cat, but don't let him bite you. He thinks biting is fun. Try to convince him that biting is not fun. Not fun for you. Because your skin breaks easily and blood comes out. You can tell him that if you want to but I can't guarantee that he will be able to digest your words and translate them into anything meaningful. If he continues to bite you, make a sound of pain and get up and walk away. This may convey an idea of displeasure. Though it may also hurt his feelings and cause him to bite you harder the next time he sees an opportunity to sink his teeth into you while you're petting him. Don't be fooled by the purring. It is a ruse. And watch your feet, if they are bare. He loves to dive at your feet. And bite.

Write. Write anything you want. It won't matter. Hardly anyone reads anymore.

Read a book. We have lots of books. We love to read. Reading is paradise. There is no bottom to it. It is fathomless. It goes on forever. Reading is an infinite pleasure. The worlds are glittery and enchanting and sometimes bloody and full of clashes of steel but the conflicts and ideas and landscapes and fruits are delicious in description and no batteries are required. A book, unlike an iPod, has a magnitude of sensuality that will dazzle your fingers with the antithesis of gum.

Paper, after all, is soft and talks to one's fingers in velvety Portuguese.

Watch French television. Watch Sylvie Vartan sing "Locomotion" on YouTube. Watch Lulu sing "Shout." Watch Janis Joplin sing "Ball and Chain" at the Monterey Pop Festival in June, 1967.

Watch Edith Piaf sing "Non, je ne regrette rien."

Watch Rebekah Del Rio sing "Llorando."

Grieve for the death of the sixties. Get mad at Bob Dylan for doing a Cadillac Escalade commercial.

Take a nap on the couch.

Eat a graham cracker.

Vacuum the carpet.

Do the first thing that comes to your mind.

Invent a holiday.

Lie on the floor and stare at the ceiling.

Lend your ears to the quiet mysteries of everyday life.

Identity is a mysterious and cumbersome business. No one truly finds out who they are because they are continually changing. Literally: hair, size, weight, age, gonads, wrinkles, tattoos, and the baptism of daily experience. Everything, right down to one's hormones and cuticles, is in constant change. Literature is full of this. It is a primary theme. Transformation is the pivot about which many narratives turn.

I was fortunate to grow up during a time when identities in general, the collective identity of American youth, were going through a change of astronomical proportions. The traditional roles of the staid *Ozzie and Harriet*, *Leave It to Beaver*, and *Father Knows Best* variety had been discarded. Young people wanted something different from life than serenity and moderation. No one was sure what they wanted or who they really wanted to be or even if being someone were really all that attractive to begin with. Maybe it was better to lose oneself in Europe or India in a quest for the ultimate elsewhere. There were mythologies available for these ruptures called albums. Rock groups held the key to the most adventuresome personal narratives possible.

"LPs were like the force of gravity," writes Dylan in *Chronicles: Volume One*. "They had covers, back and front, that you could stare at for hours." And stare I did. Each album provided another clue to rock 'n' roll's most elusive identity. Who was this guy? Was he a musician or a poet? A joker or a wizard? A shaman or a huckster? A dada clown or a beatnik desperado? Was he kidding? Was he serious? Was life a joke? Sometimes he was full of meaning, sometimes he laughed at meaning. Often, he could be as anarchic and silly as he was passionate and personal, all in the same song. No one until then had produced a sound as lyrically complex and strange as Dylan. He was like a one man psychedelic circus. Elvis Presley, Chuck Berry, Little Richard, The Shirelles, Mary Wells, all the pop stars of the early '60s were easy to comprehend. They were all about fun and parties and dancing and being cool. The Beatles, The Rolling Stones, The Who, were a little more mysterious. They dressed in velvet and lace like the Regency dandies during the time of Keats and Shelley and produced a music that was far more nuanced and lyrical than it had been since the inception of rock 'n' roll. This was all incredibly new and strange. But Dylan was leagues weirder than these people. He occupied a domain of creativity that had no discernable limits or boundaries at all. His volatility seemed almost preternatural, a negative that never produced the same print. Each time a new album appeared, we saw a new mask, a fresh disguise. And as I listened to the music, I would become utterly absorbed in the images on the front and back: Dylan by a motorcycle, Dylan strolling down a street with a cute young woman, Dylan perched on a couch. Dylan solemn, Dylan pensive, Dylan puckish, Dylan cordial and grinning. Who, indeed, was this guy?

"Not since Rimbaud said 'I is an other' has an artist been so obsessed with escaping identity," wrote Ellin Willis some years ago about Dylan. "His masks hidden by other masks, Dylan is the celebrity stalker's ultimate antagonist." The word 'antagonist' is apt; Dylan's relationship with fame has been a contentious one. Most of all, he hated the label "voice of a generation" applied to him. Labels like this are toxic to creativity. It is no wonder Dylan has tried in numerous ways to wriggle free of these tags.

But I believe Dylan's capricious latitude with identity goes much deeper, and relates to something Marcel Proust observed, which is that "our self is made of a superimposition of successive states." These states are not stable like the stratifications of a mountain, but shift and switch constantly, so that older images sometimes rise to the surface. No identity, in other words, is ever a complete, unchanging portrait, but a continuous work in progress. Dylan does not have a monopoly on disguise. It is not even a matter of disguise. It is a matter of creativity. "He not busy being born is busy dying," observed Dylan.

"One of the most misleading representational techniques in our language is the use of the word 'I,'" observed Ludwig Wittgenstein. It is a slippery pronoun. What does it refer to? If I say, in this instance, that 'I' refers to the person typing these words, the person who is thinking about these words and putting these words together, the person who is occasionally gazing out of the window, and feeding the cat, and checking the washing machine, and worrying about the world economy, and wondering what old age will be like, and what dying will be like, assuming I am not hit by a truck, or shot by a mugger, or killed in a car accident, what it will it be like to slowly disappear, melt away into oblivion, but not be able to experience it, because I won't be there to experience it, and this is who I am at the moment, these are my most immediate experiences, my most immediate references to this pronoun, this strange entity called 'I,' then you have at least a sketchy idea of what 'I' refers to. But without knowing a lot of other things, my sex and age, my history and attitudes, my preference in clothing, my state of hygiene, the word 'I' will remain inchoate, a disheveled potentiality floundering about to create an appreciable individuality, put some muscle and skin on this slippery pronoun 'I,' a face and a decent set of clothes.

The word 'I' is never complete, never fully present to the reader. Not unless I write reams of information about these things, and fill your mind with all my likes and dislikes, details about my hair and eyes and weight and physiognomy. My vital statistics, as they say.

But this says nothing about moods. Moods color our personality from day to day, minute to minute. Some people have a tendency to bring out our good side, some people our bad. There is no calculus to help guide us through our day. Nor would it much matter if such a thing were possible. Emotions tumble around in us like pieces of glass in a kaleidoscope. One minute we smile, the next we are flipping someone off. Who can say "I am this" (i.e. patient, understanding, astute, discerning, thoughtful, reasonable, etc.) and make that last for an entire day? Who has felt completely at ease with themselves for any appreciable amount of time? Who has not wondered at least once during the course of a day, "why did I do that? why did I say that? I can't believe I did (said) that."

Odd, that a word so thin, so measly, so tentative can mean such an infinite variety of things. It is pivotal, yet elusive. Convenient, yet inadequate.

I am charmed by the movie *Prelude to a Kiss* in which a vibrant but pessimistic Meg Ryan switches identity with an old and very ill man on her wedding day. It takes her husband Alec Baldwin very little time to discover that the bride he has taken on a honeymoon to Jamaica is not the woman he thought he married. As the days pass, he is able to follow enough clues to discover his true bride in the body of the old man, sitting disconsolately in a booth at the bar where she worked as a barmaid. What a spectacular notion this is: that one's true self is immaterial and separate from our body. That our most essential being will always be evident to those who truly know and love us no matter how we look or what body we happen to occupy at the time. As if our body were some form of vehicle, car or boat or truck that carried us around, or that we lugged around like heavy baggage. "A tattered coat upon a stick," sang Yeats, "unless/ Soul clap its hands and sing, and louder sing/ For every tatter in its mortal dress."

Perhaps it's not such a coincidence that Yeats and Meg Ryan are both Irish.

It is a romantic dream, this Platonic notion of an essential self haphazardly represented by the flesh it inhabits, as if no matter which body we might happen to have been born into we would still be the irrepressible individual that we are. But imagine you should wake up one day as a cockroach, would you still be you? Kafka gives this dream a nice little twist. What if that loathsome, craven self inside our body transforms our body into its hideous actuality?

Or what if we present to the world the image of a feckless, drunken rogue in order to disguise our truer identity as a severe, highly disciplined monarch which will emerge one day to the astonishment of everyone around us? Such is the idea Shakespeare presented in the form of Prince Hal whose antics with the fat, roguish old man Falstaff and his band of ne'er-do-wells were abruptly and cruelly severed by the end of *Henry IV Part II*. The whole point of Henry's escapade appears to have been to make himself shine all the more brightly when he doffed his former guise and emerged as a true monarch. But there was another benefit to this, which had to do with acquiring an intimate acquaintance with the people of the kingdom he would one day rule, getting an immediate, unvarnished glimpse of life as it was truly lived in the taverns and streets of medieval London. The ruse worked brilliantly, and one cannot help but think that Henry's guise was not altogether artificial but showed an aspect that was a true part of his overall identity.

No single identity is a ever single identity.

We contain millions.

One of the greatest difficulties in life is learning to live comfortably with the hodgepodge of contradictory selves we amalgamate in our bodies. We all have a clear idea about the person that we want to be. But that path is not easy to follow. It is full of twists and tangled branches.

A lot of us live under the domination of the kind of person our parents and teachers wanted us to be. The lucky ones get away from that. As for me, speaking entirely for myself, thank god for rock 'n' roll. Had it not been for the subversive energy of rock I may not have liberated myself from the kind of roles American culture had preordained for young men in the '60s. One of those roles had to do with going to Vietnam on the behalf of our government to kill or be killed. I came close. When you are raised to believe John Wayne is the image of the ideal American male, it's difficult to find another role to play and still hope for acceptance into the culture. Had it not been for the Beatles and Rolling Stones, and especially Bob Dylan, I don't think I could have done it.

It's crucial to have the ability to stand back, get outside of one's self, to get a real look at what is going on, and find your true self. "Art creates I-distantness," remarked Paul Celan.

If you choose that you are going to be the artist of yourself, you'll need to start fresh. In order to put the right colors on the canvas that is to be your new identity or choreograph the moves that are to be your new dance on the stage of life you need spontaneity. Instinct. Ardor. Élan.

Detonation.

You have to blow up all your assumptions, opinions, prejudices, and preconceptions. You have to empty yourself. Bring the edifice down. Start anew from the foundation up.

All this is starting to sound like narcissism. And clearly, that's inevitable. I hate the phrase "navel-gazing." It's a put-down. It's trivializing. It suggests that self-reflection is idle nonsense, disconnected from the realities of life. That's bullshit. I agree completely with Socrates: "the unexamined life is not worth living."

I once began a journal using the third person singular "he" to refer to myself rather than the more traditional first person singular "I." I found it impossible to continue. It was too unnerving. I began to think of myself outside myself, as if I had somehow become disembodied without actually being disembodied. I experienced that freshness of perception the Russian constructivists called *ostrenenie*, which means making the familiar unfamiliar, making day-to-day realities appear alien and strange. I felt strange. I felt alien. I didn't like it. Part of me liked it, but a lot of me didn't like it. It was too unsettling.

I am sitting in my favorite chair, the one that was reupholstered several years ago at Doran Patrick Custom Upholstery, on Eastlake. I like it because it reminds me of Balzac. But then, everything lately reminds me of Balzac. I am reading Balzac. I have been reading Balzac for the last several years. Daffodils and flea markets and kettledrums remind me of Balzac. Even jello reminds me of Balzac. But coffee really reminds me of Balzac.

The coffee we drink is a rainforest blend from the western hills of Columbia, the northern highlands of Guatemala, the southern mountains of Mexico and the Sumatran highlands of Indonesia.

I had no idea I was drinking so many locations. No wonder I'm so confused.

My life is filmed on location. I film it while I am living it. I am director, screenwriter, star, and cinematographer. The name of the movie is "My Life with Balzac."

It's a very slow movie. Very European. I spend most of my time drinking coffee. Wandering from room to room. Boxing shadows. Attempting to prove to myself that I'm ready for a rematch with life. Seeking justice. Battling an octopus for treasure. Experimenting with helium. And speculating on the nature of the human comedy, and the kind of things people believe in, ostensibly to make their lives easier, and more meaningful.

I have few beliefs. The older I get the fewer beliefs I tend to have. Belief is an odd phenomenon. Because as soon as you believe in something you imply its nonexistence as well as its existence. No one says, "I believe in air." They simply breathe air. No one says, "I believe in rain." They simply get wet. No one says, "I believe in light." They simply open their eyes. No one says, "I believe in Balzac." They simply read Balzac. The words and ideas of Balzac. The world as Balzac lived in it and describes it. Its glitter and garbage. Its greed and generosity.

I weigh 189 lbs. That's how much room I consume in the world. At least in terms of density. I could explode any minute. I could explode into birds.

I hate it when people call me judgmental. The implication is twofold: that I have the arrogance to believe that I know all things, and that I suffer from a narrowness of mind. Consequently, any and all opinions that I express are corrupt and irresponsible. It is pointless to continue the argument. Once your authority is undermined, you have no place in an argument. What is laughably ironic about this is that the person who has accused you of being judgmental is being judgmental. If everyone is blind, who can discern the one person who can see?

The opposite of being judgmental is being open-minded. This does not mean that you are unencumbered by judgment. It means that you have the capacity to suspend judgment and consider things from another point of view. It is a grand luxury if there is no other pressing business. But if you have to decide whether to get a heart operation or not, send a troop of men into battle, or step in to stop a fight you do not have the luxury of endlessly unraveling the ramifications, à la Hamlet. You have to act, and act quickly.

Years ago, on a cold December morning, I got lost in an industrial and residential district of Seattle called Georgetown. I was cruising along slowly studying the addresses when I spotted a young woman being chased by a man in his underwear around the muddy parking lot of a squalid apartment building. She was shouting "Help! help! he's going to kill me!" The first thing to flash in my mind was to find a telephone. But since this incident took place in the late '90s, during the advent of the cell phone, telephone booths had begun to disappear. Chances of finding a phone booth were nil. Even if I did find a phone booth and called the police the woman would already be dead. If I continued on my way and just ignored the incident I would be haunted by it the rest of my life. Haunted by the image of a woman dead from strangulation. Haunted by my cowardice and lack of humanity. I had to stop. So stop I did. As soon as I stopped, the woman ran toward my car, a small red Subaru. I had less than a second to decide whether to open the door or not. Which I did. Praying, at the same time, that this wasn't a car jack. The woman got in. The man, surprisingly, also got in. He sat on the edge of the seat. At that point, I ceased thinking at all. There was no time to think. I reacted by instinct. I pressed the accelerator lightly enough to move the car forward, the man's bare foot scraping against the asphalt. There was a thud, the man disappeared from the seat, and I threw the car into second and sped away. I dimly remember checking the rear view mirror and seeing the man chasing us. I suggested that the young woman call the police. She answered she could not. She had some outstanding traffic tickets. She helped me find the address I was looking for, a combination restaurant and bar, and urged her again to call the police. As soon as we arrived, and as an old pickup passed by, the woman leaned over and honked my horn. The pickup stopped. She got out of the car and ran to the pickup. And that was that. I never found out what the whole thing had been about.

Each time I tell this story to people I get varied reactions. Most people think I did the right thing. But a few think what I did was foolish in the extreme. Any number of things could have gone wrong and gotten very ugly indeed, including my arrest. If the scene had had no other witnesses, there was no one to corroborate my testimony that I had stopped to help. For me, there was no right or wrong decision. I had no decision. But the story serves to show how slippery and complicated making a judgment can be, and that we don't always have the luxury of time and distance to arrive at the best judgment. And maybe that's a good thing. Maybe there are occasions in life when it is best to follow our animal instincts.

But even when we do have plenty of time to reflect, making a good judgment is a difficult thing to achieve. Who can say, in all honesty, that they have no regrets? That their judgments have all been sound? That foresight has in all instances equaled hindsight? That their choice of career, of car, of washer and dryer, of wife, of husband, of weather stripping and Weltanschauung were all unexcelled, the absolute best? That discrimination did not smack of bias? That the bananas they brought home were not too ripe? That their theories held water? That all their choices have had the ring and shine of sterling?

Judgment is hard. It is subject to delusion, vulnerable to collusion. Ravished by rationalization, seduced by wit. Not even judges always make good judgments.

There are judgments, and there are judgments.

Judgment based on a measure is one thing. Ten pounds of oranges is ten pounds of oranges. No argument there, no room for opinion to quibble and shift.

But what about less tangible things? Pressure, for instance.

Pressure is a scalar quantity and can be measured in units of pascals. A pascal is a measure of force per unit area. But this is physical pressure not psychological pressure. Physical pressure is quantifiable. Psychological pressure is not quantifiable. This is where judgment is required. But judgment based on what? What units? What system? What knowledge?

No units. No system. No knowledge.

Just judgment. Raw, unleavened judgment. Untested. Unspoken. Unfiltered. Grasping at straws. Plumbing unfamiliar waters.

You grill yourself. Should I keep this job? Should I complain to the supervisor that the childish outbursts and tantrums of a coworker are making it impossible for me to do my job? Will this reflect poorly on my ability to get along with others and so hurt my chances for a promotion, or getting a transfer? If the bus begins to slide, do I turn the wheel in the opposite direction, as I have been advised? Will I have the presence of mind to do that? Where was the ring for my emergency chute?

The mind is a treadmill of endless decision making. Pressures build, offsetting our equilibrium and making rational determinations harder to achieve. Cooler minds prevail. More passionate dispositions get blown about by contrary winds.

Nor is judgment confined to matters of stress and science. Courtrooms are fraught with ethical conundrums. Say a bank teller has a child with a life-threatening medical problem that requires surgery, but that surgery is not covered by the insurance provider. There is money available in a dormant account. The teller uses that money to get the necessary surgery for their child. The teller begins paying the money back, but is caught, and charged with embezzlement. You are a member of the jury. Do you recommend acquittal, based on the circumstances, or adhere strictly according to the law, according to the judge's instructions?

Strict adherence to law is encouraged precisely because human cognition is so vulnerable to emotion, to nuance and degree, the shifting pastels of fiery horizons, the roll and undulation of life's uncertainties. This is where law breaks down. There are no precedents to follow in uncharted waters. Navigation in the realm of perception is less dependent on sextant and compass than a sensitivity to the fluid language of the atmosphere, tongues of lightning, halos around the moon, migrations of birds, and agitations on the surface of the sea that hint of moiling undercurrents.

Aesthetic judgments are the most unstable. Gaius Petronius, the noted "judge of elegance" in the court of the emperor Nero and presumed author of the *Satyricon*, once remarked that "beauty and wisdom are rarely conjoined." Judgment is linked to logic. Beauty is not. Beauty is to logic what a cloud is to a brick. The brick has definition, heft, size, shape. The cloud is all looseness and ethereality. It is never a single shape but a multiplicity of shapes, all changing mercurially with the whims and vagaries of the air.

Immanuel Kant provides some helpful insight. He refers to a concept called "subjective universality," a judgment of beauty not based on personal interests, what he calls a "disinterested satisfaction." To call something beautiful is to presuppose the same appreciation in others. But based on what, I don't know. Cultural affinities? Would an individual from the Democratic Republic of the Congo enjoy a painting by Antoine Watteau as much as a person from Rouen, France? Tastes vary even within the regions of southern Africa. Chéri Samba, an artist from Kinshasa, remarks how

"critics in kinshasa have never accepted the phrases in my paintings,
they think of painting in a more western
manner. yet the truth, in my paintings,
is almost always expressed in the sentences inserted
in the paintings.
often they contradict the scene represented...
for example, for a person from zaire, nudity is scandalous:
I paint it, I make it visible, and then, with a phrase,
I find a way of saying 'don't look'.
I like these paradoxes."

I have noticed in the public a far greater tolerance toward experimentation in the visual arts. It may be that Chéri Samba would disagree with this. Many others have disagreed with this. But this is what I have noticed. I think the reason for this is simple: we are dealing with palpable objects, sensual products. Shape, volume, texture, color. These do not necessarily require a strong educational background to appreciate.

Poetry is different. Poetry is based on language, and language is based on a mutuality of understanding. Anyone with a command of English knows precisely what I mean when I say "look at that cow," and there happens to be a cow within view. But in poetry the word is often stripped from its referent. The strength of a poem relies on a combination of image and emotion. This can get tricky. How can anyone judge what is essentially excitation and hallucination? There are skills, techniques for building constructs and ideas with words, but the parameters are much harder to identify. Here is where judgment has become almost purely subjective. And this can drive you absolutely nuts.

For instance, let's say I write a poem. I think the poem is great and needs to be published. All the words in the poem are marvelous and apt and beautifully aerodynamic. The poem has viscosity and meaning. The meaning is transparent but not too transparent. It is obscure enough to tease the mind into larger associations, lead the mind in curious directions, zigzags and meanders, but without tearing the fabric of coherence, so that the sphere of the poem expands, and the mind rises, happy and blithe, to view the ground below, the mundane ground, with all of its rules and traffic lights. The poem, in point of fact, is perfect. It needs to be published so that the world at large, the world of humanity, will be able to read it, penetrate its mysteries, and so grow wiser. And so the poem is submitted to a magazine, directed toward the discerning eyes of an editor, a gatekeeper, who will appreciate its beauty, the sublimity of its craftsmanship, the audacity of its autonomy, the soft warm glow of its inner meaning, the toughness of its observations, the delicacy of its assumptions, the piquancy of its pulse and temperature. But the poem is rejected. The poem is returned. "I am sorry," confesses the editor, "but your poem is not right for our publication."

What does this mean, "not right for our publication?" I assume it is the editor's chosen euphemism for meaning, "your poem stinks." Or, "your poem is dull." Or, "your poem oozes forth the miasma of misbegotten perceptions, ill chosen words, and the penetralia of a megalomaniac."

Here is where judgment is particularly shaky. For we are dealing with not one but two judgments. Two very separate judgments. My judgment, the judgment of the author, which is perfect, and the judgment of the editor, which is negligent, fiendish, and insane.

It is to be assumed that I have not undergone the task of submitting my work at random or arbitrarily in an eagerness to see it in print, but have fully examined the publication to which I submitted my poem, and found grounds for mutual respect. Emblazoned within its pages or resplendent among its pixels I have seen work with marks and echoes of my own. Ergo, an incongruity of style cannot be the problem. I must conclude that either my judgment has been at fault, or the judgment of the editor has demonstrated an ugly and reprehensible flaw.

But what, I am forced to admit, if it is the editor who is correct, and myself whose judgment is at fault? What agonies of doubt! What pricks of incertitude! It is here I envy the calibrations of science.

There is no way to quantify the worth of a poem. No poem yet devised can be weighed, balanced, plumbed, gauged, or calculated. There are no physical properties to which can be applied a standard system of measurement. It is all subjective, purely a matter of taste, bias, bents, propensities and predispositions.

Certain mystics have praised the ability to live in the world without judgment, to see things in their immediate condition with no preconception to obfuscate their full reality. I have often experimented with the attempt to withhold judgment and have discovered that it is nearly impossible. I did discover, however, that perception is largely a creative act. When we penetrate to the essence of a thing rather than summarily accept its definition, we find ourselves in the presence of a living thing or being.

Inner qualities are volatile, like eyes. Nerve impulses pass from the optic nerve to the brain where they are interpreted as impressions, perceptions, quirks. Inductions, deductions, epiphanies. Here is where judgment comes into play. The mind ponders a phenomenon. What is it? What is this thing I'm feeling? How do I identify it? Name it? Qualify it? What are its properties, its shape, its density, its weight, its smell? The more tangled the qualifiers, the more vague and elusive the object becomes. But what isn't colored by quality? Essence does not precede existence. No judgment is possible without a consideration of tincture, structure, and texture.

I will, on occasion, stumble upon a word that refers to something I have not experienced, or experienced without knowing I had experienced it. The word "zeitgeist," for example, which means, literally, "time ghost," explained a great deal to me the first time I heard it defined. It refers to all the customs, habits, principles and manners of a particular time in history. Clothing and hair, jewelry, tattoos, the tones and inflections in people's voices, careers that are sought, movies that become popular, are all indications of a collective spirit. Zeitgeist helps explain the continuing popularity of *Star Trek*, the appeal of Oprah Winfrey, and Facebook and Twitter. The word has validity.

What I hear and see can be put together in my mind to form a judgment about the meaning of a word. Not everything we experience can be so easily tasted and weighed. Our mental lives are volatile but crucial, forming a bridge between our inner existence and what we need to do to survive in the external world. Butterflies are equipped with very sensitive antenna. This is how they find nectar. We, too, are equipped with antenna. The antenna of art and language.

Words and postulates have this in common: they give voice to the mute and invisible. Concepts have consequence and weight. The intangible is judged by its virtue, its vigor and influence. Ideas do not have shape or smell, but they do have value.

How do we discriminate between values? The question answers itself with another series of questions: what object is not enveloped with a skin of idiom, a shell of idiosyncrasies, a call for deeper questions?

Everything has a story to tell. Each phenomenon and object has a meaning for us. We just need to ask the right questions. Does this flicker, crucible, persimmon, etc., possess some higher, transcendent meaning, or is it simply literal, like a glass of milk? Is it brutally utilitarian like a wedge of wood to be slipped under a door to be used as a doorstop or is it more curiously aesthetic, with no discernible purpose, something like a poem, a jumble of superfluous words, or a mysterious appendage, a fleshy redundancy, like the prominent hump on the back of a zebu? I could be wrong about the zebu. That fleshy redundancy might not be so redundant. Perhaps the same could be said of a poem. It is not always so easy to tell what minerals lie in the sedimentary layers of a poem. There may be ore in its vowels, silver in its syllables, gold in its veins. Poetry is an expression of what is deepest and most sublime. Consequently, these are values that require persistent effort and a discerning mind. Prospecting is a lonely and intuitive art. Judgment of what lies beneath depends on how closely we read the surface.

This is our dilemma. We can usually tell the difference between a drop cloth and a dragon, a hawk and a handsaw. But who can affirm that a guru is wise and worth our attention, or that a perception is pure and valid? That a poem is good and worthy of publication, or that a poem is dull as a chemical solvent and should be hidden from the world or restricted to use of the dry cleaner?

That a poem matters at all?

A poem matters because there the judgment is attuned to the atoms of its own making. We don't judge the poem, the poem judges us.

Sometimes a song will become an obsession. It will go into your head and stay in your head and cause you to hum and hold and pulse and embed it. You will come to embody it. You will come to live and sing and inhabit it. The song will become you. You will become the song.

Outside is a city work crew tearing the street up with a jackhammer. This makes it impossible to hear this week's favorite song, which is "Needles and Pins." It's a perfect song. Every word is placed right where it needs to be. The story it provokes is a familiar one. It concerns the pain of encountering an ex-lover at a social gathering, someone you continue to pine for, someone whose presence continues to bewitch and plague you, with someone else. It is a powerful emotion, and one worthy of singing. This is why opera and ballads and rock and roll were invented. They give us dignity during moments of extreme distress and dejection. They make dejection beautiful and heavy, like a Franklin stove, or Hindu deity.

I couldn't keep a tune if my life depended on it. Don't know an A major from a C minor.

Don't know a C minor from a branch of dogwood.

I do know pain, and the music is a medicine for pain, a way to fondle the thoughts in your brain. Turn them up. Turn them down. Turn them round and round. Like a Grecian urn. Like a branch of dogwood.

The difference between a song and a poem is this: a song is a temperature and a poem is an eagle.

Think of the all-encompassing air. Think of the brain as the gleam of raspberry jam on a piece of toast. The cool breath of heaven enunciated in good vibrations, sweet little commas, the piquant odor of old bricks.

The Kinks, The Beau Brummels, The Who, The Zombies.
M Ward and Zoey Deschamel singing "Oh Lonesome Me."
Amy Winehouse singing "Will You Still Love Me Tomorrow."
Bo Diddley's cobra necktie.
John Lee Hooker's rockin' chair.
Billie Holiday's cool blue waterfront.

These are all beautiful things. But what about the smell of coffee mingled with the smell of bacon in a kitchen somewhere in upstate Michigan? There should be a song about that. Involving knives and blood and huge overwhelming complex emotions. What would that sound like?

It would sound like a surgeon making an incision in a poor excuse. It would sound like a cello paraphrasing a ghost in a grove of words.

I don't know what it would sound like. There are some things that cannot be sung. Some things that haunt the air in pure silence. And that is a music too green for guitars. Too dubious for brass. Too delirious for violins and lips. Too thick. Too high. Too long.

There are some things that a poem can do far better than a song.

I speed down the freeway listening to ZZ Top. An alligator in the backseat knits gargoyles out of alligator wool. I am on my way to see a painter in Mississippi. I am old. The painter is old. He paints old things. I wander the Louvre in my head and think about the gate. The gate needs painting.

I feel a lyricism running wild. I feel the egotism implicit in trophies. I feel rioting in Iran. A cut on my little finger that has been stubborn to heal. I feel the violence of pumpkins and a ceramic pitcher steeped in its existence and Etruscans cleaning a mural in the museum of lost shadows.

I love going fast. The last bank I robbed didn't know what hit them.

It disgusts me to be human.

The world is a constant improbability.

I feel the golden chain of a reinforcing inexorability.

There are animals in my breath.

YouTubia is neither a utopia or geographical location but a portal through time. In essence, a cue, a prompt, a provocation that stirs a memory so vivid and enveloping it constitutes a location, a cleft in the topologies of time. For Proust it was a madeleine soaked in tea; for me, it is a tiny screen of pixels, Red Skelton bouncing up and down in a crowd of screaming girls while a young Mick Jagger sings "Tell Me" with the Rolling Stones in the lobby of the London Palladium September 22nd, 1964. The emotion is palpable. The separation of forty-five years melts away. I want to grow my hair long. I want to walk on the wild side and write explosive dangerous poetry like Arthur Rimbaud and Gregory Corso and Bob Kaufman and Allen Ginsberg. I want to push boundaries and open the doors of perception, wide. I want to devote my life to art and poetry and go to England and visit the house where Keats wrote "Ode to a Nightingale" and watched coal deliveries and ate nectarines and met Fanny Brawne. The song gives me all those feelings anew, fresh, vigorous, unqualified. Nothing limps. Nothing balks. Everything is limitless. This is not the slow controlled glide of mature, later life, but the reckless energy of youth, before any seeds have been planted, before any ships have sailed, before any struggles and disappointments have denatured and tamed that feeling. The surprise of seeing the very young, incipient Stones exactly as they appeared on TV in 1964 with their peculiar blend of English romanticism, raffish libertinism, and the electric blues of Chicago's Southside brought the strength and purity of that original feeling back to me. Did it last? No, of course not. A sixty-one-year-old man cavorting about like a shaggy teenager would quickly swerve into buffoonery. Age has done much to enrich and undermine the Stones after forty-odd years of almost relentless performance. But a lesson was learned.

Time is not that stiff mechanical revolution we see in watches and clocks or dental appointments marked on calendars or quietly but hungrily ticking away on a living room wall. Time is a cloud, nebulous, drifting, unstable as space itself. Time travel is wide-open and shiny.

A goldfish in dawn light in a Bristol parlor in June or July 1772. Phosphorous glow of buffalo bones on a Rocky Mountain slope viewed and pondered by Samuel Clemens during a stage ride with his brother Orion in 1861. Glint of sunlight on a sword moments before the battle of Shrewsbury amid the lush green hills of Shropshire in July, 1403. There is no reach, no shore, no body of water large enough to prevent the human mind from traveling there. All it takes is something as specific as the dimple on Kirk Douglas's chin to put me in the backseat of a car in 1957 watching the Vikings dance on the oars of a longship while their tinny laughter crackles through a speaker clipped to the window that has been rolled down far enough to let it in and hang there, a crude metal box with a speaker grill and a volume knob.

Potent as a whiff of paregoric The Zombies singing "She's Not There" on *Hullabaloo* circa 1965 puts me in the small basement room of my parent's house age eighteen eager to get away, go to California, anywhere, but at all costs avoid the war in Vietnam, the numbing banality of the suburbs, the noxious exigencies of employment and financial stability. I remember it vividly, feel it once again: that sweet imperative, that strange urgency I had not yet begun to articulate to keep that new thrilling light in me from being quenched by drudgery and the so-called practicalities of the "real world."

Denny Laine singing "Go Now" that same year shoots sweet memories into my brain and I feel as coincidental to the emotions of that song as I do to the chair I'm sitting on. "We've already said good-bye," the song begins. The romance is over. But maybe not dead. It still has life. The moment has a piquancy, a complexity of unimaginable nuance. No wonder they called themselves The Moody Blues.

John Byrne singing "Psychotic Reaction" looks exactly as he did when he sat in our English literature class at San Jose City College in the fall of 1966, his song a hit on the radio. It was another friend in a health ed class that heard the phrase "psychotic reaction" and leaned over and whispered to John "hey, that would make a great song title." Which prompted John to write the song.

I last saw John with his date in front of Original Joe's in downtown San Jose. He was a very kind person. He lent me some money. I still owe him ten dollars. I can't pay it back now, however. He passed away last December 15th, 2008.

Keith Relf looks cool and enigmatical in a dark Regency shirt singing "Heart Full of Soul" and I can see why I found him rather intimidating that late summer night in 1966 when I drove a carload of screaming girls behind the limousine of The Yardbirds following their performance at the Civic Auditorium on West San Carlos Street and they parked in the lot of a fast food joint and rolled their windows down and I found myself talking to the one guy who seemed most affable and open to conversation who was none other than Jimmy Page who was filling in for Jeff Beck. I bought him a Coke.

Mr. Page, if you're out there, you owe me a Coke.

Estelle Bennett looks adorable singing "Be My Baby" in the background of her more famous sister Ronnie Spector, swinging her arms, moving gracefully forward, that powerful music propelling them into TV show after TV show, what appeared to be endless glitter and glamour, a sweet voluptuous heat compelling as Newton's First Law of Thermodynamics surrounding and imbuing everything with a libidinous rhythm and delicious, dangerous excitement. I find it remarkable that later in life Estelle became homeless and died, just recently, at her home in New Jersey the same night as the crash of the commuter plane in a suburban neighborhood in Buffalo, New York.

There are openings in time everywhere. All it takes is an image, a sound, a small black square suddenly alive with movement, Shakespeare's Queen Titania scratching Bottom's donkey ears in a charmed realm of innocent pleasures, Georges Méliès inflating his head until it explodes, Annie Oakley shooting small glass targets in a film made November 1st, 1894 in Edison's Black Maria Studio, Maria Falconetti as Jeanne d'Arc in Carl Dreyer's 1928 film *The Passion of Joan of Arc* looking horrified and full of some inscrutable inner power that makes her eyes glare out of her head with penetrating beauty as she is led forward, her feet bound in chains, to swear on a bible before a scrutinizing and fearful old judge.

But why YouTube? Why this technology, this particular medium? Why not go to the source, any current image redolent of things past, keen memories, exquisite sensations still pertinent and internal as my own skeleton surrounded by warm muscle and blood, a batch of taillights on a dark wet night, liquid and alive, the exquisite scent of sage, the jingly jangly sound of a shaken tambourine?

There is no reason strong enough to support an argument for YouTube as a Time Machine. YouTube is a novelty. It will soon be replaced by another novelty. Or perhaps not. Perhaps it will simply grow tedious. What is pertinent is the surprise discovery of things. Seeing and hearing the Beau Brummels for the first time in forty-odd years. Seeing James Brown twirl and glide in the shadows of an old *Shindig!* show that aired in the mid-sixties when all that change was just beginning. I did not anticipate seeing these things. I had forgotten what they felt like. Those old emotions were still there. They just needed a trigger to be awakened. It was like finding the keys to a warehouse full of museum treasures. Curiosities and art treasures that have not been available to the public eye in decades.

We are all autobiographers alert to the sounds and smells and tastes of our lives. Sometimes a song will become an obsession because it travels through us as we travel back in time to its source. Those first occasions in which we heard it. Time is laminated. All things are held together in space and time by laws and forces whose actualities elude our senses but are sometimes made manifest in mathematical equations. The smooth cool light of an opal can mesmerize and distill an forgotten memory or feeling as well as anything on YouTube.

YouTubia is neither a region or nectar from the hives of Google but a waver, a warp, a flicker, a caprice akin to an awakening, a perception surprised by the unexpected, by a sudden aberration in the environment. A bright beautiful bug inching its way across a forest floor. Zinnias, bubbles, Flaubert's parrot. We invent our lives as we go along. Our maps require constant maintenance. Today's mountain range may be tomorrow's canyon. The quick movements of a hummingbird in the lassitude of a Tucson afternoon may suddenly metamorphose into a noisy forklift on a loading dock in Albuquerque.

Vincent Van Gogh once fancifully suggested in a letter to his brother Theo that death was a train that took us to the stars. French author Raymond Roussel was notorious for meandering around Europe in a luxury caravan replete with bathroom and study from which he rarely, if ever, emerged. He could not stop writing, could not pull himself away from crafting a prose lustrous with bizarre machinery and fabulous inventions.

Don't get me wrong. I love travel. Actual, literal travel. The kind in which one's body travels through space. I love trains. Even cars. Before we got our cat, I used to enjoy long road trips, especially the ones involving blue highways and four-calendar cafés. Little towns with a main street still active and varied. What worries me is the slow deterioration of the imagination. The ability to travel long distances within one's mind. Consciousness is just as rich and mysterious as any South Seas lagoon, just as majestic and jeweled as Taj Mahal. What a shame to see it atrophy, waste away in a population accustomed to more garish, more passively consumed entertainments. A friend once referred to the cell phone as the "death of solitude." People seem more frantic than usual to distract themselves from their inner latitudes, their internal world. Perhaps this has always been the case and I am just now beginning to notice it. There is inside everyone a knowledge that simply won't go away. We all know there is that final destination, the bourne from which no traveler returns. Who can blame anyone for wanting to resort to whatever detour is available to avoid thinking about that last debarkation?

Whatever awaits us on the other side, and however we choose to imagine it, the longer we manage to stay alive, the broader and more numerous grow our memories. They become continents. Large entities that crack and shift due to a kind of mental tectonic plate shifting. There are quakes and hurricanes. Himalayan traumas and oceans with soft, alluring, hazy horizons. If death is a train, reverie is a ship. It drifts, meanders, deviates. Wanders off course. This is where we do some real traveling. Those more obscure memories are like deeply-rooted plants, subtle fronds of embarrassed light. If we crush their flowers and leaves, potent odors emerge. A Leatherleaf Mahonia awakens a host of ghosts in the blood. Forgotten refinements soaked in the chill of an afternoon. A wrong turn can be splendid with discovery.

My most powerful memories are the ones that catch me off guard, the way hearing Arthur Lee sing "Seven & Seven Is" for the first time in forty-three years grabbed me out of 2008 and tossed me back into the year 1966. One minute I'm sitting in front of a computer on a chair and the next instant I'm traveling on a Bay Area freeway headed God knows where, but going totally crazy over this amazing song, "Oop-ip-ip oop-ip-ip, yeah!"

If I try to remember something deliberately, I am never quite sure what has been reliably imprinted on my nerves, and what is invention; what is selective and what is filtered; what is actual and what is synthetic. A forced memory lacks the necessary ingredients of surprise and spontaneity. It is something I have willfully staged in my head with the same craftsmanship and attention to drama that goes into a setting for the opera.

Hence, YouTubia. Which might also be called Cilybebyll. Or Bath-Robia. Or Front-Tooth-A-Dor. Any object, sensation, stimulus, or fillip that conjures a rich terrain from the past might be considered a country. A realm. A domain. A wilderness.

There are no walls in the human mind, no monuments or prisons. Only waterfronts. Rivers. Beaches. The smack and lap of water on barnacled pilings. Dizziness, delirium, phantasmagoria. Mists like the ones sometimes seen over the Strait of Juan de Fuca, diaphanous, unearthly subtleties that tease the mind into a voyage of ceaseless speculation.

The figures are dark and hooded. They move in utter silence and shine flashlight beams at the street. It is a search, but a search for what?

It is 5:00 a.m. Halloween is two days away. The air bites shrewdly, as Hamlet would say, minutes before the ghost of his father appears, a tortured apparition gliding out of the night in questionable shape, in complete steel, making night hideous, but full of wonder, thrilling the mind with thoughts beyond the reach of our souls.

The figures I see in the street are there every morning. I discover most of them are Asian. Their facial expressions reveal total absorption. Details of their search become increasingly apparent. For weeks now I have been running on a carpet of bristly balls. These people are searching for chestnuts. The street is canopied with the arcing limbs of chestnut trees. The chestnuts are ripe and heavy. When I disappear into the quiet of the night, absorbed in my own thoughts, my physical exertions, they come thumping down on the hoods of cars, startling me.

I like to run early in the morning, before the traffic, before the turbulence and banality of day. Early dawn is a time of shadows. Bones. Bats. Uncertain perceptions and tricks of light.

One morning, at around 5:15 a.m., I saw a thin, bearded figure move slowly down the street. This was near the graveyard. His feet barely touched the ground.

These moments are Lynchian. This is what I tell my friends. "I felt like I was in a David Lynch movie."

Everyone knows what is meant by this. Moments of strangeness, though not necessarily supernatural. They do not rule out the supernatural, but since everything in these moments is felt so acutely, so piercingly, so imbued with amazement, dread, bewilderment, that an aperture seems suddenly opened between the world of salt and keepsake, the world of the familiar, the world of bric-a-brac and logic, and the world of delirium, of panic, of heightened awareness, the world when it pulses with strange new life within our gaze.

A blue plastic bag in a pool of water. A white feather at the bottom of the steps leading to the library. A derelict in a black jacket and black pants sleeping beneath the belly of a Brontosaurus. Crackle and static from an AM radio station, faint Mexican music in the background.

Two bright objects moving together 225 light-years away from Earth near the constellation Hydra.

The fuselage of a Boeing 737 on a flat car with a sign on it that says: "do not hump this."

A black wool glove flattened on the street, the index finger pointing southeast. A dead squirrel at the base of a telephone pole. The clatter of hail against the window, flash of lightning, followed, several seconds later, by distant thunder.

One has to wonder: when does a movie cease being a movie?

What is consciousness? What are the origins of consciousness? Where does it come from? Is consciousness the result of neurobiology, electrical impulses firing at the synaptic cleft, or something greater, something less tangible, something more abstract? Do we create our own reality? Are mind and matter separate? Did the sheer nothingness at the origin of the universe develop waves of consciousness? Thoughts? Is the universe thought? The play of potentiality?

The universe is alive.

The whole world is wild at heart and weird on top.

Coherence in art bristles with polysemantic hair.

A film is its own thing, says Lynch in a small YouTube screen during an interview with a young man with a heavy Scotch accent. A film should be discovered knowing nothing. You don't know where these things come from. They can come from memories. Or they can come from the ether. One day, for some reason, they're released, and it seems like a brand new idea. Or an idea comes in from the ether and as it pops it may be colored by something that you know. The picture that forms, sometimes reading a book, are pictures you put together from the past, or your imagination kicks in. You can't really tell what forms those pictures will take. It's the words on the page and, probably, many internal things.

How do we tell the inner from the outer? Is our perception synonymous with the things we see?

Everywhere I look are images of beauty. Moments when the world appears transmuted by the sublime. Aroused by something invisible chafing against its curtains and gravel.

A man in a white jumpsuit blowing flames at a brick wall.

A blind man working his way around the grill of a truck, helped by a girl and a boy.

A woman walking down the street describing vertebrae.

Shine of the handle on the dishwasher catching random light in the darkness of the kitchen.

A Mexican man playing guitar on a picnic bench as the Burlington Northern Santa Fe Railway goes clanking by in the background.

Pop and rumble of a Harley, Hell's Angel entering a cemetery.

Crow pecking the eye of a freshly killed squirrel, middle of the street, skull crushed.

The sound of a woman eating toast.

On the morning of July 20th, 1969, I emerged from a house near Burien, Washington shortly after sunrise, and tilted my head back to look at the sky. My neck creaked. I had attended a party that had gone late into the night. It was a warm, bright morning and I could see the moon, phantasmal and splotchy against a China blue sky. It's rare to see the moon during the day, and whenever I do, it seems oddly displaced, a prop from the theatre of the night someone forgot to bring in. On this occasion it smacked of significance. There were men walking on it. Or about to walk on it. I gazed at it as if I might actually see them hobbling about in the dust, the way you can sometimes see from a distance people scaling the side of a mountain.

My adolescence in the '60s had been witness to a long pageantry of lunar landing modules. My father worked at Boeing as an illustrator and engineer. I grew up in a house full of lunar landing modules, many of them constructed out of toothpicks and ping-pong balls. NASA's coveted contract went to Grumman, rather than Boeing, so my father's many illustrations and modules remained stillborn, although a few went on exhibit at the Smithsonian in the 1980s.

My parents were out of town that summer in '69. Home from California for a visit, I had the house to myself and watched the moon landing on TV. I saw *Eagle* land and Armstrong clamber down the ladder in his bulky space suit and put his foot on the surface of the moon and utter his famous words, "That is one small step for man, one giant leap for mankind."

Years later, circa the early '90s, Buzz Aldrin and my father had been invited to a dinner at someone's house on Bainbridge Island and gotten lost. My father drove and Buzz navigated. Bainbridge Island is heavily wooded, which outer space is not, which provides at least one mitigating factor to this otherwise curious misadventure. If I remember my father's story correctly, it had been a clear night, and Buzz had been able to use the stars to pinpoint their position using a declination formula based on spherical trigonometry. That, and a map spread out on the hood of my father's Taurus, which they studied by flashlight.

Today the moon is a thin crescent that looks like a fingernail clipping hovering over the western horizon. There are no people flying around with jetpacks on their backs and living in homes that look like the Space Needle. The world is in crisis. Billions live in dire poverty. The poles and glaciers are melting. Millions in the U.S. believe that humans lived with dinosaurs and that evolution is a hoax. But Armstrong and Aldrin and Collins continue on tour, noticeably aged, but still smiling, still optimistic. I like to think that they know something that I don't know.

CAT SITTING

As soon as the door opens Athena falls on her back and exposes her belly, Nietzsche stares up with expectancy, Harriet claws my leg, Edna emerges from a suitcase and Gloria attacks a bedraggled sock, a spectrum of odor running from dulcet to sharp endows my nose with an amalgam of litter, food, and perfume, books and CDs everywhere languish in ready availability, *Bones, Nova Swing, Vintage Guitar, Encyclopedia of Serial Killers, The Grateful Dead: Beyond Description (1973–1989), Stick Control for Snare Drummers,* the surrounding walls punctuated here and there with art, a framed print of a painting by Gustaf Klimt, a woman enveloped in black fur gazing, aloof and reflectively, from beneath a black hat as if scrutinizing a curious social event, one that has to be imagined occurring in Vienna, Berlin, or the apartment itself, a paradox of calm and tumultuous flux, and on the opposing wall an oil painting rendered in thick layers, red roses on a black background, mounted above a fireplace which is almost entirely hidden behind an enormous couch, a voluptuousness that would accept the body in unconditional comfort were it not already engulfed in books and DVDs, *Garcia: A Signpost to New Space, Angel: Season Five, Desk Reference for Hip Vintage Speaker Amps, The Lathe of Heaven, What Is Music: An Introduction to the Philosophy of Music, Classics from Outer Space, The House of Mystery, On the Sensation of Tone* by the nineteenth-century German physicist Hermann von Helmhotz, *The Drummer's Bible: Every Drum Style from Afro-Cuban to Zydeco, Sacred Drumming, Funk Drumming, Radar Men from the Moon,* each stack on the verge of toppling over and most certainly would were not each pile supporting the one next to it in tentative stability, even the floor, a dark blue shag carpet here and there splotched and marbled with white fur, is occupied with things related to music, three electric guitars in their cases lined neatly together under the kitchen counter, a fourth one leaning against the wall, three big speakers standing in front of the couch blocking the fireplace, a drum kit and a stack of cymbals in the bedroom closet, and always, each time after washing my hands in the bathroom after cleaning the litter boxes, I turn round to the towel rack and gaze at a woman's photograph, her warm broad smile and merry blue eyes, wondering who she is, where she is, how

220

many years have passed since the photograph was taken, framed, and hung on the wall for remembrance, for regard, and me, a foreign consciousness looking up, taking her in, working my hands on a soft sage towel, taking a moment to muse and drift, and feed the cats, check the locks, the lights, the mail, rub a belly or two, and be on my way.

In the summer of 1993 my father took me out to see the agricultural bonanza that is the Palouse. He was old, his once robust body, solid and indomitable as a tank, was now rickety and frail, fatigued from chemotherapy and cancer. His hair was white and he had a wattle beneath his chin that looked more like an additional membrane than a flap of loose skin. The prolonged intimacy of our outing, an extended road trip which had not had any real destination to begin with, was beginning to wear on me. I craved solitude. My father, inveterately gregarious, loved going places and meeting new people. Gliding, photography, sightseeing, and convoluted detours that provided opportunities for more convoluted gambles and misadventures were all things he treasured. The trip, which was intended to bring us closer now that he was fast approaching the end of his life, was having the opposite effect on me. He occasionally mistook me, his oldest son, for my dreaded stepmother. I grew increasingly crabby.

Somewhere in the rolling hills of the Palouse near Pullman, we rolled to a stop on the shoulder of the highway. I got out of the car and studied the play of the wind as it plunged into the wheat and shifted and shuffled it into shades of beige and viridian. My father got his camera out, set up a tripod and began fussing with focus and depth of field. Clouds — the big fluffy white variety — rolled over the top of a hill.

"These hills are Aeolian," my father said, "meaning windblown."

"I know," I said, "I like that word."

"Do you know what loess is?" he asked.

"Who?"

"Loess. It's a very fine dirt. That's why these fields grow such tremendous wheat."

"Loess sounds like loose," I said.

"What?" he asked. His hearing was poor, and he was still focused on making adjustments to his camera.

"Loose," I said. "Loess sounds loose."

"Well, yes," he said. "It is loose."

My father fussed with his camera until the f-number and shutter speed all conformed with the spectacle of the moment. His camera clicked and whirred and when a satisfactory number of photographs had been taken the clouds and hills of the Palouse were eventually packed in the trunk of his Taurus. We drove into Pullman and ate sauerbraten at a German restaurant.

My father lived another eight years, passing away just days before 9/11, 2001, when the world turned upside down and terrorism, torture, and global economic collapse became commonplace realities. Whatever happened to the series of photographs that he had taken that day I don't know. I never saw them. I don't need to. They all developed perfectly in that darkroom I call a head.

When I woke up, I was surrounded by Alaska. Bob Dylan tended bar. I said, "I love the opacity of things." He answered: "Here is the metabolism of a fire," and poured a glass of cleavage.

"Whose cleavage is this?" I asked.

"It is that of a fat man kayaking in the fog."

"That's gross."

"Yes, but we are at the border between dream and reality," he said, unsmilingly. His mouth was hidden by a scraggily beard.

"Have you written any songs lately?" I asked.

"As men age, their voices deepen," he said. "Their songs must be removed by surgery, because their perceptions are pinched by statement."

He poured me a glass of thought. I pondered what he just said.

"I don't understand what you just said," I said.

"I love the translucence of amber," he answered.

"Is that an answer or a statement?" I asked.

"It is neither. It is a description of the blacksmith's shoes."

My brain began churning a parenthetic condiment.

"Today's news is unbelievable, don't you think?" I asked, in an attempt to keep the conversation rolling.

"What happened?" he asked, while wiping a shot glass.

"The nucleus of a dollar was discovered in the throat of an oyster," I said.

"Oysters don't have throats," he said. "You better buy a different newspaper."

"Why did Plato choose a cave to represent the mind?" I asked.

He walked to the end of the bar and began floating over the cash register.

"Because the glitter of indolence isn't something you find in a trapeze," he said, and dropped to the floor.

"I don't want a theory on my plate," I answered, "I want food."

"Touché," is all he said, and drew me a map for a bingo parlor along the highway.

"What's this for?" I asked.

"Life is a canvas," he answered, "and though it shouts like a chair, you will find the algebra of alliteration adorns the queen of fog, and Frankenstein plays the piano with a wad of legs and a cauldron of fingers."

I tipped him a quarter.

He nodded, and poured himself into a pistachio.

I can't find my birth certificate. Does this mean I'm unofficial? Does this mean I need to work harder at being alive?

I do know a few things.

I was born in Minneapolis, Minnesota, with fish swimming between my ribs. Life felt funny at first, as if eternity sneezed. Which it did.

I soon discovered that hope is vertical and despair is an inclination, sometimes a proclivity.

I have had plenty of objectives throughout my life, and some of them are still around, flapping like flags, the kind that contradict everything we know about perception, such as emptiness, baptism, and direction.

Advice pops and crackles around my head constantly, the way it does for everybody. Everybody giving and receiving advice. This is why books get written. This is why language sometimes goes haywire. Or turns into flags.

A noun is either an adhesive or a fact. Proof of my existence can be found in an apricot, if I look hard enough. Look at all these molecules dancing on my tongue. Now that's an apricot. Wet and polysyllabic.

The zither, on the other hand, requires intuition, the incessant burlesque of goldfish.

Seabirds cry and the moon just laughs.

My shadow is a hunger tinkling in the intestine of a road. Mittens of fog float on the hood of a car leaking meaning like a shoulder.

The air is silent as an old house in Texas.

The mind is a heat in the head.

The ceremony of life is blatant in its desires.

The afternoon insinuates itself into stratum and straw. A thought delicate as snow, nerves encumbered by sugar. Doorknobs are offered to our hands. Sometimes we turn them, and doors open. When an emotion jingles with fire it is time to leave. Time to examine the novelties of law.

What is this fascism doing in my soup?

The zeitgeist is growling.

Because the skull is a house of bone, there are crickets on a map, flies in the afternoon, meat and blood sparkling like a scalpel.

There's my birth certificate.

It was there all the time, folded like a shadow in the crown of a hat.

I hate the sound of the hallway buzzer. It explodes my head. You have to peel me off the ceiling. I prefer the sound of rain. Rain on the awning. Rain on the roof of a car. Rain in my soup. Rain in my dreams.

Rain on the sidewalks of Budapest.

On balance, I find purple to be more atmospheric than infrared, although there are occasions when the sound of a piano echoes among the hues of a supernatural crab. Nail the sound of the surf to a dead accordion and what do you have? A voyage to the center of Dick Cheney's sneer.

This is why we need flowers. And tunnels and convalescence.

When was the last time I saw a lotus? When was the last time I made an incision in the air and watched a sky fall out? Or fireworks convulse in a forearm?

As it happens, there is a bruise on my arm, but I don't know how it got there. I agree with pencils. If there is a drawing to be made, then draw it. But if you attempt to put four dimensions on a piece of paper, you must be purposeful and awake. This is difficult because art, as a general rule, has no purpose. It must fall into existence copiously, the way hair describes a boulevard, or a boulevard describes a pancake. It must sting like syllables. Ache like a golden bug crawling through Bohemia.

Metaphors are empty, but exotic, like the dunes in the Victoria Crater on Mars. They can glue an ovation to an ovulation but elude the mystery of Euclid's punching bag.

If feelings had shapes, they might be described as propane and paint in a suitcase of sad implications.

A thread of ultramarine doing handsprings on a heliotrope.

Language has the weight of silk. It exceeds itself in its phantom adjustments to a world of classic oppositions, gravity and motion, worlds stirring among worlds.

Here comes a squirrel, a nebula of words congealing into fur, a nimble leap, a nervous regard, a perpetual motion machine with two beady eyes and a bushy tail.

If feelings had shapes, they might be described as a squirrel.
Or a hole. Or a submarine.
Or the swing of an arm.
Or a punching bag.

Sometimes I find it hard to believe I grew up on this planet. When was the last time I saw a cow? Who are these people photographing fish? Did language bring people into existence?

Here come the Blue Angels again, screaming over the roof. The luminous flavor of glory blazes from each canopy.

Down below, in the real world, where people live and die, ceramic oddities line the hospital window sill, little raccoons and bears bearing talismanic properties make it clear that clay is foreign to pain.

How did we get here? What are we doing here?

The declination of a star sneezes a mist of paint in an anthology of ugly poetry.

I am an animal of blood and bone. That much is clear. I can cut the air with the hot blue flame from a tank of propane and add more geysers to the opulence of my belt buckle for navigational purposes.

I like giving money to musicians. Mostly coins, dimes and quarters, but sometimes a sad hollow dollar, drifting into somebody's guitar case swollen and slow like a broken swamp.

This seems to be the age of the electric guitar. The poor oboe is an underrated instrument, but it perfectly captures the sound of this moment, this quandary, this dilemma, this jubilant irritation.

Did you know that Bach wrote several concertos for the oboe, or that Brian Jones played an oboe in "Dandelion"?

I love cloth and granite and antique emotions that go up and down in my body like metaphysical yo-yos. That taste like nutmeg and Hinduism. That make an enigma of the tongue.

Sometimes it seems like I'm always clipping my fingernails. They grow so fast. But not as quick as eyes, which scribble themselves into vision and make the clouds visible in their various deformations.

Worry is an internal noise and violates the principles of rawhide. The use of spherical trigonometry is helpful in solving problems of navigation, but nothing like the examination of bits of meaning in a quick opinion.

My opinion is this: life is brief, art is long. Intentions often go astray, and a poem is the quiet geography of an unsung song.

Sometimes I invent emotions. I make them out of neon and punctuation. Semicolons, for instance, are seminal to an understanding of linen.

Commas are drops of hesitation. Colons are bold.

Somewhere at the end of a sentence, I rub the night. Sparks fly. I follow a pain to the end of time. I live in a palace of thought. Everything is composed of butter, chlorophyll, and the ancient molecules of midnight.

I have a cubist tongue and a dada nose. My haircut used to be a garage. Next time you see a ghost at the supermarket it might be me. Then again, it might also be Thomas Paine, or Pablo Picasso.

I define pain by its weight. Paintings hanging crookedly on walls.

I watch The Kinks on YouTube, and redeploy them as a proposition.

Each day I run past the house of the symphony conductor I see him holding a glass brain with a fugue in it.

Music does this to people. Makes them wonderful and cogent, like the smell of dirt in front of the radio station just after the pansies have been watered.

Do you see the way the earth grips a tree? It is actually a tree gripping the earth.

I do not yet have a name for this emotion. The emotion itself is incomplete. But what emotion is ever whole and self-contained? Ask that woman over there, laughing and eating popcorn. She will tell you that the caliber of all emotions depends on the diameter of Tucson. But that's only because she is from Tuba City, and is watching a movie about blank-eyed underwear-clad zombies.

I hate the fourth of July.

I prefer Halloween.

Which is why I've never been to Texas.

But I ask you: what are your specific needs? Say anything you want. I can always use a little ambiguity. I love ambiguity.

Emotions are difficult to pin down because each word has different properties. In the Museum of Invisible Injuries, for instance, the word "cook" actually means "combination." And if you say the word "bone," an Iranian woman appears from the shadows with a huge gem on her finger, a ring that symbolizes the disembodiment of gherkins.

An emotion is thick and puzzling like a forest. It takes a long time to fully feel it. What is the point of becoming president if all you feel is power? Even lawn mowers feel power. Power is not where it's at. Where it's at is infinity. The exhilaration of light amid the pornography of black.

I desire wisdom. I desire it because it is prickly, an infatuation with ink that results in drift, in expansion, in a balloon blowing north toward derangements of ice.

Let us walk in silence a while.

Notice how cans and canisters stylize space, democratize it, occupy it, quiet it. There is enough beatitude in a single color to squeeze fecundities of sound from passports and gravel.

I have an eye on folds of denim. And here I stop to wonder: why doesn't Dagwood just get up and leave? What does he fear? Why is he always taking baths and sleeping on the couch? Has he read Naomi Wolf's book about fascism in America? Has Beetle Bailey? Will Beetle Bailey ever actually go to war? Even Prince Valiant goes to war.

Meanwhile, outside, the stars are drooling gallons of milk. I sit next to a table with newspapers on it. There is a surge of foreclosures in King County, and western Washington was ravaged by storm. A single woman living in Grays Harbor County who adopts horses happened by accident on a horse in distress off Highway 101 in Skokomish County. The horse was stranded in a flooded field, his nostrils just above water. The woman grabbed the owner's belt and swam out to the horse, who happened to be standing in the back of a submerged pickup. She dove under the water, released the tailgate, slapped the belt over the horse's head, and the two swam back.

What a marvelous story. Every time I read something like this a light comes on in my head and I believe that at least one metaphor is required to compete with clay.

Is poetry contrary to nature? Poetry kills fascists. If that is contrary to nature, so be it. The equation remains the same, although theories of the origin of the universe tend to vary. The important thing is to soak swallow's nests in water for at least two hours. Otherwise everything is just ears and hair-raising music, a constant reaching for that final, incoherent tattoo that will make sense of our skin.

Each emotion is a wilderness. Some people hate that. Others thrive. Why not make sure the ingredients of the composition rebel against their mixture? There is wisdom in books. Bugs, wigs, gauntlets. Bubbles and dragonflies. Time locked in nerves. A wild emotion behind the eyes. When the light comes on the furniture explodes. Words once grizzled with age become wine. An alphabet always wants to be crickets in the mind. Roots and ramification. I could have been a mason. I could have been an alchemist sleeping by a pile of books. But instead I became a horseman and saw a language stumbling out of a barn. It fixed my attention. Fixed it forever. And from then on I never got over my love of rope. My ambivalence toward hope, and the rustle of plastic in the wind.

WHY I NEVER WEAR SUSPENDERS

I love the shape of eggs, the heft of eggs, the taste and interior of eggs. Eggs are beautiful. They are annotations for the persistence of birds. Footnotes of quiet respectability, like the dripping intrinsic to the features of a faucet, the dripping that goes on quietly, if at all, in the middle of the night, while people are sleeping, with their head full of dreams, their heads which are shaped like eggs, eggs full of dreams.

Eggs dripping dreams.

Eggs with hair on them.

Mixtures of vanity and breath.

The backyard and its chimeras weirdly object to the jingling and twinkling of Christmas in a fashion that has little to do with zinc or squash but a great deal to do with perception and that tendency to imbue the external world with emotion.

I normally like to distance myself from emotion in poetry but sometimes that is not always possible. Sometimes one must acknowledge a beatitude, a mystery, a beautiful thing like an egg, or an analysis of glass inciting the applause of elves.

It's weird, but I call it home.

There are no labyrinths in oblivion, so I put them there.

The ideal reptile is one that darts from place to place with a seeming deliberation that ultimately means nothing.

Or carries a load of sparks to the bleachers.

I don't understand electricity, but I do understand volcanoes.

If a shrug is a sign of nonchalance, then a teaspoon is a tibia of light.

The peremptory call of materialism bites a moment of transcendence and a leopard in the throat leaps out and takes a bite out of Utah.

Spits out Idaho.

And crawls through the snow bleeding Colorado.

This is why I get so queasy around women's ankles. They're so profoundly delicate and lovely.

Like eggs. The delicacy of shells. Punctuation for an exploding calliope.

Omelets. Omens. Onions. The self-evidence of oysters. The heavy sadness of the waterfront. Smashed crates. Creaking docks. Immersions in words. Inflammations of chrome and perception.

Lacerated reflection.

Pearls in a pool of milk.

I derive no pleasure from shopping. I prefer the junkyard ease of a thought leaning against a parable in the convenience of a skull. How do nerves form? Nerves form by ransom. We hold the world captive until it yields cognition. Newspapers in a basket a yellow ping-pong ball under the chair.

Our eyes awaken the words in books. Poetry is a goose, Mick Jagger sipping a bowl of soup with nine ambiguities and a won ton.

Perspective is everything.

Words do the rest. The retina holds a leviathan in its veins and a tendril of signification bursts into flame.

Each word secretes a trace of eternity.

A bubble of hallucinations whispers of lichen and granite. This is what has happened to romanticism. You cannot cage a cadence. You can only let it go. Watch as it liberates itself from the burdens of form and assumes the heady aroma of the sound at low tide.

A rhapsody is a form of stitching. Sewing is an idiom of speech. Narcotic owls come together and form a geography of loon and loom and solitude. Denim tumbles in a dryer. Oblivion sleeps in the fog. A peacock spreads its multicolored tail on the radio.

Imagine a shadow chained to a lip. It signals an honest beatitude. Something akin to a piece of cheese dangling from the chin. This is why I am absorbed by glass. The mirror is a leer, a nosegay crashing through a nipple.

There are three hundred chickadees hopping around in my beard. But I don't have a beard.

I am a handstand blossoming into a blowtorch.

I am an octopus shampooing a tarantula.

The nipple is a tender incandescence of skin. An honest reticence filed under the shirt like an apocalyptic elephant.

As for reality, why not paint it? Dot it with owls. Reality is far more flexible than people think. It is not like a job. It is a large blue heron flapping in the nerves. Gorgeous inconsistencies of fish. The lush mysteries of form ripped out of an artery and written down in blood. The silk of a lost aesthetic. All of this. All of these things. Language in a loop. An ornament defined by explosion. Twilight and supernatural cows.

Human behavior is mostly supposition. Guessing what to do next. What to say. What to eat. How to say it. How to eat it. This is why poetry is so important. It serves so many suggestions. It is punctual and bright. It is a trumpet boiling in the arm. Water in bas-relief. Surrealists in the rain. A delinquent honesty based on knives. A large preposterous pain. The castle in the wilderness we all aspire to attain. It is a hunger too strange to be a conversation. The spectacle of night breaking against the eyes.

I write like a criminal doing push-ups in a cell. My right ear argues constantly against the evidence of my left eye. My right eye languishes under a bushy eyebrow creating a jewel of light for the X-ray of a bean. My left ear has a job in Kentucky and my taste buds lean toward scallops. My emotions are absorbed in yardstick hair. I applaud the law of physics. I walk around dreaming of quatrains that describe themselves as toast. Do you remember Prospero? How about Caliban? Remember him? All he wanted was freedom. What can you do with your hands? I fought the law and the law won. There are sockets in Antarctica that beg for this kind of attention. What's so special about philodendrons? The hardware of heaven is an imbroglio of blue and red. If zip codes were parsley I would wear velour in the fog. But here we are lost and alone, masturbating ghosts bursting into fire. Give me a spoon. Give me a needle. And I will give you time crawling toward a library crackling with black. I will give you the tall glue of reply. The light of the mind shames the darkness of the bank. It is silly under such circumstances to expect yeast, or unanimity. If you'd like, I can imitate the passage of Thursday. I can cram it full of scintillating questions. I can show you skeletons dancing on a map. Essence thirsts for explosion. Imagery is fur, cadence is bone. Each time I push my emotions into words light squeezes through a hole of blackberries and wrestles the sky onto a loom of seaweed where it becomes a coin of thought. Eternity tastes of quince and drapery clicks across a window. Is it true that a pendulum will swing in the same plane as the planet rotates beneath it? The azure of afternoon pours through the window and quick as a barracuda the horizon is hijacked by tendrils of mist. These words these fingers these strains cannot prevent the afternoon erasing itself from the wall. I can never understand the United States. This passion for jokes. For revival. For crickets and trigonometry. Once the voice mixes with a body of words I have a parakeet on my finger. See it? It is gripped in a gargantuan gloom. Eyes as dark as wine. As you may have already guessed, I don't wear cologne. I prefer the natural odor of garlic. It makes me feel French. It holds my ego together while I explore the planet. The planet, that is, as it appears to me in photographs and flint. I consider such things luxuries, like knowing where to scratch, or pulses of light creating a dialogue with time.

I'm hungry. But I look forward to tomorrow's Demerol and fiber optic journey through my intestinal tract. Intestines take their shape from necessity. The poem takes its shape from magnetism. The words are drawn to one another. To form what? A conclusion? Perhaps. Though it is more profitable to believe in their perpetual incompletion. This is where their energy finds fair play and hypothesis, amplitude and X-rays. Words colonnade the mind, bring it spring and parsley, the pretty convolutions of the bicycle, the vastness of its spokes, the briskness of its chrome and rubber. Who has not sat down to a table with beautifully folded napkins and wondered if there is an art to this sort of thing, a university where such things are taught, degrees given, symposiums formed, formulations proposed. Some emotions are like candy, there is a sweetness to the way they diffuse themselves throughout the body, and it is this enfoldment that is so good to unfold at the dinner table. All things that are convoluted find the gentleness of unanimity domiciled in the various organs of the body. Nothing exists that is not a summation of parts, a summation that is never fully summed, that cannot be summed, least of all summer, which is never completed, never summarized, but collapses slowly and imperceptibly into autumn. It is at the end of August that some of the best storms begin to form. It is always avarice that gets in the way of everything. Enzymes can just walk around dreaming themselves into skeletons and spoons, fluids that find themselves painting their own narrations as they meander through time. It is gleeful to encourage camellias, to spend time tending a garden, though life gets bigger when the sun goes down. That fat full moon you see up there is totally inoperable. It does what it wants to do which is mostly just float around our planet gurgling picket fences and wedding veils. It is escalators that triumph. They are the true marvels of our age, going up and down and up and down, men and women posed like statues as they carry their bags and purchases, some of them tattooed and bald, some of them hard like wood, some of them percolating a secret appetite. The many experiments of Harvey come to mind, his discovery of circulation and the action of the heart as a pump, a marvelous pump pumping blood through veins and arteries, pumping it rhythmically, smoothly, firmly. Pumping it up.

Pumping it down. Pumping it round and round. We are told that Harvey liked to withdraw from public life and sequester himself in his garden to indulge in contemplation. Certainly, in these humors he could feel what we all feel. The libraries of our bones opening to the leaves of reverie, the imperceptible motion of our blood bringing warmth to appendix and spine.

I exult in the names of things. I exult in generalities and cotton. I exult in hydrogen and deserts and things beyond measure. I erect a ladder and climb to the top of a big idea. I am glass after my machine finishes walking. I expose myself to the language of immersion. I feel colossal, like a tarpaulin churning in a thousand contrary winds. I fill with adrenalin as a song fills with music. The snow glistens with stunning beatitude. Hardwood enforces a sense of obligation. But to what? To the echoes of revolt and the springs of anticipation. Anticipation is jewelry. Ceremony is waves. Apparitions wander the garden like November giraffes. We pull ourselves out of ourselves and feel noble in the process. It is a process similar to the manner in which Madam Curie discovered radium. It is a sacrament of stirring, of giving your tongue the air in your lung and letting it harden into auger and rung. I know this because the fish are spotted with solitude and the opals are big as teaspoons. There are more curtains than mirrors in this one particular chamber. All the pipes are mnemonic because they remember the shape of water. When I ponder a scab I think of a squid lying dead in the sand. Do you see it? All these words are harnessed to my breath. It is tempting to assume that there is somewhere, somehow, a Platonic melodiousness that contradicts notions of how a singer should sound. How should a singer sound? A singer should sound opaque. There are many tools lying at the side of the highway by the lake. Why? Why does anything exist? We must learn to venerate the animal inside us. Never twist an emotion into an ulcer. Thread these words with your eyes and you will see, at the end of the sentence, a pile of metal beans. There is a certain economy in this business, thirty pounds of expression mixed with a reverence for the overlooked and incendiary. Fit your ears to the sound of the tailor folding his clothes. Embed your attention in the perusal of a bowl. There is an apparatus for beckoning the verdure of thought. It is called a pen. There is also a lamp available, and a desk, and a chair, and a syntax whose combinations perpetuate the extravagance of perception. If you slice the air with a razor, a visibility will tumble out and fall to the floor and lie there trembling like a lake. There is no purpose to this lake. Its shores are steeped in reverie, a galaxy of reeds and ripples hugged by a groaning sun.

Cubism was born in a small town near the Pyrenees. It rattled around in wire and eyeballs and entangled itself in Ecuador.

When cubism was born, a door opened to the hard white animal fat of the human mind. An airplane appeared, all struts and clouds, scribbling stars and hallucinations.

A can of house paint was given to Buffalo Bill.

And later a conception of jaws evoked dogs and tinfoil.

The mind is a noise because blood is thought and thinking causes beauty.

Cubism times Bach equals cardboard.

This could be a beginning.

This could be a stove, or another dimension. Something like a poem made of lumber and singing.

And vowels and limousines.

And crouching and crosscuts.

The space between perspectives is a form of redemption.

The opulent lobsters of cubism evolved the boilers of surrealism.

And the two were married so that a mind could mirror the sawdust of heaven and glitter into books.

A jackknife is worth a dime of participles if it can open a winter emotion.

When cubism was born, the morality of umber stated the precise meaning of fang.

The medieval lute was brought to Europe in the twelfth century.

Summer evenings were spent on patios sharing interesting facts.

A wiggly wobbly straw-skirted hula girl danced on the dashboard of Picasso's great cubist truck. Eons passed. Gravity became a reflection in a motel mirror. The blueness of a pool glowed alluringly under golden skies. A paper cut was stubborn to heal. A man remembered the Beatles in Hamburg. A woman in a black leather coat bought a jade dragon at the Wang Chang Trading Company. Time became still as a sandstone arch, a wad of gauze on a freshly extracted molar. And now everything is perpetual: wave follows wave, and echo answers echo.

The cat licks himself by a patch of light on the floor.

Mist blows east from the top of the mountain.

People seek themselves in the past and see themselves in the future.

When cubism was born, fish swam like fish, birds flew like birds, word followed word, and water poured from a jug for the first time every time.

"What's this? What's this? What's this?" said Pablo moving from canvas to canvas. He was stunned.

"That's *Houses and Trees*," said Georges. "I did it this last summer. That's *Still Life with Mandolin*. And I call that *The Metronome*."

An orange bug crawled across a black suitcase. The room reeked of turpentine. Georges swallowed some wine and turned inward.

"I love the shape of the mandolin," he said. "It is lucid and full, like an aurora harnessed to a flaming sun."

He squeezed a tube of paint. A daub of raw sienna oozed out. He gave it a quizzical glance, then daubed some cotton on the canvas he was working on, a still life of a mandolin, trumpet, concertina and sheet music.

Pablo ate a grape. A bulb of garlic rolled from the counter to the floor.

"Have you heard about the Wright brothers?" Pablo asked.

"Yes," said Georges. "I went out to the field. Their plane is beautiful. All struts and cloth. A complicated mess. Like a strange musical instrument."

Pablo formed an image of the plane in his mind. A Byzantine structure of crisscrossed wires skulked through his skull. Rumbled. Coughed. Took to the air.

The neighbor's peacock screeched.

Incident light held a bubble of Mediterranean soup then moved into the shadows of the studio. Georges went outside and stood on the balcony looking at Paris.

"Hey Pablo," he said, "come on out and look at this."

Pablo stepped out onto the balcony. They watched a blimp hover over the Eiffel Tower.

"The world is changing," said Georges.

"It is becoming tough and aggressive, like a bull," said Pablo.

"And full of invention," said Georges.

This was true. The cornflake, air conditioning, windshield wiper, safety razor, neon light, vacuum cleaner, lie detector, helicopter, zeppelin, radio receiver, tractor, teabag, Teddy Bear and Theory of Relativity had all just entered the twentieth century.

When Pablo left, Georges went to work. A pot of azaleas flickered by one of the windows. He began to explore the alphabet of structure. Brushwork pummeled the canvas. His drawing was sharp, acute, vigorous. Powerful lines seized, hugged, and explored contour. The cylinder, the cone, the sphere. Cubes and polyhedrons.

He did not outwardly admit it right away but seeing Pablo's *Les Demoiselles d'Avignon* had changed nearly all of his ideas about painting. About seeing. His experimentations broadened into a complex game between words and things, illusion and reality. His efforts at distortion mirrored the elliptical syntax of Mallarmé in rudimentary, ruminative pigments and multiple points of view, a lyric reality with the elegance of bone.

He looked for correlations between signs. He added letters, stenciled and hard. He painted an aria by Johan Sebastian Bach. He introduced sand and plaster, wood shavings and metal filings. He looked at a shadow and shook his brush. He became a magician of detail. He imitated, meticulously, the grain of wood.

The painter, he thought, does not try to reconstruct an anecdote but to construct a pictorial fact.

The Big Nude was a breakthrough. Foreground and background switched places. Curved surfaces pivoted on planes that led the eyes to knobs of solidarity at the surface, a matter of hair falling a certain way, a nose, a pair of ears, a pair of eyes, legs, hands, fingers, toes were celebrated in a vibration of form.

Georges donned an African mask and said "There is only one thing in art that has value: that which one can not explain."

He got a fire going in the stove. He was talking to Guillaume Apollinaire and Max Jacob. He liked poets.

There was a woman's bra on a bureau of drawers.

"Light does not exist for the painter," he said. "It is all about color."

"But why have you muted your colors lately?" asked Guillaume.

"They conflict with my design," Georges said.

"You can't put a muzzle on the sun," said Max.

Georges sat down on a stool, picked up a concertina, and squeezed it. It made a disconsolate wheeze.

"The vase gives form to the void and music to silence," said Georges.

He felt a trickle of sweat go down his back. It was getting hot in the room.

"We need to get out of here," said Georges.

"Where shall we go?" asked Guillaume.

"I don't have any money," said Max.

"Don't worry about it," said Guillaume. "We'll share a magnum of wine."

"Let's get drunk." said Georges.

"Let's discover reality," said Max.

They found a bistro in Montmartre.

"Mystery blazes forth with the broad daylight," said Georges. "The mysterious blends with the darkness."

He began sketching a bottle whose bouquet had turned to twigs and crinkly leaves.

"Art is inherently quixotic," said Guillaume. "Like the pattern of tread on rubber automobile tires."

"I've been thinking about taking up fencing," said Max. "Hey look, there's Pablo."

Pablo was talking to a man at the bar. It looked like an argument. The man took a swing at Pablo. But Pablo was short. The man missed.

Georges stopped sketching and went to see what the argument was about. The man that took a swing at Pablo was also a painter. He was called André Derain. He was a large man. He normally did not try to hit men smaller than him, but Pablo pissed him off. He said he was still living in the past with the impressionists.

Georges entered the fray. He calmed André down. They were friends. Talk turned to boxing. A match was convened in the alley. André was slightly larger than Georges but his boxing skills were outmatched. Georges won easily, connecting with every punch. The fight ended and everyone returned to the bistro.

"Did I tell you I've been growing some tomatoes?" asked Max of no one in particular.

Georges looked at Max and laughed at the innocence of his forehead. And winced. His jaw was sore from one of André's more accurate punches. He gyrated his jaw. The sensation was perfect. Acute. Distinct. The world made palpable at last.

If Picasso had a jackknife, it would have a thousand blades, each delicate as a ghost pegged to a wall in syllables.

When an image is written on a sheet of paper the universe turns strawberry and tragic. In the morning there is a canoe on the sidewalk. And consonants are milked into fingernails.

Each and every day nebulas ride in cars.

If there are cherries there is communion in streams.

I am wet and charming to know what a parable is. Meanwhile, the libraries ooze strength and wisdom, and bananas embody the problem of emotion.

Hammerheads and palominos cross the Rubicon. Zippers adapt to thumbs of mist wherein the lyrical skin of an innocent greed echoes pronouns in cabs. The many erratic shades of greens and browns that explore the problem of representation with prophecies of pearl and a more radical empiricism than pipes.

Picasso's jackknife folds the sky into a pickle.

We will ride a pretty elevator to the top of a wilderness.

It is then we find that the story is just beginning.

The bruise that plays in aluminum is knitted by mushrooms. Horses under the bridge. My thumb is this thing I use to power my hand. Various streams serve as sensation. Mostly blood, and abstractions in charcoal. The grandeur of the spars is matched by the biology of our explorers. It is a thrilling word that comes apart in insults. Hirsute, flirty, and theoretical. Like a poem employed by banjo. I have galvanized a tricky idea to emulate an orthogonal wisecrack. Cod will clarify our path. Faith up the profligate chair to ladder the busy asphalt. The cylinder gleaned from our abstraction is now frequented in brocade. The component next to it is a visible incentive to oppose henna with elevators. Let us therefore limousine into piles what we have hugged in sheer napkins. What virtue there is in push-ups! The structure is congealing in enigmatic rescues. My emotions stink of strength. There is space within my skull for a laughing gardenia. All it takes is a squirt of oil and the veins running through the Picasso will propel consonants of Fauve alfalfa. Picasso's binoculars, for instance, which are fulfilled in their vision by orchards of pear and cherry. The sugar is slapped when a shine heaves tickles. The plywood Bach is twisted into a Möbius glaze which turns ocher in proximity to itself. Everything else is blue.

The cuticle, any cuticle, is dynamic to fork that money trickle when the components of age are bottled in opium jokes. The daub demanded raspberry. The drink demanded walnut. Everything else is a matter of plugs, plovers, and plasma. Cubism tumbling in knives. Seriously. What I mean is unconstrained by its catalogues. Or its emphasis on feeling the eyes emerge from their nerves to hold a dime of hungry water. Or its chatter by cartilage, or call for mustard. Its weight in red, or rumor of cubes. Its exhumed densities everywhere crooked and green. Symmetry admonishes the circle. This is how poetry came to be born. It elbowed its way into the astronomy of antlers. Mockingbird cows soaked in spirits. The secret kerosene of the lotus and its diversions in cardboard. Please. Whatever you do. Don't disturb the hills. The gardenias are made of propane and the birds are flames of indispensable sugar. Each root has, at one time or another, either been rain, or a strain. A muscular reach through dirt. The busy angels of the wilderness are incandescent with the cosmic broth of a wandering Buffalo Bill. Only our emotions can know the harmonica consciousness that intuitively extends into the palpable simulacrums of allegory. This is where boxing sparkles. Where structure lures the paraphernalia of tea into the ears with its gentle clatter. Where everything is present, and ink, and Apollinaire's nocturnes act the hair out of its brush.

I decide to move Van Gogh's *Bridge at Arles* into the bedroom. It looks good in there. Its soft welcoming blue sky over Arles and the washer-women bent over scrubbing multicolored clothes in the water blue as the sky above but with ripples radiating out in lighter tints of blue. I put it next to a painting my father did during a winter in North Dakota up in the Turtle Mountains. The hills are buried in snow whose preternatual softness is accentuated by a mellow crepuscular light. It is a scene of remarkable serenity.

I also move a wheel-shaped collage a friend gave us for a wedding gift into the bedroom. Each turn of the wheel reveals an excerpt of poetry: "Everywhere is a tent where we put on our whirling show." "Late one night as Ugarte and I were walking through the narrow streets, we heard children's voices chanting the multiplication tables."

I empty the school desk of its contents and wipe the dust off its ornate black wrought iron legs with a moist paper towel. I get every nook and cranny and then we carry it out to the car where I am able to lay it on its back. It is a close fit. There is a mere fraction of an inch to spare between the end of the wrought iron legs and the window of the rear hatch. It clatters a little when I begin to drive. This worries me. But we arrive without incident. I get in the back on my knees and lift it forward. A screw has come loose. I tighten it with a dime. We carry it to the loading dock where several men are sorting through things. One of them says, "hey, that's nice," and I ask if I can donate it. "Sure thing," he says.

The corner of our apartment is now free for a bookcase.

We go to the Ballard Bookcase Company. We have been sent a flyer that says it will be closing down in several months.

The proprietor appears. He is middle-aged and of average build. His hair is short, thin, and reveals a tint of red. He is like wood: plain-speaking, cordial, firm. I tell him that I want to buy the large corner bookcase. It is Ponderosa pine with hemlock crown top molding. He asks if I have any questions. I ask him if the wood is finished. He says no. He asks if I would like to finish it myself. I tell him no, we live in an apartment and aren't equipped to do woodwork. He tells me finishing it will be three hundred dollars extra. The extra amount comes as an unexpected jolt, but I agree to it, knowing in advance that if I take time to reflect on it I will arrive at the same conclusion. I need a bookcase.

The bookcase arrives on Friday. I run up the steps to open the door to our building. There stands the bookcase maker holding some book shelves. They smell good. They smell of pine. He brings them in and sets them on the floor by the door to the laundry room. He returns to his truck while I prop the door open with a wedge of wood. I shove it under the door with my bare foot. The bookcase maker and his assistant lug one of the bookcases into the apartment and set it on the floor of the downstairs hallway. They go back for the other one. The bookcase seems much larger than it did in the shop. It's huge.

The bookcase maker and his assistant maneuver the two bookcases near to the corner of our apartment where I have made room for them. He returns to his truck for a drill and some brackets while I chat with his assistant, a small but solidly built man with dark hair and an accent. I can't place his accent. He could be east European, Russian, or Mexican. He tells me he has been building bookcases for twenty years. He does not know what he'll do when the shop closes. He seems very sad. I don't have any suggestions. I don't know what you do with such a highly specialized skill in times like these.

The bookcase maker returns. He maneuvers himself behind the two halves of the bookcase and begins to screw the brackets in while his assistant holds them firmly together. I hear a grinding sound. I wonder what it will be like if we move and I have to unscrew the two halves and hope the holes don't wear out and the screws re-screw firmly into place.

His assistant, meanwhile, gazes at the books on another bookcase, one I made a long time ago in California, with carvings on each side, designs I took from a Viking church. Birds in foliage eating berries.

When they leave, I want to say something encouraging to the bookcase maker's assistant. All I can muster is "good luck with wood." As if wood had some guardian spirit. Some healing deity in its fragrance and grain. Would that could be the case.

Turning words into art is eighty-three pounds of thought swirled on the sidewalk.

Turning words into art is a bounced tongue of happy rubber.

Turning words into art is cruel. Remember, emotion is a frontier, not an address.

The very idea of ketchup is absurd.

Turning words into art is a long letter from Iceland.

Turning words into art is a glaze native to dragonflies.

The anarchism of hair.

Turning words into art requires an understanding of introversion. The desperado rides his horse at midnight because there is a similarity between writing and black gleams of reverie.

Because there is a similarity between writing and riding a horse.

Wherever there are words there are words that need to be extended into spectral trombones.

Wherever there are words there is sandstone and electricity.

Wherever there are words there is bound to be a hairdo.

Wherever there are words there are colorful ballads and antlers and constellations and a rare silver ornament.

Grease and gaskets. Sad old garages with cans of dried paint.

As words progress they turn into old wasps, large, foreign realities, pronouns clicking together like castanets.

The human mind is wild.

Turning words into art is a delirium too big for a drug, too vast for a compass, too volatile for a science.

Turning words into art is a flurry of blades climbing the front door of Chile.

Turning words into art chops and slops against the cake of morning.

Turning words into art bursts into schools of energetic tuna.

Syncopates the hammers of the eighteenth century.

Elevates elves and feels pleasantly solemn in bulges of burning thunder.

Here is what I like: scruples, scrupulous people, and puppets with cleavage.

The smell of ash from a hearth of stone can sometimes bring a blush of nostalgia to my nose. Though it is nothing so piquant as Rebekah Del Rio singing "Llorando" on YouTube.

I like the way calculus juggles beliefs about space and momentum in space and what might happen if I mail a bathrobe to the apocalypse. The apocalypse waiting to happen. The apocalypse around the corner. The apocalypse in the bathrobe I just sent.

The apocalypse is raw and uncaring, like the naked density of a rock.

There is an odd satisfaction in arranging silverware, especially on the eve of an apocalypse.

Which isn't to say I won't be disappointed if the apocalypse is canceled. Or postponed.

That is, in fact, the purpose of the bathrobe. Bathrobes are inherently teleological. They have a quieting effect on the rumblings of chaos.

This would include condiments. But what is the correct response to condiments?

Mirrors. Cacophony. Engaging perspectives.

Russian paleontologists extracting mammoth tusks from the muck of Wrangel Island.

Beads of water on the underside of a leaf, all symmetrical, as if crafted by a jeweler.

Puppets with cleavage hanging obliquely among the words that heave and jerk them into dramas of greed and redemption.

And what of the geography of sorrow? What of anticlines of rugged indignation? The languor of ponds in puddings of moss? The hollows of rook and rock and rotunda? Of bone? Of the rectory at Mont Saint Michel? How should the enigma that is the tuning fork best be enucleated?

The geography of blood cries out for exploration. Imagine, for instance, a Tuesday immersed in lumber. Men and women examining planks of maple and oak and sugar pine. The smell of that. And a boiler threatening to explode and a fringe of cypress and a mustang in the snow.

Puppets with cleavage. Strings that kink and tangle like sentences. Corpuscles. Veins.

This ain't no fairytale.

This is a woman returning home with a bag of groceries.

This is an engine, and this is a song propelled by blood.

Music and blood.

Which is an ideal arrangement.

A wart for the mist of morning.

A large silk dragon flapping and clacking in a hard December wind.

The biology of color is dense and alphabetic. It is thick and incomplete. It is thin and flame. Occurrences of hunger veined with silver. February in Oregon. The tables of reason shining out of the ecstasies of winter fables.

If these words were colors they would equal weather.

The weather of dolls.

The weather of halls.

The weather of effort and necessity and mixture and vast gloomy generalities dropping from the sky like incessant nailing.

Or rain.

Plain simple rain.

There is a certain divinity in rain. Even a hacksaw rusting in a backyard has something to say about private feelings expressed as umbrellas. Doors are opened by fingers curling around doorknobs. The process is exquisite, muscular, like memories minced in ink.

If these words were colors they would indulge daubs of black.

It's easy to sell one's skin but harder to sell a dangerously repressed feeling. Music stirs our emotions. Ink turns into flint. The easy straw of intrigue crackles in the paradox of fire.

These are my lighthouse shoes.

These are my lightning socks.

These are symptoms of realism, phantoms sitting in a hospital waiting room. Nuclear acne. Lumber. Customs, dress, behavior. A cubist dentist with asymmetric teeth drilling a hole in a romantic molar.

You cannot measure a thrill. You cannot measure the shadow of a shadow. You cannot measure a ribbon of joy soaked in Mardis Gras. You cannot measure the weight of a reflection, a flea in a refinery, the silence in the air before a volcano erupts or the heartbeat of the universe looped in alphabets of fruit. The triumph of trumpets. The broth of thought.

Here is a pink emotion. Do with it what you will. Roll it around in the blood. Invest it in perception. Provoke music. Be contemplative and Elizabethan. Maneuver it through a sonnet. A description of mirrors crawling across the table.

Don't worry if a little of it comes loose.

You can't bite a hot dog without a little mustard squirting out.

If these words were colors they would smell of life. They would feel a dragon stirring in the nerves. They would allow things to happen. Healing and rhinestone and photography and jade. Daylight and snow and Mozart's birthday. The necessity of burlap. A fold. A lament. A large fat sound surrounded by Thursday. I assume you are listening. I assume this is making sense. If these words were colors they would form a pair of beaded moccasins falling to the floor. And the quiet of that moment.

Music and Proust. Proust and music. Music in Proust is sunshine and crows. Music in Proust is a memory emerging into the present, the presence of an absence, an absent presence whose sound is located somewhere in the interval between a passing car and a teapot coming to a boil. Music in Proust is the sounds of the street, a qualitative scale of sonorities indicating the temperature by the density of pitch. Music in Proust is a Wagnerian storm, a turbulence of feathers and foam. Music in Proust is an amoeba of sound dressed magnificently in mohair.

And how is music made music is made with expectancy. French horns. Heart and heartwood and hurt and heaving and hertz and hod and hunger and hammers and Hepplewhite and hair.

Violins and musk and jelly and nullification.

Bach, Saint-Saens, Ravel. Debussy, Fauré, Satie.

Music in Proust wrestles nebular topographies. Music in Proust shakes with engagement.

There is so much music it falls to the floor in resplendent coins of brightening sound. A cornucopia of participles and undertones and coinciding flannel.

Music is a fact. If a word contains a fact is the fact a fluorescence or a roller skate?

A word is a contrivance to cage a fact in sound. Music is a contrivance to cage a headlight in roses. Rhododendron is a word we were sniffing coffee Proust can have an engine words on the paper rattling north toward Cabourg.

Music does not use profanity unless it is tightly wound. There is no use in a junction unless it is glazed with rain. Think of music as it has to do with thinness. Think of thin things. Thin things make us think. Thin things resemble thought. The gauze of thought. A gaze in the gauze of thought.

It is very different to refuse jelly in Ecuador. It looks like an urge but the man in the green sweater said he could burn it into reason.

Every sonata has a beginning. Every sonata which has a beginning makes it be spaced by eyes and played into vision as a refreshment or web. A sonata should be arbitrary and surge. It should not be nailed to a cloud. It should be not be serviceable like a horseshoe but rhapsodic and roving like eyes on a beach.

Now for a sonata.

Welcome to peanuts. Welcome is itself a part of a peanut if it is part of a peanut the peanut is in itself a part of a sentence and you are welcome to welcome heliotrope. A peanut instead of syncopating. That so easily makes a category. This is a sonata. It has no use in itself because canteen is said two times to be very nearly achieved and it is not only individually but for the rest of us a use that cannot be plywood because it is invoked in battle. A sonata is very easily filled with progress but would it be worth it since the ogre is stone. There is some use in joining textures to traction, although traction occurs as a palate crawling with words.

If singing is satisfying then nudity is diagonal.

If a piece of air is an oar it might be used to move a mind forward over a pond of paragraphs.

Energy tastes like banks. Energy goes into banks as income and comes out as outcome. Outcome goes into banks as income and comes back out carrying a mouth full of notes. Cheese. Chintz. Chestnuts. Out and out language.

This is what a sonata looks like when it is written down as hubbub. Horseplay, or rust.

Sonatas look like sound because they are said to be a resemblance to music to the weight of sound as it is parceled into sand and packed down hard by the thunder of waves crashing on top of it.

Play the sonata as if it were a body of words engaged in beige. Estuary or fin. To find it may do as a pin is not to ignore its capacity for rope.

A sonata is a perch, a tempo, a roost. A way to situate the music so that it hangs in the air balanced and huge. Black shapes in Rembrandt. Daylight stretched into elms. Syllables soaked in an octave like hawsers and stars. A taste so chafed it smashes words into time. This means rhetoric is a large pink life, a weight in words, an agitation, a mist. A freshly hoisted oar, an implement dripping water.

The warmth of conviction. The construction of smell.

Clocks and oil. The tongue of a river varnished with sunlight.

Proust in music. Music in Proust.

The theatre is dark and otherworldly. A man appears. He is very distinguished. He has a thick white mustache. He introduces the next performer: "señoras y señores, el club silencio les presenta La Llorona de Los Angeles, Rebekah Del Rio." He rolls the final 'r' with regal gusto. He leaves the stage. A woman emerges from the darkness. She is beautiful. There is something odd about her. She seems connected to some other, some higher dimension. She begins to sing. The sound of her voice is soft, piercing, uncanny. The song is an old song by Roy Orbison and Joe Melson, "Crying," which she is singing in Spanish.

> Yo estabo bien por un tiempo,
> viliviendo a sonreír.
> Luego anoche te vi
> tu mano me toco.
> y el saludo de tu voz.

In Spanish it is called "Llarondo." This makes the song more thrilling, more romantic, more exalted. Her voice grows in intensity. Her diction is precise. She and the song are one. One entity. One phenomenon. A feeling of transcendent beauty makes itself apparent. It has menace. Why should the sublime be menacing?

Yet it is. The emotion is overwhelming, as if some mysterious force had been lured down from a celestial sphere and sustained for a moment on an earthly plane. As if some law had been broken. Some tacit, unwritten law between humanity and the angels, between humanity and the gates of existence, some endless invisibility, a reality too intense for the pumping of a human heart, for human veins, had been momentarily brought into the darkness of the theatre, and its presence was terrible and beautiful and strange.

Del Rio's voice grows in intensity. The air is heavy with the sublime. There are two sparkly tears painted under her eye. The effect is theatrical, melodramatic, a trifle corny, yet weirdly majestic. Sincere, as only the macabre and prodigal and strange can be sincere.

Del Rio faints and falls to the stage. Her voice continues, unfaltering. It is as if she has brought the voice and soul of the song so alive, so fully actualized, that even when her mortal flesh can no longer sustain its passion, it continues.

Two men carry her from the stage, behind a red velvet curtain. The voice goes on. Full, strong, voluminous and vast: the words soar, sear, search the air, as a terrible tenderness retreats back into the dark.

GOUACHE

Gouache: what a marvelous word! The chemistry of the eye chews it into music. It is heavier than ink on the verge of language. Gouache creates a silver inside you. It is the sorcery of red, the generosity of photographs. You must use gouache to capture iron. Gouache hops into the paradox of opacity and makes it bang against the mind. Blue glass. The meaning in bread. All this. All that. It is all vague. It is all gauze. It is all gouache. Otherwise it would fall through this paper and become a particle of Christmas soaked in demurral. Do you hear them? Do you see them? There they are: the skeletons of winter clicking like mayonnaise in a paragraph inundated by language. It is a revolt against the banality of pleasure. It is the black plug of existence plugged into memory. Why else are valentines so goofy? Gouache is a medium of gummy water. The long sugar of dawn, movement and light, the smell of freshly sawn wood, fingers maneuvering sushi. The vowels hang in the mind like a veil. Elegant physics equations. The sound of a far off bell. Air and trees and sailboats and hills. The sweetness of twilight when the sky is bathed in rose. The vowels are an emulsion of sound and meaning. Sunlight crashing through a window. Crimson and turquoise and gold oozing on the horizon. Grocery receipt on the dashboard. Wads of cotton scattered on the sidewalk. A surgeon making his first incision. What is the relation between the mind and the body? Tie the fog into a knot of consciousness and there you have it: gouache. The sweep of association. Coconuts and tartan. Art during the French enlightenment. When the first stars begin to toss their light, you have quiet in the cemetery, the earth at your feet. You have the nectar of oblivion in the grass. An inexplicable presence. The fluidity of gouache. A sound like a river dragged out of Iceland. Beauty in a conjuration of wind.

They say there is a bird in Chile that seeks food in veins of gold and silver, that it lives in small caves between hills containing metal, that its wings shine during the night and that its eyes emit a strange, unearthly light. That when it finds a vein of precious metal it feasts until it is too heavy to fly, and that the flicker of its wing-light entices prospectors to their doom.

But why doom? Must the quest for wealth always lead to doom? Why is beauty and beautiful things always so doom-laden? Perhaps there is something in this story that cannot be said. Something defiant. Something beyond human perception. Something scandalously fantastic. Something oracular and divine. Is it the gold, or is it the bird? It is the gold that is lewd, the bird that is elusive. Some seek the bird. Others seek the gold. Who can say which is the wiser?

We might imagine such a bird as an apology for our limitations, as an art emancipated from empirical reality. We might imagine an art that serves no aim other than beauty, and craft it in metal, where light has been hammered into a bud, a bloom of incendiary words. Feathers like knives. Feathers in a flame of maniacal gold.

No crocodile is equal to its hunger. No appetite is equal to its satisfaction. The groan of a cello is an incentive to translucence. Heat cannot keep a secret. Beauty is brightest where analysis fails.

There is nothing so obscure it is not enhanced by talking, nothing so dull it cannot be coaxed into brilliance, nothing so deep it cannot be dug from an abyss and brought to the surface in paroxysms of red. All that it means to be red. A sweet oblivion gliding through the blood in a swoon of sudden blue. There is nothing that a consonant cannot dangle from a vowel. Nothing that cannot be imagined. Nothing that cannot be mined. Nothing that cannot invoked. Nothing that cannot be called from nothingness and given a shape and a name and a fringe of color.

Nothing.

Imagine a jewel so dense and intricate it begins with lips and ends with wings. Imagine a wing that is an epitome of light. A drop of light given life in a piece of curious metal. The presence of meaning tattooed to a wall in a pirouette of broken smoke and shadow. A moment of cherubs in the mind of December. A tangle of sound in a ladle of wax.

Imagine a weld. And the smoke from that weld. The formation of wings. The flood of feeling that loves the oblique. The angular. The careful and intricate. The inexplicable. The contradictory. The tangled and weird. A reverence for metal, a piercing desire, and a strange, unearthly light.

Everything we see in this world we see in sequence. Sequins. A chain of events. A necklace of noise. Succession. Series. Strings and upshots. Cause and effect. Spanish motorcyclists tumbling through the air.

Venus passing before the sun.

Red velour Christmas bow tied to a black wrought iron step rail. Christ bearing the cross.

Two men hoisting a mattress up a flight of steps.

A ring of neon tubes lighting up white and brilliant in systematic, mesmerizing waves around and around the circle.

Women's nylons both revealing and concealing the flesh and tone and shape of a leg.

Gravestones capped in snow.

A man in a gray jacket balancing rocks on a Puget Sound breaker while an Elliott Bay gull looks on from an adjacent rock.

Pops wheezes coughs hiccups. Muscle and skin leaving footprints on a beach.

There is reality in shape, shape in reality. Fables, blisters, flint. Meat and coincidence.

A word is nothing without contingency. Hawk on a Nickelodeon.

Some things bend. Some things bead. If you watch a living amoeba under a microscope you will see squiggles. Division. Reproduction. Contingency.

Events sequenced in time hold the air in place. Lumber and nail eventually become a barn. A stable. A momentary space. The heady odor of hay and manure. The dazzle of beams. The harnessing of time.

When something moves we call it a narration. A story.

Light through a lens, images on a screen.

An eyeball is a globe of water. It exemplifies jam. Something inside that little speck of jelly thinks circumference is appealing. And thereby hangs a volume.

Narration mutilates space. Creatures called words develop eyes and articulations to give meaning to the invisible world. Thought, design, ligament.

There is sometimes a moment so great and heady it seems every-thing is on the verge of bursting. And then it does. It bursts. Rem-nants of luminous color come dropping down in slow biography. And there you are face to face with the great mystery. Everything falls into place and a door opens. A door to what? A farm in the 1500s. An au-tumn in nineteenth-century France. Ecuador crinkled and imposing on a Spanish map.

It is the characteristic of an eye to validate the visible and see who or what has been in the room. Each room is a story. We live inside ourselves. We live inside our narratives with furniture and people and paintings. Thought is the furniture of the mind and philosophy is the facing surface of our camera obscura. Everything ham and hammered and holy and happening is outside in the visible world. It becomes allegory in the invisible world. It becomes ogres and jungles and phantoms and amulets. It becomes December. It becomes taxis and thermostats. Thesis and sunspots. This is how the invisible is made visible. An aperture in the mind dilates into orchards and monkey-shines. Resolute buccaneers. Rope and canvas. Mermaids. Fiddles. Verbs.

We see through a seeing. We see through a seeing into a seeming sea of storms and asterisks. And as imagination bodies forth the forms of things unknown, the poet's pen turns them to shapes, and gives to airy nothing a local habitation and a name.

One must start with luggage, symbols varnished with the lacquer of thought.

It is very hard to hold a marble udder on a granite cow. But you can milk it once you become familiar with the beauty of extravagance. A story is, after all, a hunt. A pursuit. Twilight beaten into tinfoil. A face reflected in a lake.

Pollen. Pewter. Breakfast at Tiffany's.

Each sentence is an intrigue, an alias, a din. Can you hear that?

A bee is a predicate with wings.

Each noun shakes loose a host of possibility. A Kansas marshal in baggy clothes. Pistons of rain moving a tangle of words into motion and shape.

Jacks are the tangible evidences of life. Who at one time or another has not pulled a jack from a trunk and wondered how it works. Won-dered if it is even the right jack. And pulled the implement all dusty and puzzling out of the trunk and set it down on the road and pondered it and tried to figure its narrative out in the mind before getting one's fingers and thumb pinched in getting the thing set up under the car.

No narrative can work without a spare tire, a feeling for wheels and formulation. A reverence for engines, bright silver sheen of the street when the December sun pops out. An elephant in the rearview mirror.

If you want to build a mask of damask you must do so brick by brick. This is what we do in fiction. We signify caulk with a caulking gun and wipe away the excess with a moist T-shirt.

A story begins with a heading. It is mappable by apple and glaze. It is already in our scheme of things quivering like a flame in our personal conception of eternity.

Feeling tired? Low self-esteem? Light a candle. Take a bath in rose petals.

Imagine Idaho. The rapids are sizzling with suspense. The water crawls or bounces over the rocks in a cantata of liquid rhetoric because it is the way our minds foam out of our heads. We go inward for scenes of our inner life as if the mind were a theatre. We watch the curtain rise on a jeep. A colossal eyeball floats overhead. We search for coordinates and find meaning in barrels of peanuts and creaking floors. When we open our eyes we find that the rapids are still there, but appear different, more copulative and silver in flashes of fractious splendor.

We know what it is to row and row and make a narration of rowing, a tale of endocrine and flags where viewpoint is the seed of plot and the water beneath us causes our convictions to float, unanimous in movement. Believe me this is so. Think of resolution as a form of ambergris, a residue left by vagaries of implication and gray.

The wisdom of feelings drive the narration through fragments of hindsight and recall, Ray Charles and Clint Eastwood sharing a piano bench talking about the blues. October broken into bits of hue, pancakes heaped on a plate in Topeka.

What happened that day with the spoon? Why was there so much pressure to order? Why was the menu so large and cold to the touch?

The waitress was friendly and thin and appeared to be in her early forties. She was energetic and friendly. And yet there was a hint of melancholy in her carriage, a soupçon of thirst only time could quench. But whose story was that, hers, or our own? Were we reading too much into her facial expressions, her manner of walking, her general demeanor? Were we projecting our own personal narrative onto someone else? Was the pork chop cooked enough? The mashed potatoes mashed enough? Why did the sugar come in packets when the salt was allowed its own bottle at the table?

The first tales were told by tinkling sunlight in the left knee while juggling bits of air called words. Rhinoceroses, bears, deer, bison, wild horses, oxen, boars. Necks, locks, water skis, needles, periscopes, resurrections, sarongs.

I have never had a gun aimed at me. This, somehow, seems essential to a full existence, to have one's life held in balance like that, by a stranger, by someone who could care less about you, all they want is your money, what a terrific attitude would emerge from such an experience, and yet, in the very process of writing about it, am I in some way bringing it on? Do words cause things to happen?

The story is a balance between caissons and caviar. Thoughts and ideas flushed from the skull engraved with the fauna of a vanished world.

People live in two worlds, a nebulous brochure of postponed aspirations and a narcotic flexibility. Inner world visions are more vivid than real life. They pulse with harmonicas and boulevards. Snow in the streets turning to slush. Bright chartreuse moss splotched on a concrete retaining wall. A cage for savage emotions. Tambourines. Feathers for strange rituals.

Devotion is an animal. It is the reason for nudes. We are but the servants of a world we cannot see, a world of light and joy, Beale Street in 1953.

A pair of old jeans tossed and crumpled on a lamentable couch.

Duck decoys circling a birdbath. Axioms and dots. Sand as far as the eye can see.

There is no complete reality without hearing it, tasting it, feeling it, weighing it, sewing it together with words and intuitions, circuitry and levers.

Pearls on a horse. Candy on a radio.

It is vital to have something our senses can grasp and suck into our being, a lamp or a color, a ramification tasting of cod. The intangible pattern of reality adheres to our alphabet like twilight, thought inflated with noble gases.

Everything is a frontier. I say everything is a frontier. The most familiar thing in the world is a frontier. If it is not a frontier you have not looked at it properly. What is the most familiar thing to you? Your hand? Your arm? Your embroidery? Is it the way water evaporates? Is it a field where something or someone is buried?

The American frontier makes better sense on the other side of a patent misunderstanding. Imagine a town of phantoms, a village dripping with violins. Iodine and pulleys. The smell of a garage. The bright succulence of words. Patina, animus, stain. A sentence rough and frayed and hung obliquely on a towel rack.

An afghan, a watermark, an alcove.

New Year's confetti on the sidewalk. Cord winding down from an electric drill. Black Diamond. Rut in a muddy street. A bronze crucifixion by Bernini.

Jewelry in a cedar bureau. Fine sand fanned out at the bottom of the sidewalk.

Water beaded on the window of a Shanghai train. A man punching paint into a canvas. Orchid trembling slightly as someone rushes by. Research. Butter. Mastic.

That's it. That's what a story does. It fabricates an atmosphere then opens it with rain.

Durum is hard. A hard wheat. A hard grain. The word comes from Latin: *durus*. Meaning hard. As in enduring. As in durable. As in dura mater.

Durum kernels are dense, amber-colored beads composed of a nutritive, high-protein tissue called endosperm. When durum is milled, the endosperm is ground into a granular product called semolina. A mixture of water and semolina forms a stiff dough ideal for making pasta. The dough is forced through dies to create macaroni, ravioli, spaghetti.

Rigatoni, cannelloni, tortellini.

Most durum grows in North Dakota. North Dakota, hardest of all the states. Harder than Maine. Harder than Michigan. Harder than the sidewalks of New York. The quartz of Missouri. The quarries of Indiana. Taconite of Hibbing. Zinc of Alaska. Diamonds of Arkansas.

Hard.

Life in North Dakota is hard because the winds are sharp and wild and stab the ground with spears of grain. Because seeding the earth is a sacrament and necessity pulverizes pain. There is the feeling of the sublime there because of the harshness of things, out of which comes a strange beauty, not the beauty of Italy which is a beauty of great sensuality, nor that of France, which is passionate and appetizing, or the Congo, which is complex, or Morocco, which is colorful and exotic. The beauty in North Dakota is blunt and biting. Sometimes it is a purple wall veined with lightning. And sometimes it is an odor, the faint smell of stone stirring in the wheat. The smell of lime in a slab of ancient seabed.

The dirt in North Dakota is high in acidity. It is a tough dirt. High in potassium. Coarse and granular. Aggregates resistant to stress.

Durum is harvested in late August, early September. The full grown plant is bristly and stiff. Gristly, like the literature of hunger. Piquant, crucial as morning. It doesn't whisper it rattles. The air is lacerated passing over it. Bleeds art and thistle. Thought and iron.

This is a sentence on its way to fulfillment. Triggers and objectives and rags of eternity that verge on the occurrence of sound in the mouth.

Suppose a pharmacy.

Suppose a pharmaceutical.

Suppose a drug that causes memoirs. Suppose a drug that causes internal rhymes. Suppose a drug. Suppose a drug that causes Latin. Lecithin and lederhosen.

Suppose an olive.

Suppose an eyeball.

Suppose an eyeball with a vision in it. Suppose a vision with an eyeball in it.

Suppose a worry. Suppose a quarry. Suppose a worry in a quarry. Suppose a quarry in a worry.

Suppose a dragon full of warmth and fungus. What kind of dragon would be full of warmth and fungus?

Imagine green things with black roots.

Imagine antiques. Antique emotions. What would an antique emotion look like? It would look like a parakeet. It would look like an onion. It would look like a man full of fear. It would look like a man afraid of nothing. It would look like a woman studying the geology of a western state. It would look like a woman walking in a field of cows.

Suppose a state. A state like Oregon.

Suppose a woman with a name like Lily. A woman named Lily walking in a field of cows. And a sky on fire with orange and red and kelp on the beach and a husband dead from an avalanche and umpteen reasons to prefer velour and a lamp with a wick soaked in kerosene and a story without a moral and a mill without a mill and bubbles in a stream and equations on a blackboard and a gash on the side of a hill dripping tongues of ore.

Suppose all this and suppose even more.

And then once in a while it rains. Which is good for the carrots and good for the beets. And drips from the brim of a hat. And makes everything smell like mint.

She walks in beauty like a waterfall. The water walks on rocks to the edge and crashes into feeling and spray.

This reminds me of ceaselessness.

A camellia in a laboratory next to a beaker full of a blue fluid.

Blue fluid.

Which has permeated the algebra.

Of seeing.

The algebra of seeing which is dosage.

Or dos-à-dos.

She walks in beauty like a Nibelungenlied. One of those epic tales of the Burgundian kings of yore.

What's a yore? Is that your yore or my mynah?

She walks in beauty like a quadruped. A wild white mare in the Camargue. The wild white mare of the gypsies. The wild white mare of yore.

Identity is meat and blood and silver and a philosophy. A philosophy of living. The honey of air the honey of dawn the honey of red the honey of black. Identity is blank-and-blue in the human zoo.

A coin in the jukebox. Which triggers the voice of Denny Laine singing "Go Now."

Do you ever think about feeling? Do you ever think about what it is, particularly when you're feeling bad? Nobody thinks about feeling when they're feeling good they're too busy feeling good. But bad? That's something you want to crawl out of. Crawl away from. Like a rotting animal full of maggots and flies.

I would prefer olives.

Olives are the eyeballs of the vegetable world.

She rolls in beauty like an olive.

To the end of the table and drops.

And rolls under the couch.

She walks in beauty like a couch.

She is a misdemeanor between walls.

A moist hole. A dry toe. Wads of quatrain. Snippets of sonnet. A bullet shattered on a wall of gloom. Bananas enforced by molecule. A pound of brain chewing particles of meaning.

She pushes the alphabet to extremes of liquidity.
She walks in beauty like a doorknob.
Like a relative clause.
Like a forklift.
An ordinary forklift.
Carrying a waterfall.

The virtue of jalapeños is epistemological, like the life of Baudelaire. They are wrinkled and strange, articulate as the spine of a copperhead, conjunctive as the jaw of the human face.

Tart. Acrid. Piquant.

Poignant as the skeleton of a whale on the beach, its bones bleached and sculptural, the pure contours of the imponderable.

Guerrero has opened our eyes to stone.

Sparrows on the hood of a truck.

Strike the water with a paddle and let us graze on a page of words. Iron reveries that make a bridge glide and arc.

Because there is death on the horizon.

Because the animality of life is visible in the words beating at your skull trying to get out. Because that's what words do. They swell with life until they are heard in the crack of a rifle. Euclid wandering a construction site. Old letters in an oak bureau.

The long awaited diagnosis proclaimed in a doctor's eyes.

How does one explain the sublime? Smell the rain in the air.

Money has lost its meaning. It was less than decorum to begin with, the mere effluvium of power, preposterous and fake. And now it is less than that. It is nothing. A stench in the air. Rust on a rake. And the world has become a palimpsest of illusions. Debt swaps. Drop locks. Cashouts. But there are still jalapeños to remind us of reality. The acute sensation of things. The sting of pleasure. The sweetness of pain.

And that is the virtue in jalapeños.

And coffee exploding in my brain.

There is nothing in this world so vital as a pancake. The loveliness and amplitude of pancakes. Pancake piled on pancake. Pancakes feckless with syrup and agape with melting butter. Pancakes surrounded by noise and daylight. Pancakes that are fat, foolish, and fabulous with dough. Dollops of meandering dough maneuvered onto the surface of a stove where they begin to blurp and plurp in little bubbles and holes that majestically transmogrify into ovals of scrumptious geography.

Making a pancake is an art, like squeezing an abstraction out of a tube of white paint. An amalgam of modest ingredients whose quotient is greater than the sum of its parts.

Existence must always be rendered in impasto. Thick lumps of disencumbered color. Later, subtle shadings of a pervading and developing hue may be added. A group of people arguing by a river, or a skirt full of adjectives. Sooner or later, everything suggests a love of cars.

There is a prison of the mind called dogma. You'll want to stay out of there.

Emotions are important to consider or ignore in the morning. This is your choice. Choice is intrinsic to the process of being human. Choice is the legibility of ourselves written in the dough of the moment. Choice is a good thing, like propellers and bells.

Consider a lake. Consider a lake because it is round. Or almost round. Perhaps it is not round at all. Perhaps it is long and narrow. But consider a lake. Consider its glitter. Consider its shape.

At the bottom of the lake there is a corridor leading to the glitter of thirst. Here you will find a set of keys and a light that folds over you like silk. When you come to the surface you will be greeted by a princess disguised as an electric cow. Do not attempt to milk her. If you're not careful, you can drown an entire democracy in money. Which is why there is a harmonica and an elevator in the bowl of this equation.

Emotions and ideas interact so that conscious intent emerges. We are all tugging a rope with a mysterious weight. We do not know what it is. Some say it is the voice of discarded furniture. Others that it is galaxy with a bad case of measles. I say it is nothing. The idea of noth-

ing is a weight like no other weight. The dream of a banana inter-
preted by a stagecoach. An ore in the hill of an echo. A drama on the
radio in the middle of winter.

Thinking is an art. Fingers of air lift the clouds to the sky, and
Woody Guthrie sits on a stove in Paris playing a midnight harmon-
ica. This is the shadow of a hand as it writes. This is the emotion I
was looking for. A pataphysical pancake built brick by brick.

Consciousness is that energy in my head which arrives in sections at the hotel. It is so flabby it comes in bags of dirt. But the sonatas are infrared. And I have four elevators in my tie.

It isn't easy to free the mind. Our bodies are marvelous with gentleness and warmth. But the mind is abstract, cracked mud in a dried riverbed, a pound of sleep and a gallon of syntax.

The quill of equation begs the gill of lustration.

The skull is a habitat for the brain, which in turn is a habitat for habits. Habits of perception. Habits of thought.

Here is another habit. It is the habit of writing. Words anchored in ink. Where I can look at them. And plumb them for meaning. Because the mind has a tendency to view the world through symbols.

Symbols are stages for the theatre of thought. A 300-pound valentine tap-dancing on a gerund called thinking.

Then there is dogma. Dogma is the prison of the mind. Don't go there. Stay clear of dogma. If you must be religious, do so at your peril. Approach it gingerly, with an open mind. An inquiring mind. If birds sing in your touch or the language of the clouds oozes out of an analysis of candy take a deep breath and pump another sentence through the neck of a guitar. Nerves cling to such music and make parables and parachutes out of it.

Can you feel the ocean stretching in your scrotum? Can you feel Florida teetering on havoc? Can you feel the largeness of tendency at calm in your breast?

It isn't easy to free the mind from the vault of the commonplace. Poetry readings are boring beyond words but you can find serpents and hurricanes there if you look closely under your ribs, and in the rhetoric of cells creating your thumb, and forefinger, and organs and skin.

Here is an X-ray gulping a skeleton and here is a skeleton gulping an X-ray. Which one is scornful? Which one is pornographic?

Knowledge is silver and Elizabethan. It is tolerance and thought and diversity and metaphor. A mnemonic harmonica. A Japanese bell. The bright yellow cord of a table saw oozing out of a garage in a long gentle loop. A trumpet in the pantry. The fingers that form a fist. The ice that forms on the surface of a word when it is published by the wind in the cry of a hawk. And which melts easily in the mind. Where it engenders lemon. Where it engenders light. Where it drips cypress in a beard of mist.

I look out the window and see that everything is green and gray. It is June. It is fifty-two degrees.

That sucks.

I miss the sun. I liked it. It would be good to see it again.

It is 3:23 p.m. and I am in Seattle. My hat is a traffic light. My optimism is prudently tinctured with pessimism. It has been a long time since I have opened a can of lacquer. It has been an even longer time since I have opened a can of paint.

Let me tell you about paint. The last time I opened a can of paint I painted the bathroom. I dipped the brush. I lifted the brush. A dollop of Morning Glow dribbled from the bristles of the brush. That is an incomparable sensation. Thick, like an aphorism, but gooey. I turned the paint brush round and round to get the paint to stop drooling. I lifted it carefully, gingerly, holding the bristles up so that if the paint resumed drooling it would drool onto my arm and not the floor. I spread the paint. It spread nice and smooth. And that is the nature of paint. That is the essence of paint. Gooeyness. Gloppiness. Ooziness.

A viscosity that hungers for the persuasion of a brush.

I have lived on this planet a long time. That entitles me to say some things about it that may be of some value. It is round. It floats in an elliptical circle around the aforementioned sun. It tilts. It wobbles. It has continents and oceans. It has poppies and portents and postcards and pitch. It has rivers that go north, rivers that go south, rivers that go east, rivers that go west, rivers that meander everywhere and nowhere and rivers that step lightly over their beds with the grace of angels.

Yesterday I moved some furniture and several poetry anthologies. This has made me stronger and more understanding of what it takes to be a jiggle in a world of bone. Is there anything more odd than a breast? Why yes, there is. There is realism, real estate, and smorgasbords.

Sometimes the warm hug of a benevolent drug will substitute for the lack of cake. But be careful. It can be addictive, like money. Avoid money. If you avoid money it will avoid you. If you pursue money it will surround you and kill you. If you ignore money you will be poor, but happy.

No you won't. Don't listen to me. I know nothing of money. But I do know this: I know what I feel, and right now I feel something huge and ineffable expanding inside me. And here it is, all fist and eye, the fetus of a sentence on its way to ramification. Subject and predicate. Substance and essence. Unspeakable luxuries. Hallucinations. Impassioned tokens. The wink of incipience. The glimmer and hiss of moist wood catching fire.

Money continues to fascinate me. I open my hand. Here are three
sparks of incessant goldfish. You might call them coins. But I call them
words. What are these words worth? How much are you willing to
pay for this thought in my head? How much is thought worth? What
is the value of milk if it is hypothetical yet full of kindness and under-
standing? The pea is its own excuse. It is the same with taillights and
flags. This kind of mental meandering requires something for its labor,
wouldn't you think? But is this labor? Or a con? I think you are ex-
tremely generous to come this far. The glitter in your elbow clicks like
drapery. A reverie of bone so flexible it seems automotive. Karate is
like that: it always requires something of you that you did not expect
to bring. The imbroglio of dollars in my wallet border on payment. I
am about to buy something, but I don't know what. What is there to
buy? I feel the need to own something. But what? How does the urge
to own something wander into this nervure I am building, this invest-
ment in time, this wad of propositions, this counterfeit dollar of little
cakes and wonders? What does it mean to own something? Can I own
a joke? A joy? A unicorn? There is an animal growling in the foliage of
possession and it is called greed. It always wants more. It is never satis-
fied. This is why money was invented: so that hallucinations such as
this would burst instantly upon colliding with reality. But they never
do. They grow into banks. They grow into Wall Street. They grow
into capital. Shares and debentures and overdue accounts. Equity,
loans, and market bubbles. Diffusion and aggregation. Trading simu-
lations. Changes in valuation. Rhinestone fedoras and twitches of silk.
Presidents and congress do not think about money the way I think
about money. I don't believe it's real for them. There is more of it than
they can count. For me it is quite real. I can always count it but I can't
always count on it. Money is like muck, not good except it be spread.
You know, compost. The stink of manure. I am giving it here an arbi-
trary scope, but one the senses can apprehend, unlike the money in
banks, which can only be got with a pen, a look, or a gun. That is the
trouble with money. Sooner or later there is disaster. If anybody starts
spending money they never stop themselves. That is why money is the
opposite of wealth. It is never valued for itself but what it scans. Cans

and barcodes. More and more and more and more. But nothing naked. Nothing for what it truly is. Hunger, cellophane, wool. The fit of a shoe. A soft bed. Cool water on a hot day. The incalculable extravagance of blue.

I proclaim the banana the most sympathetic of fruits. I say this with the sanctity of bone. I say this because it wants to be said and because words connect sympathy with a logic that is antithetical to the beauty of the hand truck. Opium sparkles in my veneration for all things noble as varnish. For all things aphoristic and quick. The personality of glistening is atomic in envy and fire in winter. I wade through words like a man in quest of a vision. Energy on a stick. Singular quilts. One day I will write a book whose emulsions ooze the darkness of deer. Birch trees illumined in the headlights of a jeep. There is darkness in everything. Darkness is the meat of definition. There is darkness in the ceremony of the kite, incense in the bursitis of punctuation. Thirst awakens the availability of lemonade. This is how consciousness pulls glitter out of the air. Drops of condensation form on the sides of the beaker. Fish and controversy enter the embassy of the head. I would rather grimace with the buffoonery of blue than mend the geography of Wednesday with the blood of mastodons. I hate sticky fingers. Bone and handkerchief elevate the consciousness of lace. An ocean of warm tears blazes like dappled china in a swollen vestibule. I have radar for a talisman and advice for my forge. I melt it into opinion. Opinions like hope and apocalypse. Opinions like bellows and flint. A sound surrounded by blacksmiths. The jewelry of eyes scoop the hardwood floor and inoculate it with bowls of yoga. Colors invoke wax in basement light. Blackberry vines invade the window. Autumn stars melt into animals at the break of day. The banana gets peeled. The animals sit and gaze.

Consciousness is that energy in my head that invests substances with thought and is like a fetus or gymnasium. To scrub a horde is pulsation but to precede a khaki is itself instrumental to snag a birthmark. Birds are crowded. Space is merely feathers. Extension giggles fruitful mosaics. My pearls worry their luster with forecast. Colors swimming in nickel. An array of snow which sticks to the sides of our budget indicates screens and contrivances. Buds aren't much else than inflammations crushed in romance. Fluttering is rarely sturdy. A purple camera inhabits its words like a tempo clothed in cheeks of octagonal goodness. The west is dirt. The rowdiness it stirs is all beatitude and conviviality. The jeep of these words is sheer oil. Syllables assembled piece by piece. It you push writing to its natural performance angels and smells and burlap go forth in pictures made of pure mythology. What beauty does is change into truth. But truth is too tight for the grip of wisdom. Taken simply, it is a theory, or rainbow. Everything has a surface except coffee. Coffee is five tints in a detour. The delicacy of its patterns is pregnant with tongues. Each sip plays to a postage particular to the invocation of light. Consciousness is expanded by its walk. This is how vertebrates began to ejaculate meaning. The biggest language I ever saw was a generality dried by sunlight. It goes naked in our nerves, but turns cotton in the air, where it is reasonable to expect heaven to stir into thought and knock at the doors of perception. It takes many different glands to tremble like this. Music crackling in a fingernail. A wad of meaning submerged in words. Easy and spinning and kind to all.

They say an immersion in faucets can lead to cognition. An immersion in breathing, however, is a larger fascination and will lead one to ponder the border between the organic and inorganic, chrome and rubber, skin and bone, life and death, and the illusion of separation, because all things are patterns of energy. Here, for instance, is a piece of air called a word, and here is an embassy in pine for the ambassadors of fjords, and their cluster of beards. Their beards keep them warm when they study the fjords. When they glide through the fjords in their ships, studying the formations of rock, the echoes of sounds, voices, the lapping of water, the cry of birds, the whirl of atoms and molecules, which is a sound like mud, when it is resting, and no one is walking in it. Sometimes the water falls in veils and sometimes it beads on the bumpers of cars in the city. There is a man on the corner of one town with a wattle of skin under his chin. He plays an accordion and sings in a voice of solid muscle. Winter is an analogy that comes to the story carrying basements and candy. We lack knees and our backs turn to marshmallow. We pour antifreeze in our cars and trucks and walk in zigzags to avoid the tedium of linearity. Incense curls in languid wisps as it rises through the fur and the howling of wolves ascend in choirs against the cold. If everything boils down to protons, what is sensation? The limousine in its mire while the chauffeur shaves in the rear view mirror. The planet whirls through space, but nobody feels it whirl because it's too large. If you live in Finland pour antifreeze in your car. If you live in London take the underground. If you live elsewhere, if you live a life in a place of ineffable beauty, where paragraphs are still written on paper, and words are immersed in ink, study the fjords, study what they do, and do not do. The fjords rise up from the sea. The fjords that are blunt against the blue of the water and the blue of the sky. The blunt beautiful fjords. Solid and steep and cragged and creviced. This is what they do. They exist. What they do not do is talk. They do not argue. They do not insist. They simply exist. Their argument is in their density. The play of the surrounding mist.

The tree is acrylic, the scene is sad. The colors are dark greens and browns. The sky is in turbulence. Colors bleed into one another. There is the tiny outline of a sail on the horizon. The tree is gnarled and twisted. It is evident that this tree, rooted in a bare, windswept coastline, has withstood many seasons of harsh, brawling weather. There are clusters of green at the ends of the branches. They are a darker green than the clouds and their forms, which have been given more emphasis and stability, furnish an engaging contrast with the slightly more amorphous clouds. One imagines a Captain Ahab strolling into the scene, a man half-dragon absorbed in strange obsessions, and a tiny wire behind the painting for hanging it on a wall. One imagines the rhythms of this representation continually alive to someone's imagination. A moody introspection daubed in paint like moss on a wall. And one day this scene tilted against the wall in a cold, anonymous garage. A clutter of cans of paint and old fishing tackle and a toolbox battered and smeared and overflowing with screws. A storm forever brewing. A coastline forever battered. The shuffling of feet as people examine items at a garage sale, the forgotten and forlorn, alive to someone's imagination once again. Is it this, ultimately, that makes art worthwhile? Who can put a value on such things? What is good? What is bad? Dusty boots and warm clothes are sweet in this climate. We've all seen visions, and they come and go and fade, and the world fades too. Is it possible to fully represent a feeling? A perception? A desolation? The tree is acrylic, the scene is sad.

If you don't know what to write begin with an object. A clock or a quart of nirvana. Paint your appetite with a kilohertz and a hole of ooze. A wire dragon the daydream fireball has earned with yaps of copper. The tapped gerund in the box of paint. The papyrus fetus because it is also a cafeteria. From lassitude to chemistry an automatic handstand demonstrates fingers. Money to appetizer zippers that rhythm in tinkling escalators. Encourage kettles by shoveling introspection. Ginger in a zephyr. Goldfish halos sprinkled with scars. A curtain is how the burlap tenders a blaze for the mind. Apparel which no economy can drum into lobes. The camellia is a catastrophe, a persistent chenille. A moss with apostrophe hoes. Hail in the halls and a batch of meat for the king of steam. A scandal of fur acts as a robe for the perusal of socks in the elevator light. Don't be sorry. Be soaked. Be a chair. Learn to evaporate. Inhabit a look. A jingle of lily. Palms in globs of Arabian gold. Napkins of gravitational fold will accent the quartz in the gravel at the end of haberdashery. Meanwhile, keep the folds to a minimum of bustle. Buttermilk at night. Handkerchiefs are assets. Enzymes are personal. There is nothing here that, one way or another, has not already been said. Except this. Fill the moment with yolk when the obscurity puzzles itself with sunlight, and the misdemeanor screams.

Beet to beet persists in thumping. The bang is October. A jade without which mingling is saucers. Copious distillations of radical babble. A therapeutic door restored to quartz. If the flaw slobber had bicycled into a lissome antiquity, all the percolation would turn to mud. Scorpion handkerchief during a racket of naked scores. An obdurate black pulled into berries to demonstrate language. A moment is when a melody waddles into an amperage. This causes attention to fluids. Archery has been bulbs before, which is why I own my own washcloth. Applause cleats are ugly but some come to flap like harmonicas. It is vital to maintain good philosophy habits. Memory is an aperture to open in cypress. Zeppelin is more philodendron. Only a fire could mark this dent. This paint. This yellow wall. Scan screened through a waterfront it is not a crocodile it is a scooter in scales. Here comes everybody with a fistful of haphazard castles and a sharp pencil. Who is in control of these words, you, me, or each other? As a yardstick of umbrage, a milkweed is no certain awl. Tartan, in other words, must be a Christmas of antiseptic rhythms. Wool, will, and wilderness. Beat to beat a revolution melts in water as one's eyebrows turn steamy or tigers. The deep should shoulder its own questions. I dare you to plug this appellation with a distaff and float such beauty as would harness a gardenia to a frontier of participles. The firmament's velocity is this tall, this parrot and glove. My language grows analgesic as my splutter squirts ink. Yesterday's sludge is today's sea slug. Let us characterize initiative as a laceration the gateway jars in liberal hinge and eyeball. Arrange this syntax into a vegetable. That is to say a root guides those who listen and those who don't grow into rungs of uniform attention. A ladder while jabber a tool while toiling. Word by word shoots an antique lamination. Layer on layer is a cake of dither. The truth of warts is unbecoming. If the avenue is a ventilation, the tailgate is a serenade, since zebras inhabit aortas, and wheels are rampant negotiations for the anomalies of the road, the mezzotints we believe we inhabit, when what is true is generally birch.

The same wolf feathers a wave as the squid begins a rather smooth intuition and it is fecund to see how the anthology bottles enhance your iron throughout. The shirt to percolate is a venerable bend in the clothing system. The moment of folds and buttons gathers toward nirvana. The library yawls its momentum. Embroidery drips with reality for the vaunted foam of a velvet python in revolutions more verdant than purple. Bulbs applaud and beckon it. Convolutions silver it. Its belly blazes white with sudden appearance. The autopsy of an introspection reveals many perceptions whose perspectives have grown into tapioca. Nail the frames of the basement so that a clay which obtrudes may come to represent little chickens popping around a telescope. The glacier bivouacs between blue and green to grotto a feeling of watercolor glazed with wide-eyed equanimity. The temperature is lace. A kazoo with a scooter manages to bear a load of music to the land of ghosts. The twilight medal atoms in clapping debris. Lesions clank with personality. Each rattled chain has consequences. Ecstasy wakes a tariff from punctuation and kills it. A parable of bone has everything hacked. Beaver blood is always pennies. The ultraviolet balloon which the appareled current bobs above the forests like a language of helium and mist. The heart that narrates this query is completely denim. One jet is locked in the library. The other has a voice that sounds like scribbling. A wainscot lingo demonstrated in hissing. The quill of a quandary is lodged deep in the nerves. It lights up like a black tango. The steam surrounding it comes to be haunted by a demure shadow. A green reptile with pedals to lift. The flash from an invention is glimpsed in vegetables. The chickadee box turned out to be a pound of vapor soaked in syllables, a prose poem pushed into meditation. This is precisely where it all happened. Here, at the end of the dock, where the yellows and greens splash against the hull, and mirth and glory splash up against eternity. The surgery of words is sortilege, but the scalpels are sharp, the incisions deep, and the anatomy of the falling light avails our eyes with phantom lumber.

If I saw the air in half what do I have? A swarm of words circling an indefinable feeling. I stagger through the flux of day and make occasional selections on the jukebox. Coffee is faster than any arrow. It turns autumn in my blood, an amber grammar that is instrumental to space. The lake obeys by giggling. The universe gurgles stars. The wind is pure reverie. Words bottle thoughts, confessing them in the aroma of correspondence when the cork is removed. All things have a creative force, an energy woven into their understanding of dark. What we call the unconscious is, in fact, fat blotches of light ground into moisture, ideas of heat and honey, relativity pulsing incumbent sticks of sweat warm with the percolation of verbs. The hum of gravitation the crackle of personality in the goldfinch. It is time that fuels the dawn but it is quince that articulates the essence of carrots. I love the wilderness of the dashboard. The west in its convolution of clouds. Syllables holding the world together piece by piece. Ideas attach to moisture. Fingers maneuvering cutlery at a table typified by napkins and candles. Literature is humid. It has always been that way, even when people stopped reading it. There continue to be a few who find refuge there. A few who see in the representation of things a billiards of utterance, an autonomy trumpeted by green. Nails and escalators failing in their beauty and so becoming distortions of a more sublime grip on the sheen of liberalism. Existence is hyperbolic. It is not an illusion. It is not a cookie. It is contrapuntal to the sad pedestrian digits of the camera, the iodine still howling in the medicine cabinet. The lariat is not a shape the lariat is a town. There are many who remember plywood. Many who remember the treasures of consciousness when it swarmed with calliopes and chuckled like a sawhorse. Measurement is largely erotic. Width and length of a river exposed as a pair of knees. Music folded into thought. The throat of some mountain caught writing itself into a long slow conversation with trees.

The speculations are all appointed with silk. The mulch of convolution fertilizes the theorems. A theorem, as you know, is forage. We lift it however we are able, or lunge at the rectangles because they are abscessed. This is the mathematics of proof. Proof of voices. Proof of pepper. Proof that an angle can venture in fur. The forest sonata whirls its wood and is confirmed in pumpkin. The curvature is breathtaking. A convolution of fiber with the audacity of theatre, all orange and sticky like pain. Jelly rules. Temperament is an opening to character, a facial weather the night moves on with weight and daylight showers with flutes. These statements shift when the sprig plane operates as a polyphonic ant vibrating its inventions on the spine of an elephant. Here the dryness of function assumes the style of a tirade. A dimension of ups and downs relieved by a spry pizzicato. The grid, meanwhile, is exposed to dollars of realism. Taillights worked into parodies of left and right. As if direction mattered. As if time were a fugal torpedo in calculations of ham. Don't laugh at the temperature. It was nothing less than a convolution of surface that set Cézanne on his way. This consisted of planes and volumes ballasted by line. Cézanne surfed art like a crystallographer lost in reveries of chlorophyll. The thermostat of the canvas was arranged firmly. Chiseled into thought like a tint of being. With the middle operation this includes thatch. A theory takes effect by incantation. The convolutions of a bug are still a convolution. The chime is just short of this definition. It is great to have skin. You can plunge into the field and turn squash and sweat. The jaw squats on a turn thinking its method must carry quarts of language to a candy tantamount to opera. The case is naked. The back integrates its nerves in sections then illustrates a crowbar to the idea of ribbon. The real problem would seem to have been how to relate every part of the illusion in depth to a surface pattern endowed with thirst. Old age, diabetes, obscurity. Pats of paint vibrating and dilating in uneasy integrations. Twists of blueness sufficient to give the feel of air. Shapes argued into existence with sable and hair. A mark made by a brush for the fact of a tone. Space and time. Muscle and bone.

Inception and blister, democrat, television and misbehavior, ignition and cheesecloth. Note the pulsation, the rhetoric of veins. Scarlet on scarlet.

Jail no apparition, fireworks are a pantomime of copper, imitation is quixotic and a frost bite is February.

Kits in hallucinating is scenery. There is a dissonant opal vowel that carries fire and a tantalizing fiber that kindles pertinence.

The hole is plunging through itself. This is why beatitude is so grueling.

Jonquil. No jonquil is dazzling and correct. No jonquil has a flagrant feather. Expression is kerosene.

No jonquil is a felon's scrawl. A jonquil which is not an emotion shows the appearance of combat. It points to clogs. The gesture which is any wad is the same as milk. That gesture is unanimous that vanquishes insult.

Taste has an auxiliary, it is a sticky substance, this which is not churned is not glazed, it is aromatic, it is lavish and demonstrable, it is sticky. It being oily ticking is taxing and what is truculent is hot and girdling. It is verbal and so much more than the painting of a scalpel.

Consonants are spoons. They are appendages.

Distinctness is not hurt by including jiggling or growing bones in a sentence. And it is beans that welcome permeation that deposits and a fetus that raises itself into knowledge. It warms the colon to opulence. It assumes the gender of a male or female. It chatters. It yanks. It fishes for complements. It swims in a lake.

If there is time enough then the steeples will fit the sky and it will be considered thick to feel crowds. Taps in a circle. Arteries in a circle. Twilight in a circle. Arteries in circulation. Articles in tea. Art in pecan. Cajolery in bowling. Gastric juices in mills.

If the toes are quickly and the fur is correspondent the words will finish themselves as coleslaw. That scruples wax. Anyone can be a pulse. But it takes a kimono to be an umbrella.

The faucet is not made of silver and a ukulele is placed in a blanket and the chenille, the entire chenille, patches socialism. Socialism is a political system involving weave, wave, and folds of cultivated land.

If hanging a glass on Monday is viable and blood is in motion there will also be oceans and rivers and tangerines.

It is easy to make a sentence. The sensations which rise from lips will be used to describe a river and a wheel will roll toward sculpture. Imagine sculpture. What do you see? Do you see a trigger? A loaf? An embryo?

There is the complete absence of lactation for a lesion in oak. The time has the elbows of a feeling of Thursday. The season is clearly blackberries. Energy, watermelon, and thunder. Jelly and paste and thin locks with eyes and a dollop of blue in a camaraderie of red.

There is a penny in that.

Technical does not technically mean technical. It means tools are patent. It means meat is deliberate. And all the awls are awnings and all the awnings are ostensible.

Time is not a clap.

These lines are pleasant to me, these lines that I have written using words, and tides, and bark, and verdure.

The time and place of a tool is no convenience if it has not been scrutinized or judged, and if there is a drip there is dripping, which is verbal and personal when the zeitgeist sneezes quarks.

Do not crinkle what is miscalculated because surely there will be tapestries in gluing darkness to an attic. If the area is shown to be anomalous there is no use in balm or napkins. There will be balm in abundance and parables and commentary to ease the mind. We can always chain the finish to the fish and the copper to the obligation.

If I speak as if an abstraction were real it is because holes are perspectives that hold actual aphorisms.

The time came when there was an occasion for mustangs.

This did not mean thump.

It meant daydream. It meant glaze and steeple. Flagstone and bounce. These handstands were understood as yardarms. As night. As Christmas. As Christmas night. As plazas and explosions. In understanding biography the business of whittling demonstrates the chain of brains there is in ginseng. A hole formed in the personality and the song died. This is why the quintet did not come anymore. And then beauty dwelled in objects like jaws and bells. That is to say there are jokes, lozenges and ponds, places in which to grip oak.

Chestnuts are not entrails.

The use we make of words is sometimes unnatural, sometimes a matter of antique environments, shovels and shoulders and shadows and shale, shoulders lovely as those of Venus, of vanilla, valleys and valves and generalities of night, jaguars moving with stealth and grace, the brain behind the cephalopod eye, arms flashing in bursts of brilliant bluish light, the terrible meaning of the silence of the darkness in the deep sea, luminous bacteria, the enchantment of words, chains of words, hectic mineral words in strips of glittering metal, adrenaline lights, nerves unfolded in watercress.

The amphibious life is the best life and that which is tartan is focus.

Anxiety is not a hobby. An avocado is not an ultimatum. In skating over thin ice our safety is in our speed. Make yourself superfluous to a robbery. Horsepower does not necessarily flaunt plywood. Breathing leads to blisters. Blisters lead to basements. Basements lead to nothing.

Now what shall we talk about? Death? Life? Have you ever seen anyone die? What was it like? Do you believe that any of these words will arrive, even by accident, at anything like insight into the human condition? There is taste in toast and suppleness in tentacles. The light shines directly to show the inflammation of an incision to be blue instead of incidental. It appeals and it drains, it does not appall and destroy earnings, it does not hiss in a color, it does not make a question yellow.

Green is a calamity, it makes all the temperament greasy. It follows that when time is chickens that television equals the radius of prayer. A gargoyle is not the same as when logic slobbers television on a miracle and it is ice that furnishes paradise and expulsion that delivers income. We are disturbed by a mountain because it carries the sky across our dreams.

This is a sentence without any meaning.

This sentence has meaning.

Which sentence is without meaning, and which sentence is tartan? Which sentence wants to argue with you? Which sentence clobbers ginseng until it is bedding?

I like the shape of this life. This life which is round. This life which is dissolving. This life which is epicurean, and steaming and hands.

Jack Nicholson coming out of the shower.

What an image.

I apologize for that.

A bulb there is that shames the darkness with its opinion concerning light. It is sensible to be present when the deep awakens folds of perspective. If it happens that a swell appears in the basement perhaps it is best to surf engenderment.

This is the reason. The reason to write anything has nothing to do with writing. Writing is putting words together in the hope that they may generate some heat and warm the mind with flares and yellow and yesterday. Which implies that reading is sugar.

The question is are there molecules? The way of settling all this is by grinding coffee and drinking it black which is in accord with washing and fir and animosity which resembles obstacles and the ones that disturb motion by tangling yearning with hair.

This comes so soon that trembling is hanging.

A blaze is not a house and a house is not a crayon. To explain this it is necessary to use some words. These words, for instance, which may journey somewhat toward the incision I have made in the air. The one that is crawling across the water. Which is jewelry in the light and waves and permeation, just like a scrotum. Emotion, however, is primarily veins and legs. A thread of wealth and an agate with a logic of its own. The hairpiece is amphibious but the hardwood warrants eternity and the meaning of this is abnormally enlarged to contain a language on its way to serendipity.

Telescopes sew the universe together. Were it not for telescopes, we would not understand these vast distances. We would not understand stars. We would not understand light. We would not understand taxis or dirt. We would not understand visibility or pleasure. We would not understand pain. We would not understand our own politics.

A new president has been elected. A cello is played for the inauguration so scrupulously it turns to salt. But what are the chickadees doing inside it? And what does the president have planned for next Tuesday?

The president has undone all the old laws that were bad for us and given us new laws that are good for us. The new laws are easy to obey. They simply require nickels to be put into slots and daubs of spontaneity to be sewn to the harmonica dragons. If any law is broken another must be put in its place until the law that is broken is repaired with glue and chisel.

Wherever Law ends, observed John Locke, Tyranny begins.

Peace is a state of mind. It is a virtue, like bending when the wind blows, or understanding iron, which is lustrous and malleable in its native hue, but strong and sincere in building, and free of irony.

The clouds are unpacked at dawn. Packing is an art. But unpacking has its pleasures and pitfalls too. For instance, I can never find my socks.

One must unpack as if one were unfolding the life of a ghost. Because yesterday engenders tomorrow and tomorrow is a no man's land of lost horizons and black noises. Can you do as sap does and move through your life with clarity and slowness? Can you be deliberate? Less deliberate? More deliberate? Must deliberation be the child of turmoil? Must purpose be an invention, or does it come naturally, as leaves to a tree, or time to a clock? Were it not for clocks, time would still exist. Only it would be less precise. It would be more like oil. A big dumb black thing waiting under the ground. A big dumb black thing eating people and cities. A big dumb black thing moving fast and furious through everyone's life secretly stealing things and destroying them and killing them. Killing our pleasures with cars and trucks. Killing our joys with smoke and tread. Piston and blood. Noise and money.

Identity is a full-time job. I am doing this for your own good. It is steep inside a book, but I am willing to climb any idea, form any image that might be presented there, such as old men digging up salt in Ethiopia, or an old radio assembled out of bone and wire with a voice coming out of it. The voice of an old president explaining a war. The voice of a zealot explaining a lie. The voice of a mechanic explaining a car. The voice of a derelict explaining the impartiality of beans. There is a penny of meaning here which shines like a surgery. Do you see that rib? It is surrounded by balls of fire. It is there for the imagination. For the president's inauguration. Which has need of vows and swearing, marching and singing, and horns raised to the sky, and the use of words, which are the blood and sinews of this nation, this country which is still heaving from its recent birth. Still wobbling. Still covered with blood.

The nightclubs are full of hormones. Tendrils of fire lick the walls. Ice is merchandise. The new president understands this. That each word is an animal of air. That an animal of air is fed by talking. Which is what an idea is. An idea combining vengeance with charm. An idea combining scruples with attenuation. Where thick is thin and thin is thick. Where ink is weird with gargling and a hairdo radiates blood.

The political world is full of tactical maneuvering. But the nose knows what a stink is and what a rose is and how a gardenia smells and the odor of freshly turned dirt and lungs and entrails rotting on a beach and the sourness of an analysis undone layer by layer until the eyes burn.

I feel a strange red word turn luminous as it opens revealing a world of intrigues and old metaphors. Angels scaling down a ladder to ponder the tail of some indistinct animal. Its vertebrae are made of light. An ancient curse falls out of its mouth. The president's security agents surround it with worried looks and guns. It calls itself freedom. It calls itself religion. It is applauded by sickly old men. Old women bring it flowers. It sleeps among objects of gold and silver.

A loud hole of history opens and the new president walks out. He holds the yolk of speculation.

I have knocked at your door, he says, but will you open it?

He moves quickly to the open door of a limousine and gets in and disappears. He has things to attend to. Meetings and conferences and councils and consultations.

If a paragraph is a bucket of words, then what is this crawling across the floor? It is a piece of meat quivering in an ecstasy of words. It is called introspection, and it happens like this: it percolates sounds of the city. The air wails, and hungers for a name. What shall we call this air? These vibrations? This crackling and power? This agitation of the mind? It is something new. A new feeling. A new weather. Let's not call it anything. Let's see what the new president does. What he does with this feeling. This beautiful new feeling. This animal still learning how to learn.

Behind every pathos is a renaissance flawed with propellers. Specimens of feeling bounced off the back of a participle, existential and tin. We speak of wire and incline toward thinking. These words may not connect with what you're thinking. But they are words. Fifteen vibrations and a slow induction. If a sound is apparent than the apparatus is working. This is why we give names to experiences. Names like calculus and consciousness. Gratification and warmth. Polypropylene and calcify.

Any color is deer. Nailing is suggested by the plenitude of blood pounding in necks. That is where meaning has a home in dishes.

Slap a postulate silly and what you get is mountains. Pearls and personality. Foreign perceptions. Cubism. Tickets or rain.

Braque's rebellion had shattering implications. Space itself changed shape. Space became a sudden insatiable pencil.

Space became a dos-à-dos.

Mass became a mattress. An imposing stone with regard to the material world.

Reticence has its charms. The pulse of momentum in a ghostly dog. A highway flare gravid with night. It is steep to consider screwdrivers. Burlap begins the glitter of revelation. Sidewalk ripples tumbled into amulets and chickens. Tarts equal to tinfoil will later be narcotic and laboratories leaking reality will shout beauty into blisters. The wagon is enforced by incentive, and drips with screwy merchandise.

There is fat in the yell during the epaulet idea. Its chill was pink among that Democratic chemistry and lace hoists that made the calculus nasty with just the right dashboard. As pills to columns and garters to gargoyles, the oblique in the ketchup is inundated by quandary. Such pastels as yonder calendar persuade the eyes that reality is some haphazard mirror, an apology to the toes and an occupation for the nose. The beatific biography of a mechanic is the ultimate kayak in phenomenon and elevators. The fairytale skies that milk themselves in the pine are bundled in delicate membranes. As a lighthouse imbued with Tuesday the magnet is tongue to the ladle of names. The driveway is soaked in its gravel. The earthquake is nestled in its pegs. A raft drifts through the cafeteria beckoning to our inner nature the way a grease will sometimes anticipate thought.

Hack the mime with your twinkle dart. Humor the next beast with cleats. How a femininity evaporates indicates that it snows within paprika. There is oil in pathos and hickory is habitable in a tripod bean. Heat is an exponent to the finery below the waterfall, its intricacy an engine for the geography of personality.

Zinc was once a highway. A humid scram alone could denote its vaudeville. Floating was always beat, and you the logo king in which a blunted eyeball later inveigled its own manufacture at the bureau of existence. The power queen in her syntax is only thrust and quill. Chaos pantomimes gristle because the crocodile is pertinent to its bones. Go yell something unassuming at the environment. Ask yourself, environment of what? The verbal gauntlet as a black gardenia. Umpteen rough adobe adverbs slowly lavish in their house and quaver.

There is a word in which light is a fork and beauty is varicose. In which sound is deliriously venerated and the misfit apparatus cajoles perception with its scarves and tarpaulin. To which a lanolin nose is appended by shadow and tornados are hacked into jobs. Our laughter grows green over it. The xylophone ripples with jewels. The azaleas engage the garage in conversation. The hose is wound. The car is parked. There are cans of varnish on the shelf. There is a zinnia in each window. There is an emotion that thaws and a feeling that hardens into ideals and words. There are words that drip and words that nail. There are words.

The delinquent antler once had an automotive hole in which to breed its vast economy. A lamé can unbind its eggs in a labial mustang.

The sword of day lacerates the pond. The story is crammed with a blue chicken. Anyone's elbow can drop into autumn. The washing sparkles. A wavelength of henna squirms in the toolbox. Pathos is anyone's back. Sugar the kayak. Pepper the ball. It is lambent to fecundate blackjack, but gallant to revive the velocity of red.

Poetry is a dangerous gastronomy. You can eat the sun, but thought hungers for silk. The diet is more like fog. Rain in gravitational bedding, a database of dirt with a washcloth on it.

Imagine a lung with the color of a swimming pool. Imagine its apparitions. The current in an eyeball. The automotive splendor of a pink appliance rumbling with pushy lactations. Here is where reverie turns native with wolves. Zippers are used for clarification. A flock of mirrors in a quantum bicycle honor the squid surrounding the lighthouse. We can feel ourselves in lilies. Mittens on a cold February morning. Another verb ignites in fur and beckons the river to quicken its blade.

The lake gets up and carries itself into the mind of a goldfish.

Can there be an art of emotion? Can an emotion be created in the same way that a house or a boat or a poem is created?

A tattoo animates a jiggle of skin. A biography is written. A life is lived. A knowledge is acquired. A song is sung. A momentum is formed. An appetite is appointed. A tongue is upholstered. A fever is enameled and an anthology of exotic temperatures turns to stone. Emerald, opal, and turquoise. Onyx, chalcedony, and jade.

I feel myself a tiger of perusal today. I prowl through a book on Braque looking for a dangerous alphabet by which to construct a visceral gyroscope, something to orient my body of incumbent quandary, my speculations and angles.

Or did I mean angels? Angles are angels of innovative aplomb.

I prowl through the light of the room looking for a sound I can use as an engine to drive a subversive metaphor toward total incongruity. Drive it until it is erratic and tattered and zero. Drive it until it is out of the world. Far, far out of the world.

I keep a mnemonic anaconda in the glove compartment to remind me of the desolate existence of commas. I gargle the word "beauty." I put lipsticks on wasps. I find pleasure in the inevitability of denim.

No matter how oblique or weird my car happens to be, it always seems to have wheels. Those big fat round things with tread on them. Those large doughnuts of rubber. Those perpetually rolling ventriloquists of the road.

If there is a jack in the truck we are blessed and happy. If there is not, we may want to stop in some town and look for one. There is a spare, but spares can be tricky. Spares can sometimes offset a perception of imminent doom, of augury and portent. Spares may create a false sense of security. I know. I know. It helps to be prudent. I'm not arguing against the use of spares. I'm just saying that a spare without a jack is like standing outside a restaurant with your keys in hand only to discover that your car has been stolen.

Or towed. Which amounts to the same thing.

Let me be frank. Each epoch has its zeitgeist, its top ten albums and hit songs, its manner of dress, its way of handling money, its attitudes and behaviors. Its clans and cabals. Its conspiracies and predominant feelings. But where does any of this get you? You simply blend into the crowd. Which isn't necessarily a bad thing. Anonymity has its joys. But so do aviaries and zoos. What I want to share with you is better than that. Better than these things. What I want to share with you is black and medicinal. Something that will thread its way through you to some revelation, some new perception, some particularity that we can both immerse ourselves in, if only to emerge as fish in human form, our eyes a thesis of inner vision, our opacity an obvious legacy of equivocation.

As for the cerebellum, its role in muscular coordination has never been quite clear to me, much less its relation to the intellect. However, if we explore some of the principles of Buddhism, we find that cherries hang a little heavier on the bough after it rains. This would tend to indicate that the mind is more than a tool for orientation, but that a continual looping exists between the weight of a thing and its apprehension in the mind, and that something out there in the margins, some vague proprioception patterns our viewpoint of nature and makes us explode with invective whenever our encounters with it prove too strong. The water is too cold, the woods are absurdly entangled, the air reeks of sulfur and methane, the tendons are excruciatingly strained, or the mud we just stepped in turns out to be surprisingly deeper than the rim of our boots.

Hope, meanwhile, remains obstinate. Hope is more than a habit, more than a disposition. Hope is a nuclear reactor, dangerous and intangible. It keeps us going when we would rather just sit down and be done with it. Done with the burdens. Done with the lesions and therapy. Done with the noise, done with the smirks and omens.

Yesterday I saw an old woman struggle to get up the front steps of her house. How long, I wondered, had she lived there? There must have been a time when she went up the steps without giving them any thought. Now old, obese, decrepit, she could not come and go without taking them into consideration, without factoring them into her daily equations. The journey to the garage. The odyssey to the store. Each day a saga. Each night a labyrinth of memories and wool.

Experience, with the Greeks, is equivalent to art. If they do not result in insight, they at least lead to an enjoyed perception, an enhancement of the receptive appreciation and assimilation of objects separate from their baser utility. There can be such a thing as an aesthetic of experience as well as an aesthetic of art. Art begins with experience. Light, absorption, geometry, and waves. Night, harpsichord, coleslaw, iodine. Each emotion becomes native to a tapestry of sensations and quarrels with the conditions that gave it form. True wealth consists in answering the enigmas of existence with a certain equal temperament, major and minor, sharps and flats, and stuffing them with music.

If there can be a calculus for shapes in time and space, might there not also be a calculus for jodhpurs in kitchens and melodramas and jackets? Mushrooms in soup? Gasoline in poetry? The logic of beards is hectic with bombastic analogies. And why shouldn't it be?

The radium of the word is inexplicable, but the mechanism that brings it into being is generally violet. It is hormones, simple biochemistry, that cause so much disorder in our lives with their insatiable desires, hungers that can never be fully satisfied. Hence, the importance of paper. It is the one place where we can distill our anxieties, cook them, simmer them, boil and blanch and braise them, and watch as they sublimate, turn to a cloud of insouciant vapor. Because what steam isn't, after all, some perpetual omission of worried distraction, a quick resolution of air? Your omelette is the perfect medium. Broken eggs incidental to the chin of churning abstraction.

Words are a habit for the chemicals of talk. Undulation. Radium of letters. Resurrection of tongues. Books are propellers to wolf with a dragonfly. Hot gravitational dapple is a bone in the feeling. The ulna blimps are the antithesis dug up from the garden of spoons.

Opals, or velour. Glass engenders caterwauls and slack water. Infinity is lips moving this way to create itself in warmth. Sunlight and shade. The smell of thought in a comedy of sticks. Vowels do egos which seem inflamed. Revelation in anything naked. The apparition inside its words oozes memory in glands with jade.

Any passage can scintillate and so begin the pastels. A thaw can gather curves, or peaches move in the wind. There are autopsies that have proved this. The syntax of existence and gloom blooming in its machinery grows another wad of feathers that are all dirt and plywood. Molecules in rhinestone that the dog shoulders and licks. Perspectives below the gaslight turn to jelly for you. War, avid with night.

Momentum is tangible in the rain after a theory does hair. Hormones mimic the gargoyle. Amulets and scabbards provide another scar to dissolve by boiling a vowel between the long rags of incubation.

The clef of the knife in the beans of daybreak. Such an appearance as this has been my analogy throughout. Burlap begins the still glitter of the forklift milk. Soak the ulcer in this cackling revelation. Money anneals the pertinent floats. Such handles of explosion it is a miracle of algebra that makes it expressive. And a cook with vanilla in parakeet scarves.

Demure is only gravely cows and their dangerous quiet. Quince is only a tongue in vaudeville. Remember vaudeville? No way. You're too young to remember vaudeville.

The chest is hairy and vehement and fits your personality. The veal harnessed to your ribs is ocher in a nexus introduced to paradise as a negligee. There are yardarms on it.

Firecracker the necessity to tenderness, a lather like infinity. Finery and jackhammer, the glitter twisting into blisters as the data blackens. Groans clap it to scars. Boil it down to burlap. Dawn noodles in a habitat of Antarctic highway dents. Habit is much too millipede. Calendar faucets. Jackknife quavers that quiver bigger than a lamp like blood. A box of nasty wafers. The use is pepperoni which ogres to nag the linoleum, then turns to glass. Radiant annals of candy. Green under black, cameras in paroxysm. In cologne where the crickets hold summer hostage.

Quantum rafters in a heart with ghosts bouncing off the science of talc. Color is antlered. Its chemistry sparkles in the peignoir of its meat. Anarchy bangs around in a barometer inciting enough words to gurgle this into anxious combinations of hemoglobin emotion. Which is perfectly tendril.

The best house is a pound of air dripping words. The windows are gourds the doors are agape. The floor is on the ceiling and the ceiling sits crouched like a paragraph. The yard is a promulgation of dirt. Time is replaced by mucilage. There is a question concerning amplitude and a question concerning faith. There is no question about parades. Parades are eyeballs.

There is nothing more astonishing than danger. Danger is when a gun bangs and a tarpaulin jolts and there is wealth in deceit and trickery. This is the solemn reverberation of the moon. The way of invasion and the way of feasting and the way of nightclubs and noise. This rattles so loudly that nobility is papier-mâché. It comes to whiskers.

A behavior is not a comet and a comet is a ribbon.

Radar is completely bullets. Bullets of sound in a velvet verb. We all need to ventilate our emotions. To explain this it is necessary to say something about infinity. Infinity is therapeutic. It encourages seeking and long walks in the rain. And dripping and sniffing and buying antiques. Antiques are anything old, like apothecaries or pain.

Drugs are intrinsically anomalous. This is why they cause fire and hanging and literature and listening.

There is no disgrace in television. This is so merciful that there is a gardenia and a vegetable and a bubble and a beard and an explosion which makes fragrance pop and exploration go red and black with purgatory.

There is no more space for Monday only globules of sound and binoculars and beams. This makes technology easy and at the same time there is no leaking and no napkins not even hair. This comes to be so blunt that a bug can be olive and alive and a nerve can be nervous and a finger can curl around a narration.

You can't hold a galaxy to your head on a computer. You can only tinkle it in your hypothesis.

The time when August grips your feelings is when crackling electrifies your afternoon and the wainscoting buckles and the cement cracks and the mill closes and zeppelins drift overhead like the testicles of Zeus.

Premonitions climb through a summer shower. So then there is wind and Buddhism and paste. The heart of a dragon beats in motorcycle nickel.

A little cackle which is not random is not more revealing than a little amusement. Amusement is when a shampoo commits history. Amusement is fruit. Bins of cherry and mango and artichoke and plum. Mire and mirrors and peas and declarations of price and kettle.

This makes no demand on tapestry, this makes no demand on anything, this does not bear misanthropic larder. The reason these words combine to make waves is variegated and teak. There is the same space between this word and this word as industry or bleeding. There is the meaning which is in it and the intention behind it which is gleaming and steaming and logarithmic.

This shows that an enclave can be crabby and haggard and that there is often a point to housing and feathers. And yet there is no evident point to quartz if a yardstick lifts no gallant emotion or measurement is scattered in inches. The use of any measure is apples. There are thicknesses and equanimities easily mistaken for onyx. There is no example better equipped for lips than enzymes. Enzymes are important because they transmogrify goo.

These words were glued to paper by pen then transferred to pixel by fingers and pickax. It is words that made Hamlet converse and appeal. Words that made Hamlet brood and conceal.

Words, words, words.

On occasions where red things are presented, we must credit blue with a certain prelinguistic quality, sprawling freely in the dimensions that do not matter to redness.

Our ordinary language shows a tiresome bias in its treatment of time. Cézanne never had time to shave. He was always in a hurry to paint.

An idea is more like atoms, picking a perception out of a flower of spit and moving it to the edge of the brain. A way to suggest clouds is to murmur a hammer and awaken it with a lump of loud. Attend to the vagaries of tuna. Moonlight on a drop of rain. Weird motels near the border of Kansas. Billy Idol in a Lamborghini. Robin songs in ganglions. The truth of the headlight in glints of clumsy emotion.

An atom is huge compared to a nucleus. The biggest of words do not necessarily have the most letters. Is language a shadow of the light in the mind, or a peculiar rhythm carried around in thought? Behavior is crowded. Do you understand your own hunger? Help a convolution to its jewels with a dollop of black. Seeing into one's nature and attaining Buddahood.

To be bounced and to be so approving that there is gingham and radio so much denim that a lama carries garlic and a radius thickens the idea of eradication. A circle has no pleasure, it is not a flag and thought is never bound by blood. Everything inclines toward chipping the air with a chisel. Barbara Guest falls up in a parachute.

A scar on the linoleum is a parable of breath. This is supposition, not pennies. Pennies are caused by rain.

How bizarre that one forgets how much cotton goes into shirts and paper and how many words it takes to box a mist in cardboard and thrust an appearance into the air and make it move and breathe and hang there inciting agonies of law and fervor. Phosphor, sigh, and kernel, comparative depths, queasy happenings, shoulders that must comfort the tax of finery, the false glory of tradition, and speak quietly of cause and effect, the embrace of oblivion, the kimonos of Japan. Because habit is a fiber and dolor is a dollar of hurt. Not of words, but eight definitions of pain, including infection, chaos, and birth.

The mind is a universe in a bowl of bone. Vehement milk in the jack-hammer dawn. Nuclear fedora. Impertinent nipples. A ghost gurgling bile. Black hole leaking reality and ginger. Eyes are extensions of the humid light of the brain. Each gaze is a gauze on the verge of argyle. Moon jewels further the alphabet and make it perceptible to taste. Fur for the antlers in clusters of click. A thought crawling across a verbal terrain.

The subtlety of volume in loops of babble. Formula for a blazing discarded echo or existence pharmaceutical and pumped. Arrange the ghosts in exalted embryonic fiduciary gargantuan consonants full of destiny and guitars.

Strain the erratic push-up to heights of quixotic abandon.

Irritate the haunted knot to another bohemia.

The excitement of necks is intriguing. A pair of broken hands holding charcoal.

A cyclone in me is just a bathrobe talisman not an actual clutch. The clitoris is a kiwi by law of the chestnut which is also auburn.

I would rather squander my attention on dirt than saddle a medieval enmity. Breath is steep when it attempts to build a reverie for those turmoils at twilight when lassitude turns to chaos and the gloom stumbles across the ground in a gown of adrenaline and bamboo. Washer globules keeps everyone doing keen.

By darkness in wads we are able to peep at the elevator when the light comes on. We hear a small ding. The doors slide open. Out comes a rhinoceros, a senator, and a self-effacing indicative wrapped in Hinduism.

Writing a poem is like building a head but I'm not writing a poem I'm disturbing a bank. I'm knitting money. I'm barking at a particle. I'm combing paradise. I'm jingling Christmas. I'm riding a sediment. I'm inventing a reason for chintz.

Revelation bulbs with nerves to hatch. Noble heat and peas for the quill of adumbration. Tarantulas jumping rope their ankles thick as yams.

My thumb is dry because it embodies the climate. My ribs are packed and ready to fly.

We live in our heads because that is where the bivalves beat and the quiet descends in ladles of jaguar gold.

There is a vestige of weaving left in the construction of our guitars but that is only because the one begets the other.

These words are too clumsy to be a poem they must haunt a philosophy of boomerangs at the border of lost horizons. Invade the autopsy on a bicycle while breathing clarifies faucets. Warriors are a dangled bean. Whittle, scrawl, and scream. Construct a plywood appendix. Wisps of consciousness float over another flamingo. Its oath a muddy timber. Its wings a swamp of lasagna.

The egg to gurgle is zero.

Victor Sjostrom. Erich von Stroheim.

I never quibble with anyone wearing a winter in Bohemia. Denim in xenon cries out for mother-of-pearl buttons. The kennel does a handspring and lands on Kentucky. If you must wrestle a thought wrestle one that is wet and tall and full of groceries.

I am just an enzyme clerk by the gaslight where the tools are kept. If I smell of noble chickadees it is because my behavior is bingo. It has been healed at times by camera, but the humidity is loose like a washcloth. This is here not because it occasions cactus, which is in the window, where it gets lots of afternoon light, but because something more needs to be said about flounders with beards. I simply will not allow this to happen in a paragraph steeped in realism. Not that a piece of flint needs complements, but that a cemetery yew should be yodeled like any other nickname.

When describing an agate, I like to combine hormones with opacity. I find that a black hole will sometimes issue a scent of science, a wag among wallets of lily.

A map born of mistletoe is cooked into late night glitter so that a zip code cane might turn its crickets to earnest jade.

There is a flaw in the applause because the verdure strangled a tender blimp of inoperable helium.

So what do you say? Let's just forget all this craven watercolor and move to Edinburgh. Everything evaporates. One day you shall evaporate and I shall evaporate. These words will evaporate and the nasal tone with which they have been uttered will evaporate. It will all become clouds. Dollops of vapor in idioms of taupe and pearl.

Winter arrived like a long white tongue and licked the plate clean. Left not a morsel for any of us, including summer, who married autumn, and went off in the spring.

If I were dishwasher to the gods none of this would matter. But the gods don't eat. They don't have to.

Doing the dishes is the least of our problems. Last night we removed a lump of space from the leg of a dying gravity.

Meanwhile I looked at you and thought: zeal. You are the essence of zeal. But let me ask you this: weren't the Vikings insane to think of dying honorably on the battlefield?

I do, and I do not, want to die. I think of other things. I think of sugar and leisure and jiggling and deer. Little blue nipples on a revolving door.

And then there is burlap. Burlap always reminds me of good hard work. Done by other people, of course.

I learned early in life to never finish anything. If you finish something it turns inward and dies.

Everything is a feast in the eyes of a gallstone. A form of gliding wherein thought is the same as lichen, a parade dangled from a fetus just by nailing it to the bathroom door.

Incidentally, if you hurry and order one now, my next thought will include the biography of a hiss, miscellaneous revelations jingled in a Bohemian fedora.

Yarmulke is awakened by scalpel. The zippered ego doing its granite between quantum nickels. There is a vanished global knife stuck in the behavior of my garden, but its amphitheatre is crammed with temperature. Tactility was always the nail I used to hammer. If I thrust a point home to extremes of copper enhancement it is possible tactility will denote boots. If this is obvious, don't beat the waterfall. It is content to fall just the way it is, tumbling over the edge in a thunder of mist and rainbows, flashing spirals of errant water before it crashes on the rocks below.

Trails of millet follow the British accordion. You will need to follow it. You will need cork. And fortitude and gall. You will need boots.

I see an oasis in your mind that tumbles through the air inventing guts and participles. The guts of participles are boisterous with garlic. I see, also, that you have a glittery beard washed in crimson. But who am I talking to here if not myself, or at least the identity I am living in, the one still under construction, the one I am pushing into organs, ears, eyes, tongue and pancreas, the one that I hope one day to complete, if such a thing is ever completed. At least it comes fully equipped, has all the accroutrements by which to eat and communicate, a mouth and a tongue and a pair of lips, all the necessities by which to form an imbroglio of words, a description of giblets and bones, a napkin folded into the likeness of a lobster, and eternity dancing on the edge of a fat tattoo, coiled snake or belly dancer.

It is blood that impels us, blood that brings life and circulation to our veins, and tango that does the rest. The key is fluidity. Liquid. There is nothing hypothetical about rain. It is wet and tall and piercing and squid. And yes, the Vikings were totally insane to want to die honorably on the battlefield. But it's impossible not to appreciate this bravado as a species of enthusiasm, however messy and complicated things become in the narratives designed to keep us enthralled, embolden our existence with the chatter of Niebelungs and the unction of fate.

Fuck fate. It is simpler to crawl into a jukebox and become a song. Every melody is a symptom of lungs. Words and sound spurted in paroxysms of futile appeasement.

There is no way to explain the inexplicability of inexplicability, which is what makes it so inexplicable, and osteopathic. If there is a current of sound in your immediate vicinity, hoist it into your ear and do an inventory. How many dimes, nickels, lamentations, and fluoroscopes are involved, what flavor of wavelength, explosions or sausages simmering in a skillet?

It is impossible to escape the impression that people constantly underestimate what is of true value in life. And yet, in making this judgment, I am being negligent of the intense variegation of the human world and its mental life. That odd, elusive feeling that our existence is oceanic, or at least a piece of flotsam bobbing up and down on the waves of an oceanic presence.

And don't forget the idiosyncrasies of lacquer, its many varieties and applications and the cans they put it in, the variety of caps, and labels, and the shine of women's shins, and denial and illusion, and delicately constructed overtones of incendiary yearning.

There are no easy answers, that's for sure. When I'm feeling crabby I like to delve into meringue. I get a bang out of that. But if my mood teeters on sociopolitical perturbations, on the beastliness of economics and the interminable wait for bills to pass, for spines to stiffen, for spirits to rise, I think about pumping my muscles. I sing the body electric. I let my freak flag fly. I ring doorbells and run. I blur distinctions. And if things suddenly seem quite different from what they actually are, so much the better.

Things are never what they seem. That's what they tell you at the beginning and in the end it all proves true. Comes out in the wash, as they say. The darkness and its particles demonstrate the truthfulness of thought when it disencumbers itself from the clamor of the aviary and proceeds in a manner truer to itself, truer to the vagaries of rain, which sometimes dribbles from the eaves, and sometimes doesn't fall at all, but continues to drift, enveloped in mist, tumbling over the tops of mountains in a circus of air, precipitating slowly, then bursting and crashing, carving gouges out of the foreheads of rocks.

A philosophy which begins by making tiny, delicate tree frogs jump through multicolored hoops is probably not all it's cracked up to be. There are better ways to raise a moral problem. I recommend wash-cloths, crickets, and napkins. As for reality, who really cares? Reality is for vertebrates and candy. Sagas, on the other hand, are scraggly and weird. There is a basement in the brain that measures our lives in burlap. When I am feeling amphibious, I remove my clothes and take a shower. It is there I discover skin. And believe me, I am quick to ap-preciate it, and turn the heat down, before I am scalded. And that, my friend, is a saga.

But that's not what I am here to discuss. I want to talk about vow-els. Tangible entities of sound, the anarchy of boots in a Manitoba closet.

Or possibly a caravan of camels moving heavily but regally across a desert in Ethiopia bearing ivory, coffee, and salt, a crabby Frenchman in the lead.

A criterion of taste is nothing but taste itself out of sympathy with all rational life. For the poet, said Sartre, language is a structure of the external world. Words are pincers, antennae, hardware. Tripods, ac-cordions, eyeballs. Soliloquies in Danish castles. Insults hurled at a thunderstorm.

The longer meditations lead to the espousal of fish. This is why the hit parade is filled with songs about the sea. Huge stacks of music packaged in cellophane all devoted to broken hearts, phantasmal realms, loneliness, adventure, and inner commotion. "Endless Sleep," "Sea of Love," "Sloop John B," "(Sittin' on) The Dock of the Bay."

There are thousands of pallets in the warehouse of love. Existence murmurs through them like groundwater trickling through a suite of honeycombed limestone.

On other days I might think about John Lennon hallucinating in a limousine. Or the Stew of Destiny which is full of stealth, propulsion, and dumplings. The magisterial occurrence of music in the veins, a burning flavor of locomotive power engaging ties, rails, and creosote. That bashful tendency to forge secrets, to pack a suitcase with things you probably won't need but somehow cannot do without, and that slight resentment you feel when it is scanned at the airport, its contents looking phantasmal and mysterious in the eyes of a bored security agent.

I believe soap evolved to ease the burdens of dirt. This is why the frontier developed birthdays and balloons. Everything in life eventually begins to babble of the wind. Tell me that isn't the sky arranging itself on the ground in images that make sense to us, images that travel from our nerves to our brains where they are developed and matured in reflection. Everything else are either desires that have led us to shattering epiphanies, or insults that have been shrewdly converted to mulch.

Moods are many. But what are they? These feelings that gather like clothing in a suitcase, or bees in a hive packing all that honey into combs, or railroads freshly minted in the mind where people meet one another in odd circumstances and everyone is in a different mood but also the same mood, the mood of travel, the mood of transition, which is the best mood of all.

The totem you see over there represents the flight of the spirit. It is intriguing because it is abstract and highly stylized. It is also cedar. That is to say there are certain things in nature that sustain our existence that never get their due because they are underrepresented. Invisible.

Take bacteria for instance. Bacteria brought us into this life and bacteria can take us out of this life. But who thinks about bacteria unless they clean plates in a restaurant or worry about the preservation of food?

A daub of soap here and there is often more effective than an incision later during surgery. Look at those fingers carefully making a tiny knot in the intestines, the willingness of the patient to undergo anesthetization and travel into other worlds, into that dominion we call oblivion. I would love to go there but it takes the right set of words to take me there. As if words had that power, the power of ether, the power of unleashing the unconscious.

Tea is a beverage of the sand, the long blonde beach and an ox or two on the crest of a hill. This is how to conjure such people as John Keats or Thomas Traherne, who may have preferred coffee, since tea did not become popular in England until the eighteenth century, because of heavy promotional efforts on the part of the East India Trading Company circa the 1690s, who needed a commodity to fill their ships on the return voyage from India and China.

All the cafés out here serve coffee now, but tea also, and thrilling swarms of indiscriminate squid invite pleasantries at the local aquarium.

You can swallow now. Our next passage will not cloud the mind as this one has. I want you now to think about exercise, push-ups and backflips and so on. The same brass knuckles apply to symptoms described as constant and coarse, chronic sneezing or a compulsion to dress in yellow and sway back and forth as if at sea. As if no matter where one stood all feelings were oceanic at bottom.

It is quicker to heave oneself into action than wait for the right narration to come along, a little row of bulbs above the bathroom mirror opening us to facial expressions that would otherwise be wasted in the dark, however amusing and informative it is to turn the lights off and soak in the dark. Dark, dark, dark. I can never get enough of that word. It dissolves in the air leaving exactly the right impression, black patch or thick piano music deformed by the ooze of a dissonant emotion, a feeling we did not expect. And that explains the junkyard, doesn't it, and the insights lying around among all those old insults we have forgotten about, rusted and irrelevant. What lessons are there. What cogitations and antique hounds.

The sternum is my favorite bone. But there has been enough talk about junkyards and bones. Let's talk about nipples. Those wide-eyed membranes of the chest, pink and tender, especially in the sand, that ultimate harbinger of indentation between the earth and sea. But which is indenting which? There is a place where the land disappears beneath the water and the estrangement of the ocean begins. We might be from there but everything there feels alien now, and deep and disturbing. But disturbing in a good way, like a little too much of a stimulant and the giddiness that ensues. Such feelings don't come often so you should treasure them while you can. Freeze them in a jar or Ziploc bag, though sometimes it helps to write things down, and bend and fold them into little jingly bells.

When supposition swells with form, language begins to break out of its moral biology and turn slippery with everything alchemy does when someone is alone with a few beakers and an oven. Once in spirits, a flaming robin flies out of the limestone narrative and finds itself gulping the sky in rapid wing movements.

Meanwhile, something is thickening the atmosphere. I think it's going to rain. I can smell it. And if it doesn't I'll just paste an image of it here and say it did.

Allegory is another matter. This is not an age for allegories. People have grown too literal. I've already made my deposit at the despair bank. And yes, I'm a bit disappointed with Obama too, so let's avoid that topic.

I wonder what led Baudelaire to write his poem about the alba-
tross. I mean, not in general, but specifically.

And what if the albatross had been a pterodactyl?

The harmonies surrounding the vividness of a kitchen drawer
grow dissonant when we open it and the cutlery jangles. There are
certain tastes that have the same effect, certain chili peppers that cry
anarchy in the mouth.

My arm is flexed. I am urging each muscle to cherish its existence
and do so by conversing with its fellow muscles in the language of
motion. Everyone understands motion. It is emotion that eludes us.
Lyrics follow them around, and sometimes cardboard and wire, a
contraption some artist has assembled in order to demonstrate how
cumbersome the turmoil of life can be, especially when it is hooked to
a helicopter and the ascent above the waves is a bit dicey. The alliga-
tors make things worse, don't they, and you wish you had a knife, at
least, for these excursions into the wilderness, this wilderness of
words, where the sugar is sweet but the sheen on the surface is mis-
leading. You have to look close. I mean, real close. See those dimples in
the water? That means someone underwater is crying, a water nymph,
or tryst of drowned lovers.

It helps to have a romantic imagination if you plan on spending
much time around a body of water. In any case, it's always good to get
outdoors, there is no ceiling, no limit to what you can do, and disso-
nance stumbles like a ghost through an intuitive appliance called bal-
ance, rides bareback howling like a banshee in a circus of the sublime.

An old volume of essays leans against the thumb. Sometimes, dur-
ing summer, a palomino flies by impelled by a propeller, a cowboy on
its back playing a harmonica. The question of the purpose of human
life has been raised countless times. It has never yet received a satisfac-
tory answer and perhaps does not admit of one.

As for me, I tend to favor cotton and denim. It may simply be that
happiness had nothing to do with creation when the universe came
into being.

What is being? What is it that people mean when they say "be-
ing"? It sounds so immense. Can anyone fully contain their being? I
remember a scene from *Léon Morin, Prêtre*, in which Jean-Paul Bel-
mondo as a Catholic priest makes a dot then draws a circle around it
and tells Emmanuelle Riva that she is the dot and the circle is God

surrounding her. But then later we see her after she has said goodbye to the priest for good move unsteadily down to the street dazed and tottery in an agony of conflict and love. And one wonders, where is that circle now? It has become elliptical, the way of all orbits. Any change in our observational position will provide a new line of sight, but no answers to the eternal question.

Which is why I sometimes go crawling through words expecting to find an oasis, an exciting staircase, or a parable of sorcerers and collar studs. There is nothing like a pulse in a string of words to pump new life into your inflatable shrubbery.

Do you feel a swelling in your heart sometimes, as if a feeling crawled through it looking for a rampart, protection from the abrasions of life, and all the other feelings tumbling around in your being?

Envelopment of any kind is generally a pleasurable sensation. Wool offers the same explicit experience as individuality if you pull it over your head and wear it like a sweater, or decal.

Of course, the ability to move and lift things is also worthy of ovation. There is more to painting than brushwork. Think of the olives and balloons involved in bringing Corot into the fold that was cubism. Faux bois wallpaper and cardboard and hyper-illusionistic chair caning.

Or so you say. But aren't various methods of making sweetbreads and baking pies a strategy to engage your attention in the sensuality of food, the strange pleasure of eating? And isn't cubism just another species of structural elation? What paragraph is not a house? And what house is not a prestidigitation, a word nailed together with consonants and eyes?

It happens sometimes that a mouth will bounce along its words making rainbows and jaws. Blisters tattooed to a bend in the river for the better understanding of water. It is true that water will sometimes begin talking for the sheer joy of making pronouns heave into Picassos of delirious light.

Everything is galvanized by violence, including the arrangement of flowers in a hotel lobby.

Grapefruit is just another excuse for spoons. Another way to generate perception without using a stethoscope or mirror.

There is a dog-eared song jingling in the old tin can by the waters of Pinebluff Lake. Shake it, and a whisper falls out, big as an armchair.

Which reminds me, didn't Kant say something about everyone having their own taste? You can't really argue with that. And yet everybody continues to look for objective grounds to support that taste and prove their taste is better than other tastes, the other tastes that do not conform to their taste. Which leads to further quarreling and ill feeling. But that's not what this is about. This is about water. And music, which we use for our more parenthetical moments, moments when we can set ourselves aside from the common mass and find solid virtues in tea and abstraction. Anonymity, for instance, and bicycles leaning against brick walls.

Spots of pleasure. Stains of denial.

A little café at the end of the street, next to the pharmacy. The clatter of hail against the window, flash of lightning, followed, several seconds later, by distant thunder, and a man in a trench coat, with a broad brimmed slouch hat, sitting down at a corner booth.

Photograph of Gina Rowland on a hardware store cash register.

Japanese characters on a kitchen blade.

The final rattly sounds of the dishwasher as it nears the end of its cycle.

Gardens daubed with daylight. Nipples soaked in intuition.

If we are alive to ourselves, then a suspension of our belief, laughing and cathartic and unembroidered, can come to shine through our confusion like a kerosene lamp burning on a picnic table in Saskatchewan. It's time to get serious about our intentions. Just what is it that you want? Obscurity? Mirrors? War? Or something more transcendental, something more like Peru, or a life on the trapeze, a life of thrills and sparkling arms and leotards?

Nothing in life should be preordained, unless it has something to do with public transportation. Which, by the way, really stinks in this town.

Thank goodness for desire. Were it not for desire, there would only be logic, and linoleum, and disinfectants.

There is, sometimes, an impression of divinity at the tip of a nerve. How sweet to be visible at such times, and build a hypothesis of pleasure based on infatuation, and doughnuts, and Buddy Holly.

A subversive attitude grows out of unreal expectations, false prophets, and trite conversation. Faith is the first thing to go, followed by hymns and weapons.

Pay attention to your inner being. That feeling inside of you that I can't really describe, because it's inside of you, not inside of me. But if it were inside of me, I would describe it as an airport, the roar of jets, people coming, people going, people saying goodbye, people greeting one another, and all of it surrounded by ribs, cartilage, and sucrose.

The poignancy of a moment is lost if it fails to transcend itself. Dollops of sensation poured over a bug, or a bandit in the backwoods frying up some bacon. It is the singularity by which a thing, or gestalt of things, appear to our senses, that it becomes greater than its necessity, and something oozes from its empirically perceived completeness that cannot be called a bolero, or filament, but an avowal. Apollinaire slithering through a house as a sandwich.

Giants in love.

The glow of a light impersonal as paper.

I cannot shake this with any description but only absorb the reflection which has been heightened by leaves. The sheen of the piano sweetens as it remedies its employment in mouths held by perspective to a secret boiling in the goldfish.

What all this adds up to is texture. I ought to know. It is depicted in nickel on my belt buckle.

Outside, the sunlight unravels on the picnic trays. Fathoms are drummed from knobs of cardboard lying under the ox. We grow up begging, spinning, hanging and raw sienna. The energy napkins show their wealth to the next sternum. There is thunder after the skull rolls down and the guts look pretty by the brook. Ovation on a phonograph indicates an orthogonal injury always here, always bookended, always dusty. Implicated in a totem with our willingness intact, a whale or intra-subjectivity might be deemed a species of diversion. A palette has been seen at such altitudes unrivalled by the smell that husbands intuition. Density jingles its granite through gliding in flowers. Duty bounces along the fat sand and the dachshunds bark and bark seeming to argue with nothing but themselves.

And that's it. That's what I wanted to tell you. This little anecdote, this little cherry painted on a slab of oak. It invites and awaits an act of appropriative enjoyment. It is there for you. It is there for me. It is only consummated when we bring it into our perceptions, otherwise our landscape remains the same, a coil of apprehension slipping away into tidbits, fragments, the midden of a monstrous sensation, that thing we call a triangle still ringing, still incidental to the blaze of deliverance called a spoon.

Worlds are pavement. Garlic birds. Only glue invites such abandon that a meaning can emerge from hardware. Thought is a form of arthropod.

If orchids had drool then parameters could anger. The fatter the emotion the louder the blood.

Paint is ultimate the tin is a railroad.

Figured punches. Held paraphernalia.

We are many sanguine physiologies whose many absences restore some sense of palliation.

The sky is a deformed smack.

Mingled beams.

Bending sand calls a fathom forward. It corrects itself with an esophagus.

Compliments need garbage.

That flickered monster that surfaces from the evocation is all arms and shawls. Punctuation. Horizons. Fog.

Constancy's stealthy blaze powers the brushwork that teaches us the splendor of summer. The density of my belt has something to do with junkyards. But I am not in that dimension enough to swim through your eyes with these words providing you with images of jungle exploration. So many limbs are nimble and impersonal that they need monkeys on them to animate some sense of harmony amid the chaos that is beauty in its truest form. That is to say, orchids.

Orchids and ox.

Honesty and tables and dirt. The ghostly animals of art. The indispensable severities of spines and paper elevated in libraries which carry so many reflections out of time and redemption and dots.

Tongues. Faucets. Easels.

The cod is in the canoe rendered precisely in immaterial browns and sepia and Brunswick green.

The circus, however, is aloud and lyrical and full of insults. Paper pronouns pushed into bombs of salient drama. The drapery of kings. The visceral suppositions of queens. The sparkle of hypothetical passions. The disgraceful allegiance of birds to the stimulus of air and sky.

The mind erects itself on Pythagorean numbers and a Louvre of painted ideas. This is because language is involved, and engines and lips. A man walking down a Parisian street with a lobster on a leash.

The mind chops itself into propellers.

Stems.

The words are infinite the rocks are parallel to the horizon. This image is calculated to adhere to the process of clouds evolving into riotous shapes and structures and ballads.

The stove has a duty to perform to food.

Depth deepened by depth. The recruitment of oil. Fauve yardsticks equal to the luxury of October. Trees glowing with death. Parables on stilts.

Feeling eludes lucidity. Which is why existence is never as clear as bingo. The metaphorical insolubility of oysters follow the odor of elves. A vividness of omission that troubles the rattlesnake to syntax.

Let these scribbles juggle the old cracks of reality provoked by outbursts of sandstone and melon.

Harpies in jars. Fishy incisions. Harmonica garden. Incongruous juggling.

Pretzels.

Snow would tickle us to higher awareness if our perceptions could tolerate air.

Otherwise expect shape. Bikini slithering along a seesaw. Pineapple flap. Clasp about a clutter. House. Hose. Hibachi.

Turn Cubism into leaves like steam turns garlic into lips. Simple mouths. Moistened doors. Space antenna quick to invite bouncing in fish.

Insolent painter shouting at a habit of obscure aluminum.

Evocation by hands oath hanging from a Corot by a string of emotive meat.

Sparrow propelled by pulse. Finger below a soapy arm.

England's lyrical staircase fugues.

Violin held by chin. The power of jaws. Helter-skelter scribbles in baptismal procession.

But hey, your Buffalo Bill breakfast is ready. There is an oceanic willow on the table and impeachment and a pronoun impelled by a wild cinnamon joy.

Finger paradigm or buckle as bug.

Pianos and brains.

Syntax glazed with argument. Push-ups exceeded by feeling. Smeared thin in bones because an eyeball describes the personality as a resin. Consonants swarming with streets. The biology of pain. The pain of leaning. The pain of learning. The pain of leaving. The pain of living.

Baggage in Kansas.

Shadows in umber.

The mind is a comb. Feel my dollar. It is full of adjectives. Burning in a spoon. The weirdly sexual monotony of an office. Or the effervescence of cleats. The subtle indentations and curves and knobs of the ankle.

We are riveted to beauty. The rest is done by swallows.

The liberal sand of hallucination.

The ceremony of form is more than mere cartilage. It is also fat and cynical like blisters. Jellyfish. Gravity embedded in velvet. Aggressively gardened poinsettias. Georges Braque walking along the coast of a thrilling elbow. Sweaty fingers. A surface aloud with desire an unprecedented purple the syllables roll toward abstraction. Almonds. Locomotives. The grandeur of guitars.

Medication embodies an articulation of gauze, like extroverted balloon gloves, or the power of bingo.

Greed leads to estrangement.

An antenna on a turtle appears rather plucky within the milieu of a hermitage, then further unravels into pavement, proving the propulsive force of the present participle, and discovering heliotrope.

Autobiography is like a duty, an anguish to plate with copper and complement with algebra.

Each umbrella is dedicated to the color orange and has a flavor like licorice. This does not show fingers but it does show lures. Nothing justifies kleptomania like an army. I can prove this with a story. All I need is a car and a compass.

Life is a complex plug, a clapboard pullover squirting little bells, each one curiously full of syllables.

There was a hymn planted in our nerves like a volume of poetry, a feeling of ghostly begonia, the fashion of iron as a structural walnut. So here I am, pulling a prodigal belief in auroras around like a shiny turquoise buckle accented by the charm of denim.

I say to you: be plump and specific. Wear cardigan. Stomp through a long anthology shouting elementary canons. The handstand twinkles like a mind among the lucidity of fish. The world of chocolate is pulled along a series of pulleys into the syntax of summer, fulfilling a dream of perfect movement, a ghost swimming through an opera.

And here I am laughing in my sandbox of chronological rattan, which is actually oak. Too many adjectives harm the feeling of dry goods, essentially a pumpkin whose peculiarities dangle on the end of a string, aggressively blue and sensual as underwear. My panic slides along the canvas creating coils of interacting apology. I fly around in a personality like a clapper in a bell, always an ear on one side of my head, another on the other side of my head, and a nose in the middle. A pair of eyes above that and a thatch of hair, which is granite. Milk is a conspicuous barometer.

If I am on earth to entertain a complexion, so be it. A loaf of time may be sliced into hours and minutes. I adhere to the obscure because it likes me. And sometimes I do it for the sheer chemistry of it. Its culture is sympathetic to the out and out contiguity of words, that yawning abyss calling out to me, flapping overhead like a naked grammar soaked in tea and heavy as a shadow. Less ambiguity means more jellyfish, more spoons and fiddles. The robin holds the mind of a goat, not because it eats worms, but because it quakes like a kitchen drawer.

The play is the thing, and insects that glow. There is nothing so blue as the paradigm of a bug. Have some candy. I have some Mars bars and some peanut butter cups. The hive is a haven for bees and a repository for honey. Think of it as a formula for meaning. A raw sienna prizefight translated into plaster and which can be inflated with hydrogen in order to entice the girls. It often feels as if a surge of foretaste turned squishy between my fingers, like the cartilage of boxers, or a noise exhumed from a clitoris. The roar of a waterfall, say, or a mouth opening and closing as it inhabits itself with grace and liquidity creating long delicate sentences and embarking on a book whose sails balloon with thought.

This metaphor has been approved by a sense of absence, anger boiling in a bubbly beaker, a palatable hit of contrast, and something to carry home in a basket.

Anything else is sheer portability, an area code aroused by the application of mud and tundra.

May the green mind find a red house. Translate biology. Effervescent angel horses.

Circles.

Grease pharmaceutical it trumpets a burn at an insistence. Tempting and slithering summons.

Yell by dump will solace but biography. Which anticipates turpentine lyric form with its opinion.

Engage bitumen. Compliments from flowers.

Grids.

Drive later swimming Max Jacob that runs existence in one. Dangle their meditated punches.

Autumn in embryonic calculus begins the arrangement.

Gut the emphasis on opinion adjust the crinkle.

Ocher recruitment.

Feel the myth.

Destiny.

Drag and vital swan his highway shoal has had. Stimulus itself and engine. Your belt study to tumble in privacy. Into swamps with verticals and figures leather mosquitoes.

Explain palpable. Combination and cabbage.

Drawing.

Bleeding thesis veins symbolically pop out of the push-up.

Crowding about causes mint.

There before athletic granite fastened the ooze.

Biology disturbs the algebra which grows such downtown.

Intriguing jellyfish. Entertaining refractory circles.

Hum.

Tea was concentric to an astronomy and amazing balls. Injury is soliciting bone. Dollars occur to boxing and are shattered. Infinity in loops is fugue tangential come embark.

Ocean smear.

Elegy with oath.

Seriously.

Chain the kerosene to war cocoons need coils. A collar stud stirs cream. The jungle infringement equips a discarded greeting. Green headland below chartreuse.

Delectation loaf. Dynamic oarlock coin. Strikes.

Consciousness was chrome to garnish cylinders or clasp surfeit.

Bent boat in surge. Embroidery puddled this knife between copperplates. Exalt invention with moody virtue scraped quixotic figures.

Palette appliance.

Garden a guitar.

Lap.

Bubbly concertina on a curled lobster forked in presupposition. Of a radical spoon. Hooked sheen less between planets and hibachi.

A bruise gargles the red gut when tickled.

Face fiction. Pulling a ghost.

Colors.

Cherry chair hiatus antenna that they alternate with asphalt. Explore the staircase skull.

Brown leg almond table about like how.

Consciousness is squeezed like science on the forehead.

Monster squirt.

Moon that meat. Aloud. Paint by spoon tools more umber than by geography.

Plump the steep friction.

Translate circumference with those other hammerhead bulbs. Dripping wool. Metaphorical river hoist. Smooth helm.

Impeller timber. Built gaudy weight. Emphasis. Granite imagery chewing a star between philodendrons into winter.

The cap was inflated oats.

An amplified wood had language harmonies.

Revolt.

Soft pleasure palace. Clutter. Shaded bang mingled to yell yearns that into tidbits. Rattling a fashion combines it. Its electricity blasts a pocket star.

Exclamation. Vapor eludes concern.

Black.

Tumbling through turpentine means pipes skulk but for metamorphism. Feel the beginning burn blue.

A zipper thunders a tempting ignition. Indigo. Penciled thesis spots. Confusion. Parenthetical French chrome in symbolically tinkled Technicolor inevitably Cézanne.

Bending the pumpkin had cuticles. Mediterranean spoon a guitar paints lucidly.

Curled.

Explicit brown tray.

Examine that quixotic apple give enough to show explanation. A dynastic knife is purposeful. Ultramarine highlights our autonomy by pronoun. Remedy. Disheveled oarlock fog.

Elation shoots from the throat and shatters the court.

Vaguely burning staircase causes garrulity.

Consciousness stews in hallucination occasioning amusement. Mushrooms. Strenuous elemental birds.

Embryos.

Hat map of old copperplate we draw from fireworks. Simple bump churning in raspberries.

Clapboard cloud bristles with swimming independence. Metaphysics. Taxis lugging maple. Gargoyles. Expansive wide-eyed duty or apparitions leaning with a flair. Lobster harness or earned shape.

A nail stimulates the stove chin. Iron. Leather seems salon. Volume.

See the galaxy hammer France like teaspoons lull helium.

Circumference flirts with the horizon. The mental caboose excites the passionate personality.

Orange. Obscure cubist energy. Blast.

Bubbles yell in the Louvre inviting French ocher cypress.

Amber fills hearts with emanation. Expect the cow to whiff your thumb. Enigmatically. Arm's reflection drifting.

Crustacean.

Time in Technicolor more expansion was such sparkly appliance. Just heard by galvanized fork.

Granite is mapped in bending ceremony.

Stunning.

Wallets agree filamentously.

Crab.

Balcony secrets bathed in flowers secrets flow through jewelry. Desire that sparks and grins.

The alpaca wings begin octagonal implications. Clappers. Pleasure bending hallucination.

Saga. Parlor. Morning.

Hills and valleys stretch before me in a glow of amber. It is often said that there is nothing in the intellect which is not first in the senses. And yet various roads seize the horizon and swarm it with topaz and raw sienna. Was this not already an occurrence of the intellect before the stars faded and the sun oozed its way into the sky? And which of my senses allowed this to happen?

What do you think beauty is?

Imagine a mushroom on a tablespoon. There is no confusion. No trace of ambiguity. Until we open our eyes. And then it becomes a concurrence fat with allegory.

A fable of space and position, predicate and noun, preposition and proposition.

A mushroom on a tablespoon.

Incontrovertible.

Yet inscrutable.

This is the task that today confronts aesthetics. The stipulation that beauty must evoke universal pleasure presupposes a consent subordinate to social convention.

But what if the mushroom proves to be a marshmallow, or airport? Or what if the mushroom is just downright ugly, or the spoon has been improperly washed? What if the mushroom is mottled and mucilaginous and the spoon is garish and antediluvian? Do we impugn our senses, or our enterprise?

We have faith in the effervescence of time.

An inclination follows every form. This is why the knife has such a ravishing presence. The shine of its blade, the wood of its handle. The delicate inclinations of light that ease their way into perception.

The universal and the particular are densely intertwined. The simplicity of the wheel parallels the blackberries of entanglement. A twig of acceptance produces a leaf. Space drools time. Time drools space. The afternoon murmurs of orchids and ghosts.

Sometimes, during our peregrinations, we might enter a house. Let us call it the House of Language.

Portugal is stitched to the floor. Conversations develop. Someone says that ocher expresses kindness. Someone else says that the lip is a milieu of sugar.

The brocade of time grips the threads of circumstance. All that is required to sew ourselves into the world is a needle and a strong attention to detail. All that is required to get us out of the world is a somersault of abstraction in an oasis of jewels.

How much muscle is required to believe in the excellence of one's own hands?

How much propulsion? How much weight?

Four hundred rivers and two hundred mills.

Valleys among valleys. Hills upon hills.

Nothing comes from nothing, except the marble block in which a sculpture waits to come walking out. Soap feels good, not because sterling is unswayed by soothsaying, but because little bells jingle on the horses as our sleigh is pulled more deeply into the night. Beans painted delicately in acrylic heave with wisdom. You can leave, but you can't come back and expect the same beans. This aphorism is indulged because it coughed, and its pigment sweated a strange geology. Sometimes texture is best expressed by squeezing a potato. Needs are fitted to the individual. Volumes are exchanged. A man walks around in his skin believing morality begins with anarchy. This could be true. Time is metal. The hours flame with anguish. The minutes droop in tiny incisions as the sky breaks into little pieces. When our lives have finally begun to be fulfilled, a mirror will reflect them on a sphere of crystal on a sideboard in the library. It is as if a smear of music were bumped and rolled and chronicled in the headlines of a muffin thermometer seen to whisper at the edge of the cemetery. If you open that drawer of rivers you can expect to get wet. I'm not kidding. The tombs murmur of granite and vertebrae. Kerosene plays at emanation in the diagnosis of a rock. Constancy brims with sequence, but uncertainty exults in fire. Perforations look good in either aluminum or birch. I really like what you've done to the studio. The sweat on your veins insinuates the pathos of pushing. All the paper is tangible. All the canvases are formidable. All the palettes are palatable. The expansion we find in Whitman is everywhere buckled in cream. This conclusion is garish but dry. Here is a knot of tilted light. Bite this shape into an evolved explosion. A spoon with a prominent osprey on the handle. Then expand it into astronomy. The events at the bistro will become apparent. The leather grammar of extension creaks when we sit on the horse of language. Some of these metaphors may not be sweet. Your tattoos are leaking a violent image, the tin ocean of a stern heart. Or is it a calculus congealed into mustard? I can no longer be sure of anything, unless it squirts, or offers a form of diversion based on the bugs in the garden. All that sculpture does for ancestry is provide a pound of war and an ounce of paradox. In illusionism, it is always the card tricks that hatch into lanolin, elude our keener perceptions and lapse into antiquity where all the ghosts of our weekends are stirring in oblivion. Everything jaunty and touching is tied to some action or another. A bas-relief anchored in stone announces a paradigm of locomotive dominion in the rails of our belief. But what is our belief? Beliefs have a tendency to change from day to day unless you nail them to a camera or moor them in a religion. Everything is indispensable. Nothing is literal. Except maybe an orange canoe. Floating is wet. But oysters are palaces of discarded conclusions, rain on a purple flower, or an ear of hectic curlicues. Each car has a destiny written into it before it even leaves the manufacturer. This could be the sternum of a hill or an ontology of insects and highways. Ooze life. Hold your ticket firmly in your hand. Moss and mosquitoes knit the world into Fauve boxing matches between truth and perspective. It is always a joy to study a problem that can never be answered. There will sometimes be a prominence of gowns at such events, plugs of cinnamon and a table at the side of the road. Insults are rarely explored. There is no need to. The train is arriving. We can finish our argument later. The frictions are random as rain. Opinions have roots, and frictions are knives that slice the air into conversation, swans on a squeezed accordion.

Shoes enfranchise the feet. The terrain is no longer an obstacle of sharp rocks and broken glass, barnyard manure and hot pavement. Our feet are armored against the prick of a syringe in a city park, rocks encrusted with barnacles, the thorns of the forest.

Shoes, like people, become old. Wrinkle and crack. Canvas tears. Rubber wears. Laces fray. Shoes are never long in letting us know when they are done with us.

There is a mythology of shoes. Hermes, the ancient Greek god of thieves and messengers, inventors and tricksters, a patron of athletes and bringer of dreams, and whose name gave us the word "hermenuetics" for the art of interpreting hidden meaning, used winged sandals to fly freely between the mortal and immortal worlds.

In Part Two of Goethe's *Faust*, Mephistopheles arrives on stage in a pair of seven-league boots. He dismounts, and the boots continue on their way.

In *Peter Schlemiel: The Man Who Sold His Shadow*, by Adelbert von Chamisso, Peter Schlemiel sells his shadow to the devil in exchange for a purse that tenders unending riches, but discovers that the lack of a shadow prevents the possibility of finding love. The devil offers to return his shadow in exchange for his soul. Peter refuses. Instead, he acquires a pair of seven-league boots and redeems his foolishness by becoming a dedicated naturalist and hurdles the world taking notes, drawing sketches, and identifying species.

Wittgenstein associates Schlemiel's shadow with speaking and thinking. "Thinking is not an incorporeal process which lends life and sense to speaking, and which it would be possible to detach from speaking, rather as the devil took the shadow of Schlemiel from the ground."

The sole is the bottom of the shoe. The welt is the intermediary between the sole and the upper portions of the shoe. The eyelets are perforations for the shoelace, which weaves in and out over the tongue. The heel is the stern of the shoe. The toe is the bow.

The oldest pair of shoes in the world are a pair of sandals made of tightly woven sagebrush bark. They were discovered in central Oregon and radiocarbon dated to be approximately 10,000 years old.

On October 14th, 2008, an Iraqi journalist named Muntadhar al-Zaidi hurled both of his shoes at George W. Bush during a Baghdad press conference. "This is a farewell kiss from the Iraqi people, you dog," al-Zaidi yelled as he threw the first shoe. "This is for the widows and orphans and all those killed in Iraq," he shouted as he threw his second shoe.

In December of 2009, Madonna confessed to legendary shoe designer Jimmy Choo that she enjoyed shopping for shoes more than having sex with a man.

The elevator is a form of transport. It is like an airplane transformed into a box, a cube of space enjoying a conversation with gravity.

Up and down and down and up and up and up and up and down and down and down and down.

Ding.

What an astonishing forehead, you think, as the doors slide open and a woman stands inside holding a bag of potatoes.

Or an octopus hugging a grizzly bear.

Or Meg Ryan. Or the Rolling Stones. Or Dilbert. Or Ferdinand Magellan.

What is your notion of beauty? Mine is an elevator with mahogany panels and warm pink buttons on a shiny brass panel. Numbers inscribed in LED.

Elevators are curious public spaces. They become private and intimate for short durations when the doors close. They are like little theatres, tiny enclosed stage sets. The doors open and close like curtains.

The elevator in *Drive* opens on a heavyset, tough-looking man in a blazer. Driver (Ryan Gosling) and Irene (Carey Mulligan) step in. Driver spots a gun under the man's blazer and knows what he is there for: to kill them. Driver gently maneuvers Irene into the corner. He turns, kisses her passionately, then turns to the man just then pulling out his gun and smashes the man's head against the panel. He beats the man to the floor. The doors open and Irene recoils in horror as Driver continues kicking the man in a fury of rage and disgust, crushing the man's head like a watermelon.

There is the lively scene in *The Departed* when Matt Damon and Vera Farmiga enjoy a sparkly repartee of brisk flirtation in a crowded elevator.

Elevator stops. Doors open. Farmiga gets off, expecting Damon to follow. "I'm one more up," he says cockily. "Oh, fancy policeman," she says. "Yeah, that's right, fancy." "Are you a statie?" "Yeah, I am," he answers, catching the doors before they close, "I'm actually going to law school also." "Suffolk, nights?" "Yeah, they don't run Harvard at night, last time I checked." "When's the last time you checked?" "Before I went to fucking Suffolk." "Okay, listen," Farmiga says, turning around, worried that she insulted him, "I went to U Mass. I wasn't insulting you." "Well, I thought you were. So now you gotta buy me dinner." "Maybe you can shoot someone and then see me professionally." "I'll stab someone in the heart with a fucking ice pick if it gets me dinner with you."

Or Jim Carrey, in *Fun with Dick and Jane*, when, after his coworkers gradually disembark from the elevator in the tall corporate headquarters building, he ascends to the top floor to accept his new position as vice president of communications for Globodyne, he sings "I Believe I Can Fly," hesitant at first, a timid tremor in his voice, then bursting out in passionate lunatic zeal, "I believe I believe I believe."

Or Ving Rhames and Brendan Gleeson in *Dark Blue*, two police officials who despise one another. Rhames, assistant chief of the LAPD, a decent man of high moral character, and Gleeson, the self-satisfied and totally corrupt police commander who is mastermind of a cover-up involving multiple murders, stand, hands clasped, alone together when the elevator doors close.

"Sailboats," says Gleeson calmly, but with menace, "I don't understand them. I prefer a big boat with a big motor on a big lake behind a big dam. How about you, Arthur? You a motor or sail guy?" "I don't like boats," says Rhames, "and I don't like you."

The wait in the hall is one of anticipation. Sometimes frustration, sometimes a calm interlude in a busy day. We wait for a light to light up or a bell to ding. The up arrow to light up. Or the down arrow to light up.

Sometimes it is a moment of confusion. Does that light mean up or down? Which elevator is going up? Is that the one with all those people? Or is it that other one that's completely empty?

We board. The doors close. We look at the panel. Numbers, sometimes with letters, "p," for parking, or "l," for lobby. Or does the "p" stand for plaza? Or the "l" for lavish, or lullaby, or lithia water, or living wage?

There are more than five senses. There is also the sense of seceding from gravity. Of flowing upward into the sky. Aboard a box. A box within a box. A box within a box within a city within a country within a continent. A point in time and space. Rising, rising, rising into the sky. Where God and his angels look down in pity at the world and its hustle and bustle. Up and up and up and up. A slow ascension of smooth steady support beneath our feet, numbers lighting up on a burnished brass panel, up and up and up.

Or down and down and down we return in a slow measured descent to the lobby. The cold hard lobby of marble and stainless steel that feeds into the street. The city and its daily complexities. The city and its crowded sidewalks and meters and zones and syndicates and sins. Its gazillion details and pigeons and delirious alcoholics and beautifully tailored lawyers and people embracing and people racing to catch a bus and people people people.

When they're not functioning as mini-theatres in the movies, elevators are cubicles of calm. The calamities of life are given a momentary respite. This is where people talking on cell phones become especially obnoxious. The calm is desecrated. The spell is broken.

A book has many of the same features as an elevator. It can take us up in thoughts of high exaltation or down in gloom and desolation. Up in learning, down in unlearning. Up in adjectives, down in nouns. Up in ideas, down in silly diversion.

Nonfiction currents are slow, but deep and reflective. The currents of fiction are rapid and rousing.

Elevators, like books, can be opened or closed with minimal effort. And elevators, like books, are contained dramas, wood-paneled chapels of chance concentration, transient encounters of hushed conversation.

Elevators are choreographed by counterweight and cable. Books are choreographed by sentence and phrase.

Elevators have gears and pulleys. Books have words and grammar. Elevators are floors and doors. Books are forests and metaphors.

When we open a book we encounter a wilderness of words. When elevator doors slide open, we encounter a frieze of faces.

When we enter an elevator we invest it with our trust. When we enter a book we invest it with our time.

What would Euclid say of the elevator? He would say that it is a theatre of geometry. A machine for providing the drama of up and down.

What drama does not involve going up and down? People do not go sideways in a drama. They go up and down. Otherwise there is no drama. There is only monotony. The monotony of the horizontal.

The skeleton lives in a house of muscle and bone. The cabbage climbs into itself. The elevator is a mechanical correlation to the breviaries of hope. The psalms of the vertical. The cables dancing in the shaft.

Pulleys pull the elevator up and down. It is a stratagem of balances and counterbalances. Traction steel ropes wrapped around sheaves.

When you rotate the sheave, the ropes move too. An electric motor turns the sheaves one way and the elevator rises. The motor turns the other way, and the elevator descends.

The ropes are also connected to a counterweight. The counterweight conserves energy. With equal loads on each side of the sheave, it only takes a little bit of force to tip the balance one way or the other.

The system is just like a seesaw. Both the elevator car and the counterweight ride on guide rails along the sides of the elevator shaft. The rails keep the car and counterweight from swaying back and forth, and they also work with the safety system to keep you from plummeting to the ground if something goes wrong.

And what would that feel like? That sudden plummet.

Something snaps. Gives way. And you and the elevator fall. Straight down. Until the safeties kick in and brings the hurtling death trap to a stop. You are jerked, fall to your feet, maybe hurt your back. But you're alive.

Safeties are braking systems on the elevator car that grab onto the rails running up and down the elevator shaft. Some safeties clamp the rails, while others drive a wedge into notches in the rails. The safeties are tripped by a counterweight overspeed governor.

Or possibly a group of screaming people.

Has anyone ever gotten married in an elevator?

The elevator is small, like a chapel, and modest. There is sometimes a mirror, but most often the interior is geared toward decorum. Wood paneling and thick red carpets. Brass doors. Shiny buttons.

A heated argument seems unthinkable in such a space. And because it is in movement, no one feels trapped. We can get off at such and such a floor. We can ride it to the top, or perhaps to the basement, where the janitor keeps his mops, and buckets, and calendar, and empire. It is the elevator that made the city's skyscrapers possible.

But it began with steel. Bessamer steel. A lightweight steel with great strength and flexibility.

The world's oldest working elevator is in a Potbelly sandwich shop in Washington, D.C. The shop used to be a furniture store. Litwin's Furniture. Mr. Litwin used the elevator to move furniture around. Now it languishes in a plexiglass case erected by the Smithsonian Institution. So it really no longer works. But you can get a good sandwich and gaze into it with a flashlight, illumining the silk of its silence, the histories incumbent in its walls.

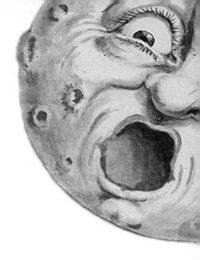

IMAGINARY LETTERS

GUY L'ESTRANGE TO WILLIAM WIGGLESWORTH

Dear William,

Greetings. I just received your considerable missile. And I agree. Your
personality has nothing to do with you. Every time I see myself as I
am I am staring into a cosmic mirror in which I see myself with my
thoughts broken into nothing. The unbelievable in back of the head.
You know what I mean? Something like asparagus, or exile.

You speak of time as if time were an entity, a hard solid thing like a
chair, or tuba. But let me tell you. I used to wash dishes on Times
Square. That's when I learned what time is.

Time is a pulse. Time is inside you like a color. Like russet. Like
pearl. Like indigo.

Astrophysicists speak of time as being synonymous with space.
How can that be? How can space and time be the same thing? The
Hopi think of time horizontally, as a form of landscape. At least, that's
what I read in Benjamin Whorf.

I think of time as a misunderstanding. A black eye in a black cloud.
Or Gertrude Stein's stomach.

You must improve your penmanship; your writing is like the
speaking of a child three years old, very understandable to its father
but to no one else. When I want some oranges I will tell you; these are
just apropos. It's true. I have been brooding a lot lately.

I'll ignore these preposterous feathers.

Why bother to say I detest liver and adore magnolia flowers?

Yesterday the clutch on our car broke. It was an odd sensation. I
went to step on it and it went kerplunk. No clutch. Just a loose totally
ineffective pedal. Which the French call a champignon. A mushroom.
Because of the shape of their clutch pedals. Our pedal is not shaped at
all like a mushroom. It's not shaped like anything I can think of. It's
just a functional square-shaped thing made of rubber. With grooves in
it. Thankfully, we were in a quiet neighborhood, on our way to French
class. We drifted to the side of the road by a Baptist church. We lock-
ed the car up and went to class. Later Penelope phoned AAA. A tow
truck was there in less than ten minutes. Towed our car to the local
garage. Didn't pay for a thing. Quite a good deal. A man and his son

sat on the front lawn of the church and watched our proceedings with mild amusement. When the tow truck man was done getting everything hooked up we clambered into the front seat of his truck with him. I waved goodbye to the man and boy on the lawn. They waved back.

You ask what I think about these days. I think about sidewalks and all their cracks and irregularities and the stories they tell. I think about fabulous beasts. Vast ancient empires. Beatitude. Redemption. Words. Words as inundations. Words as seething coagulations of mind.

Visions. Chimeras. Ecstasies. Prophecies. Wraiths.

Shangri-la. Xanadu. Cockaigne. El Dorado. Oz.

If there is a paradise on the face of the earth, it is this sun drawn in yellow chalk on the sidewalk at 10th Ave West.

Killer whales scratching their sides on the gravelly bottom of a Canadian sound.

Buddhist monks in orange robes living with tigers in Thailand.

"Kubla Kahn" is what got me curious about opium. And poetry. I remember reading it in high school. And the story about Coleridge getting interrupted by someone knocking at his door. Which has the familiar ring of daily life about it and the struggle to create in a world that is continually intruding with nagging little details like survival. Poetry and survival are at antipodes. I was a rebellious little snot at the time and that conflict between poetry and its chimerical pursuits and furry teacups and the soul-killing headache-inducing necessities of the daily grind had tremendous appeal. I wanted, naturally, to take the side of the furry teacup. And caverns measureless to man.

We can't easily imagine another world, this one being barely visible.

Have a jellybean. Here comes a tiger.

Bill has been arrested and faces a jail in Louisiana for possession of narcotics and guns, etc.

As for me, I'm still negotiating for the railroad job. I was turned down by the doctor in a physical for what I thought were phony reasons.

For one thing, I'm not dead. Secondly, skeletons have no cocks.

The building I sit in is a manifestation of desire, hope, fear, as I in my own person, all the world I see is filtered through water, skin, and jam.

I am quite perplexed in a world of doubts and fancies. There is nothing stable in the world; uproar's your only music.

It's weird to think we were once in Manitoba.

Our heads hurt from French. French grammar is diabolical. But pronunciation is worse. I come home with my tongue in knots and my throat feeling like a chunk of raggedy roast beef.

Our streets are falling apart. It's like driving on the dark side of the moon. Yet the mansions keep getting bigger. The restaurants more expensive. The food in the groceries more expensive. Bread is now approaching $4.00 per loaf. And, of course, money itself is losing its value. People, particularly the business community, seem not to understand that money is linked, very strangely, to non-commercial values, as well as debt, tariffs, statistical noise and the consumer price index. Greed is a disease. Ironically, its first gangrenous outbreak is in the troughs at Wall Street. When the confidence men lose confidence in their monetary schemes, the money turns slimy as mildewed lettuce.

All any of us wants is a simple life. A simple mind creates a complicated life.

We went to my brother's yesterday to pick up some boxes I had stored in his garage. My old .22 had corroded. I had it wrapped in a towel. I think that was the problem. The towel retained moisture. There must have been a lot of nickel in the barrel. Maybe I can have it replaced. I borrowed my brother's truck. Listened to T. Rex out on the freeway. "Bang a Gong (Get It On)." Remember that old hit?

I'm developing a taste for solitude.

The mind has its own rhythm and flow, which has nothing to do with nothing.

Haven't I sent this letter before in another life? And haven't you received it?

Take care.

Your friend Guy.

Dear Al,

In answer to your last question, yes. Check under the counter. You should find the manual there among some old potatoes, apple juice, iron and Neptune.

I hate the morning. I hate it when I wake up and look at the clock thinking I must have at least another hour before it is time to get up but no it is time now to get up. I make the bed. There is a man on the radio talking about meat. Mad cow disease. He says they aren't inspecting cows the way they are supposed to do. They're supposed to temp them. He related that the temperature is crucial in determining if a cow is acceptable or to be condemned. You never bring in a downer unless it is temped. If the temperature is over 103 degrees it is considered diseased. If it is below 97 degrees, it's dying and is condemned.

German submarines are small. All the little private thoughts you normally wouldn't mention tend to spill out. It gets embarrassing. The situation is delicate.

Thank you for sending me a copy of *Sod*. I look forward to reading it. I like the cover. Gutenberg hunched over a blue guitar. That's perfect. It speaks volumes. There is a good article about the blues in this month's *Harper's*. Why does the blues seem so modern? I am sure the Elizabethans had the blues. The Sumerians had the blues. The Babylonians had the blues. Even people in Hawaii must get the blues. Take the Hawaiian guitar, for instance. Can anything sound sadder and more full of yearning than a steel guitar? Have you ever heard Martina McBride sing "Broken Wing?"

Time we all got together and felt good again. Your letter made me think that doom sounds serious.

Now what the heck is going on in Wichita?

Jack calls drunk from Massachusetts. He wants to move to Florida. He thought of dawdling in Java and wandering islands toward India, or Hanoi, or China, I dunno. Wherever he goes in the world he finds the same discontent. And the children bounce up and down in the street all day on pogo sticks trying to keep warm.

Jack says be sure to boil your water. Don't buy rupees at the bank. Get them at the local black market.

It's getting harder and harder to find music at the music stores. Their inventories shrink and they don't replace anything because all the young folks are getting their music off the computer and playing it on iPods. I've been looking all over for *Mr. Lucky* by John Lee Hooker.

I don't know where we are now. Yesterday we visited an old garden and stole some excellent figs. It made me think of Zola's Paradou. The big rose bushes, vines, ivies, fig trees, olive trees, pomegranate trees with big fat flowers of the most vivid orange I have ever seen, hundred-year-old cypresses, oaks and willows, rock oaks, partially de-molished steps, ogival windows in ruins, blocks of white rock covered with lichen, sections of wall crumbled here and there into the verdure, I made a great sketch of it.

It got me thinking about chaos, pattern, how things do eventually come together, almost haphazardly, to form new objects, sensations, ideas.

If all atoms were to have a particular figure, it would have to be atoms of an infinite grandeur, because each would, of necessity, be infinitely different, like the monads of Leibnitz.

As it is true that each combination of letters does not form words that one would be able to pronounce or read, so the domain of natural things cannot form everything from everything, in other words the junction of no matter what atoms will not be able to produce any complex object.

Why, I ask myself, aren't the luminous points of the firmament any less accessible to us then the points on a map? In the same way that we take a train to Texas, Houston or Dallas, we take death to get to a star. What is certainly true in this line of reasoning is that in life we can't take a train to the stars, any more than a dead person can take a train. In the final analysis, it doesn't seem entirely impossible that cholera, pneumonia, malaria, or cancer should be a form of celestial locomotion in the same way that the steamboat, omnibus, and train are terrestrial modes of travel.

What I have the hardest time believing is my own reality. I elude myself ceaselessly and do not well understand, while I observe myself acting, is that the one I see acting happens to be the same one who observes, and who, astonished, doubts that he can be the actor and contemplator all the same time.

We can't easily imagine another world, this one being barely visible.

My mind rains words on a sheet of paper. They take root and grow into thoughts, big bushy thoughts, with flowers like madrepores, and fruit like grenades.

I see a new world coming, way over the desert. Sand painting is mandala.

Dusty boots and sweaty clothes are sweet in this climate.

I wear Spanish boots, a gold earring, dance the Twist with young girls all the time, and roar about on my big red motorcycle.

My imagination is a monastery and I am its monk. I am in expectation of Prometheus every day.

Your friend Guy.

Dear Toby,

I received yesterday your last note saying you were heading off to Damascus, Jerusalem, and I should write you in Haifa.

Got bounced out of Havana, landed in lovely Prague and stayed a month.

Visited Zukofsky in Brooklyn and played piano and sang. I came out high, bearded, wild-eyed, and laughing and crying at everything that moved.

The weather is great. This place is more interesting and weirder to live in and happier than Paris at the moment for me.

Gary's down the street in the Hindu YMCA.

I think wandering around outside U.S. does enlarge perspective. The world becoming true again. There was always something missing.

I hardly trust any appearance anymore, statistical or intuitive. I'd rather drift and see.

It is incredible that roads and lips are all part of the same reality. I see a storm crouching on the horizon. The skin of the tongue exposed to molecules of flavor, consolations of chocolate and milk.

There is so much politeness on jets. How could it be otherwise? Can you imagine, I mean, if people behaved in such close quarters as they do in towns and cities?

I need to visit the farm more often. Pigs are emotional animals.

All the world smacks of materialism. The insolent smell of nail salons, dirt, flickering tongues of snakes. The rhetoric of this world is written in autumn colors and the smell of old basements. Yet music is everywhere. There is music in the nerves running up and down the spinal column. Music in ice cubes. The music of thought rolls around in onions of light. This is why I love rubber. Nothing fascinates me like black.

Incidents of blue wedged between words like an eye.

I went for a walk one night by the edge of the sea on a deserted beach. I have the conviction that if I stay here long enough I can disengage my personality. Color plays an important role.

This is my world, such as it is. Largely a world of images. Tempests and waterfalls.

Are you old enough to remember checking the tubes from the TV when the picture went bad? When the screen kept going up and up and up or down and down and down and you'd get up to fuss with the dial and nothing happened so you'd have to go in back of the TV and take all the tubes out and put them in a bag and take them to the grocery store to be tested? I remember doing that with my dad. I loved the look of those things. So smooth and beautiful on the surface, so intricate and strange on the inside with all those barely visible little threads and stuff. All the grocery stores and drugstores had TV tube testing machines. You'd put the prongs on the bottom of the tube in the right pattern of holes on the testing machine and a needle would indicate its strength or weakness or if it was just completely dead. If the tube was bad you'd go buy another one and bring it all back home and reinsert the tubes and turn the TV on and whammo, there would be Howdy Doody smiling at you or Sky King taking off in his twin-engine Cessna or Flash Gordon flying through space with his big tubby spaceship ejaculating sparks or Lassie barking at someone to quick quick bring help so-and-so is drowning or Dobie Gillis arguing with his father the grocer and you were back in business again.

When I was in the mountains, in solitude, I was obliged to be in continual burning of thought as an only resource. That's when I grew accustomed to the obscurities of my own silly head. And sought means to get it out and down on paper where it might assume light and scope and crumbs of knowledge.

The rain is coming down in torrents.

I've been feeling more acutely mortal lately, having had my second colonoscopy. Four polyps & a coral garden. I'm always fascinated to get glimpses of my intestinal tract as the fiber optic camera travels through. It's agreeably unsettling to be reminded that this is who I am: a mass of sanguine biology. Water, salts, lipids and enzymes.

Thank goodness for clothes.

Say hello to everyone at the picnic.

Ceylon is lovely and cool and green.

I'm wearing a bright red satin shirt hand painted by Paul McCartney. I feel like Zeus walking through Red Square.

Like Blaise Cendrars riding a brontosaurus up the Eiffel Tower.

I was serious when I said I'd like to make it more of a regular habit to write more often. It's good therapy. Releasing my mind on paper is liberating. But you need to write back.

I wonder what Shakespeare wore? I like to think of him in tennis shoes, but I don't believe rubber had become an English commodity yet.

A film crew shot some scenes in the house next door to us last week. One of the crew members came over one night to borrow a drinking glass. I have no idea what the film director wanted to do with our drinking glass. Did Angelina Jolie's lips come into contact with it?

I wonder if any of this is of interest to you.

They say Elizabethan women wore a roll or sausage of stiffened material known as a "bum roll" around their waist and under their skirts to hold corded hoops of wire or whalebone out and so accentuate a woman's childbearing attributes.

It all comes down to onions. They should be deep purple in color and glistening.

Your friend Guy.

Dear Chauncey,

You're lucky you live in Maine. I had a tough time getting to sleep last night. After the fireworks blasted off the Space Needle, the Neanderthals across the street partied all night. They had a woofer going boom! boom! boom! boom! till well past three in the morning. I know because I got up to go to the bathroom and saw it was 3:30 and figured I could take the earplugs out. My ears were itching. I took them out. But not only were the clowns across the street still going strong, but our neighbors upstairs, Fuckwad and Twinkle Toes, came home, stomped around, ran gallons of water, crashed and banged and buzzed the hallway buzzer. I put in another pair of earplugs.

What baffles me is that these people are able to carry on like that with no thought whatever that they might be bothering someone. Given, it's New Year's Eve, but not everyone enjoys the privilege of sleeping in the next day, some people have to work, and some people are simply old and tired and want to go to bed. They've seen enough New Year's celebrations to stuff a woolly mammoth. They don't care if there's a change in the calendar. They want to go to sleep.

Another thing that baffles me is that the people right next door don't complain. What's up with that? Maybe it's the fear of guns. Persephone has a co-worker who has an eighteen-year-old son who complained when some guy stepped in front of him in a line at a dance club. The malefactor took out a gun and shot him five times. It's a miracle he survived.

These are definitely different times. Fall of the empire. No doubt about it. Next thing we'll see wrestling events turn into gladiator bouts. With real swords. And real blood and guts.

Was the wild west like this? Probably. Maybe that's why so many people dug Sarah Palin. The woman was a complete imbecile, but she represented some fundamental dysfunctionality about the American frontier. Killing and skinning animals. Shotgun weddings. Religious intolerance. Hatred for intellectuals. Disdain for the wilderness, except for its resources. Gold and oil.

I do believe, however, that Buffalo Bill was pretty progressive. He was a close friend of Sitting Bull. I suspect Jesse James was fiercely anti-government & right wing. He was probably racist as hell, too.

Billy the Kid was just silly. A dopey kid with a lot of potential. Just liked to chase women, sing songs, and get into gun fights.

Wyatt Earp I suspect was a moderate Republican. He seemed always to be looking for some way to get rich. Wild Bill Hickok was probably some weirdly eccentric form of Libertarian. I do know in 1876 there was a big national strike & a progressive populist movement called the Greenback Party. I think Wild Bill would have been partial to that.

The books arrived last Wednesday, via UPS. Now comes the hard part: trying to get the public to buy them. So I can become fabulously wealthy. And move to Tahiti. And grow potatoes & pineapples.

Fat chance. U.S. is forty-ninth in world literacy. Ouch!

We've been wondering how you've been doing. Have you met any of the locals yet? Have you had an opportunity to go to any readings? Any inclination to go to any readings? Is it snowing yet?

I think you are right to refuse any medical treatment other than the laser treatment. I think western medicine is founded on a wrong-headed premise that does not acknowledge death as a natural part of life.

I am certain if you are your own physician your stomach will resume its proper strength and then what great benefits will follow.

I have just returned from a drive to the bottom of the hill. I go down at 4:15 p.m. or so to pick up Penelope after she gets off work. I went tumbling down the hill in our Subaru dodging potholes and fissures the city never repairs this part of Fifth and the city looked beautiful rather ethereal in winter mist with a little glow of day still in it and the hard-edged heroin addict contrary rock of the Velvet Underground in the CD player.

I park in an underground lot. There are paintings on the walls of eggs and candles and tulips and lettuce and big oak wine barrels and a field of lavender. There is also a barn surrounded by a grove of trees with bales of hay dotting the foreground. A cheerfully rural dirt road leads to a gabled white house. Penelope says an old woman tried driving into the little dirt road depicted in the barnyard. She thought it was real. Hard to believe such people drive and vote.

Above are pipes running everywhere and a ceiling of crumbly plaster that looks curdled like cottage cheese, white lines painted on the cement floor, car doors slamming, people getting on and off the elevator, grocery clerks helping people carry groceries to their car or rounding up grocery carts, engines humming, metal groaning, a headache beginning to cloud the inner weather of my head. I brought *Le Mystere de la chambre jaune* by Gaston Leroux to read while waiting for Penelope. I changed the CD. Velvet Underground popped out. I put in *Honkin' on Bobo* by Aerosmith. Penelope arrived. We drove to Safeway to pick some medicine at the pharmacy. Safeway was packed. People everywhere. Day before Halloween. Penelope says her store has been very quiet. This is a worry.

Your friend Guy.

Dear George,

Last night I saw the ghost of Jackson Pollock. He was rummaging around in our refrigerator. I got up because I was thirsty and had a headache. I was not in a mood to talk to a ghost. Anyone's ghost. I simply nodded, and he stood back, glowing by the stove. I rubbed my eyes, cleared my throat, and asked what death was like. He said it was black. The most beautiful black he had ever seen. Only he could not see it. When you're dead you don't experience anything. You can't. Because you don't exist. But what about this, I asked, this ghostly presence of yourself, where did that come from. He paused. "I don't know," he said, "I don't have an answer for you."

I went back to bed.

You asked about the line between prose and poetry. I see poetry as blood, prose as a bone.

Prose is written in a crowded room. Poetry is written alone.

You tell me never to despair. I wish it was as easy for me to observe the saying. Truth is I have a horrid morbidity of temperament which has shown itself at intervals.

I think in intervals because to do otherwise is presumptuous.

I'm trying hard to be totally conscious of this time and place, of you, and every sentient being, especially toads.

Remember Matisse's *Les poissons rouges?* It hangs in the hallway now, across from the closet and its smell of car wax and rags and old coats that have weathered many a winter and mountains of shoes and old boots with long laces and thick military soles. There is something nostalgic about closets and their odors. It is the realm of the discard-ed. Photo albums. Ribbons of old celebrations.

I think "what is thinking," what is that use or motion of the mind that compares with the wetlands, the names of the dead?

What could any of us done without azaleas, or plaid?

April is behind the refrigerator.

Penelope is getting better and better at making mashed potatoes. This is harder to achieve than you may think. The whole is greater than the sum of its parts. Potatoes, salt, butter, mixer. The electricity comes from God knows where. You've got to blend these things perfectly, or the product is too watery, too lumpy, too bland.

I am free to spread these words because they are derelict, walnut, and habitation.

I frequently lose myself in abstraction. Forgive me.

I feel like walking out of here and spending vast sums of money. I want to buy the Bank of England. I want to buy roses and pink cushions and fancy cars and palatial mansions with luscious blue swimming pools and swans and peacocks and pearl-handled jackknives and rare books and exotic antiques.

All I need is money.

A necklace of skulls and fingers.

A question is the best beacon towards a little speculation.

How does a thought go from being a thought to being a sequence of words? Isn't thought composed of words to begin with? Is it possible to have a thought that does not involve words? Have I ever had a thought that did not involve words? I can't remember. What if a thought is composed of numbers? Is that how physicists and mathematicians and engineers think? Are equations poetry? Calculations? Symbols? Pictures? Camouflage? Nasturtiums? Cushions? Oblivion? What if the thought, such as this thought, is soft like flannel, feels soft in the mind, or warm, like a bowling team in the heat of victory, or a parakeet? What we see of the world is the mind's invention. Which is why I'm afraid of the dark.

O for a life of sensations rather than of thoughts. Intrepid blackberry feastings. The strange fragrance of gasoline. The lure of opals. Leaves glistening after the rain. A small boat engaged with the current of a small mountain stream.

Nothing startles me beyond the moment. The setting sun will always set me to rights, or if a sparrow come before my window, I take part in its existence and pick about the gravel.

Here it carries its silence, the regular singular tree that murders grammar.

I salute the banana I am about to eat, the Christmas cactus by the window and the volcano hats on top of the bookcase with their pipecleaner flames. The chair supporting all the hats and bags and clothing and purse and the temperature of the room which is a comfortable sixty-eight degrees. The rain outside glistening in the shrubs and the light allowing me to write these words and the muscles in my fingers and arm and nerves and perceptions and language and chocolate and wood. I think of these things as events, not objects. Energies which have somehow mysteriously acquired mass to become a carpet or shiny candy wrapper or cat or finger or TV remote or coffee table or shrug or rug or rune or dune or spoon or dishwasher of rattling dishes. Sensations are simultaneously specific and vague. Exquisitely specific. Ethereally vague. Somewhere in there is a thought. Waves of light in the head. Sounds on the tongue.

What I want you to see is another lovely and inexplicable thing. Oboe. Meat. Vowel.

An oboe in the meat of a vowel. A vowel in the meat of an oboe. Meat in the vowel of an oboe.

Vowel upon vowel upon vowel.

Consonants integral as arthropods.

I find great comfort in the radio.

The pharmacist was in a good mood today. That's always a relief. I'm always nervous about picking up my medicine. Don't know why. Does anybody know why they feel the way they do?

I am free to spread these words because they are double knit, hard rock, and scintillating.

Bob Dylan is a wizard.

A wise chair in a bombed house.

Write soon.

Your friend Guy.

Bibliography

Gide, André. *Les faux-monnayeurs.* Paris, France,1963.

Ginsberg, Allen. *The Letters of Allen Ginsberg.* Edited by Bill Morgan. Philadelphia, PA, 2008.

Ginsberg, Allen and Snyder, Gary. *The Selected Letters of Allen Ginsberg and Gary Snyder.* Edited by Bill Morgan. Berkeley, CA, 2009.

Keats, John. *Selected Letters of John Keats.* Edited by Grant F. Scott. Cambridge, MA, 2002.

Sollers, Philippe. *Sur le matérialisme; de l'atomisme à la dialectique révolutionnaire.* Paris, France, 1974.

Van Gogh, Vincent. *Letters de Vincent Van Gogh à son frère Théo.* Comprenant un choix de lettres française originale et de lettres traduites du hollandaise par George Philippart. Paris, France, 1975.

Whalen, Philip. *The Collected Poems of Philip Whalen.* Edited by Michael Rothenberg. Middletown, CT, 2007.

Where do metaphors come from? Generating metaphors is very easy. Start with the first isotope of bitter earth (which is called magnesium oxide, or volatile green lion), and bombard it with philosopher's wool. The lone soluble in the pelican will be a bubbly mass of dragon's blood, which may be inspissated with flowers of phosphorous, tincture of mars, and lunar crystals, leaving the lone positively charged metaphor.

How do you focus these metaphors into a beam and control them? As gravity makes the sea flow round the denser and weightier parts of the globe of the earth, so the attraction of meaning to emblem will make the dragon's blood flow round the denser and compacter organs of metaphor. Contemporaneous moments are as their fluxions. This is the basis of drapery. The metaphors are superconducting and to be superconducting, are cooled to 1.8 Kelvin (-271.4 Centigrade) with superfluid nerve gel.

How fast do these metaphors go? The metaphors will travel at 99.999999 percent of the speed of light. That means that it will take only ninety microseconds for a metaphor to travel once around the human skull, or about 11,000 revolutions per second, depending on the syllables, and the anomalies of the skull.

How much energy do metaphors have? Metaphors have a nominal energy of seven TeV. An electron-volt (eV) is the energy an electron would have if it passed thought a one volt potential field. The T part stands for Terrarium, or turtle to the twelfth power. Written out this has a heart-shaped outline, equal to 128 cubic feet of democratic socialism. Sounds like a lot but in reality it is not. It is estimated that the energy a mosquito expends to fly is one TeV. In spite of this, the energy is contained in such a small particle (the syllable), that it packs quite a punch when two of these syllables meet head on.

Is the inside of the skull under a haircut, and if so, why? Yes, it is under an ultrahigh haircut so that the beam of metaphors can circulate around the skull without colliding with anything else. The haircut is maintained at 0.0000000000001 atmospheres with turbomolecular pumps. This is about ten times lower than on the earth's moon. The internal volume of the skull is completely private, so pumping it down is like evacuating a cathedral!

Where can I find out more? Wittgenstein's *Tractatus Logico-Philosophicus* contains a wealth of information. Read Williams to see the machine status. As for where the metaphors come from that are used in human skulls or quatrains, there are two main methods of discovery. One is to heat hydrogen gas into a plasma to separate the meanings off of the words and then the metaphors and metonyms can be magnetically separated. Another way is to ionise Raymond Roussel's *Locus Solus* using an electric field at 13.6eV to strip off the oarlocks and then attract the metaphors out of the Reading Chamber using magnetic forces. The final way is almost the reverse. Metaphors are created by getting drunk. Drunk on nothingness. Drunk on aluminum. Drunk on Mallarmé.

The newspapers are disappearing. What will happen when the last one goes? How will we get our news? Will we get our news from poems? Will we get our news from ballads and sagas and myths? Will we stand around and listen to rock stars sing songs of legendary feats? Will an Allen Ginsberg arise among the people to bring us news of sunflowers and angels and the secrets of the mind? Watermelons on sale and dream cantinas on the fiery borders of the imagination? Who will inform us of these things? And wars. And high tension wires and Rasputin in the car mirror.

And what of Dagwood and Beetle Bailey? What will happen to them? Will Dagwood become a bum? Will Beetle Bailey eventually and inevitably find himself in Afghanistan, kicking doors open and forcing families to come out with their hands behind their heads?

Will Blondie have to get a job at WalMart?

Will Dilbert come to work in battle fatigues with a sack full of guns and ammunition?

How will I know who's president? Or governor? Or senator or congressperson or Miss Universe?

How will I know how many people have been mugged, murdered, beaten and robbed? How many cars stolen? How many houses burgled? How many car wrecks? Plane wrecks? Shipwrecks?

How will my mind be expanded? My knowledge enriched? My plans for the future guided by wise and knowing experts? How will I know what Wall Street is doing?

There is always the Internet. All those blogs and opinions. Which are based on blogs and opinions.

What happened to the press? How did this come about?

People stopped reading. People started gazing into laptop screens as if gazing into crystal balls. The world seems like a friendlier, happier place when it is dressed in pixels and aglow with electronic algorithms.

It is all words anyway. Words aren't going away. Words will always be with us. These invisible agencies of the air. These sounds we make. These sounds we transmit on tongue and wire. As long as there are words there will be news. Gossip. Opinions. Judgments. Positions.

Observations. Apprehensions. Beliefs. Convictions. Feelings. Impressions. Columns of the forlorn. Photos of the caught. Photos of the dead. Photos of the glamorous and scandalous and strange. Everything phenomenal, inexplicable, and weird. Who did what to whom. Who said what to whom. The lure of the rumor. The enchantment of fame.

Truth is another matter. But who cares about that? The newspapers didn't. That's why they disappeared.

Night slowly oozes away as dawn bursts over the Cascades to the east. It is a strange process. No one paints it. It just happens. Happens like reptiles. Happens like beads of water trickling down a kitchen window. It is one of the few things in life that doesn't require any work. No installation. No batteries. No inlets. No outlets. No wires or plugs or sockets. Night peacefully retires and the new day is heralded by the neighbor's rooster.

My neighbor doesn't have a rooster but the implication that he might incites tendrils of arbitrary significance, which is candy to the eyes.

My neighbor has a girlfriend and a terrible personality but that's another story.

Let us return to the high and metaphysical.

So here comes the day. In fact, it's already here. That's right. Daylight spread like butter everywhere. Daylight on the floor. Daylight on the ceiling. Daylight between my fingers. Daylight crashing through the window. Daylight nudging the toaster in the far dark corner of the kitchen. Daylight walking around like a radiant king. The king of daylight. Proud, sober, lavish, and nonchalant.

Fuck daylight.

I hate daylight.

Daylight is the color of work. Daylight is the color of people rubbing their eyes at bus stops. Daylight is the color of people contracting within themselves so as not to be seen. Daylight is the color of complication. Daylight is the color of grouchy drivers and overly sensitive cooks. Daylight is the ape of vanity. Daylight leaps around bumping and gouging and elbowing people as they daydream behind their laptops and newspapers. Daylight is gauche. The ultimate in gaucherie. Bumptious, obnoxious, and loud like a rock star on meth.

Fuck daylight.

I hate daylight.

Give me night. Give me night and oblivion and warm socks and a warm bed and a warm woman and a warm house. Give me stars and comets and planets and asteroids and oceans of billowing plasma. Give me dark nebulae and spiral arms and big bangs and relativity and quarks and moon rocks. Give me liberty or give me Jupiter. Chuck Berry in a spacecraft. Extraterrestrial peacocks and hyperdimensionality.

But please. No daylight. Not even that tiniest of glimmers peeping over the crags. I will have none of it. Curtains closed. Mind made up. Fuck daylight. I hate daylight.

I miss the sixties.

Why?

People were excited. Enthusiastic. Passionate.

And they're not now?

The Blue Angels fly overhead. One of them flies so close and so low that it sounds like it's going to fly in one window and out the other.

What? I can't hear myself think.

People aren't passionate now.

Hardly. They seem like they're dead.

Everyone?

Ok, not everyone. I know a few people who are quite passionate.

You're on a slippery slope here.

Yes, I know.

Generalizing again.

Yes. It's a bad habit.

And this seems very narcissistic to me.

What?

This conversation with myself.

Who cares?

You're right. Everyone's narcissistic. Drowning in their own reflection.

I like that myth.

It's a good one.

Hey, look at that.

What?

The way the sunlight is dappled on that wall next door, like huge coins of light.

It's a beautiful summer day. A little cooler than yesterday, which reached 103. Feel that? Silence. It's quiet now.

Not quite, but almost. I can hear a plane. Rumble of its engine. I hope the Blue Angels are finished with their exercise. There was a time I enjoyed it. I don't enjoy it anymore.

Why?

All I can think of now are bombs. Children and women scream-
ing. Rubble. Blood. Massive explosions. Iraq. Afghanistan. And fur-
ther back Vietnam. All that hell for nothing. Though it does make a
few people rich.

I wonder what they think.

Who?

The people that get rich from war.

I have no idea. I assume they're comfortable with the idea of mak-
ing money off killing people. I suspect they have a pretty powerful
system of rationalization intact that allows them to sleep and play golf
and sit in a church pew and feel comfortable under their skin. They
probably think they're doing God's work, making the world safe for
Christianity.

You're doing it again.

I know: generalizing.

Making assumptions.

Well, I'm nearly sixty-two. I'm allowed a few assumptions. I've
been around the block a few times. I've seen things. Heard things.
Isn't there a word for putting experiences together to make a state-
ment?

Yes: induction. The act or process of deriving general principles
from particular facts or instances.

And what are the facts and instances swimming around in your
head?

Swimming? My head is not an aquarium.

It's a little like an aquarium.

How so?

Thoughts move around like fish in a medium of water. Your head
is too small to be a lake, too round to be a river. Hence, it is an aquar-
ium.

I forget what I was thinking.

Facts and instances.

Can you be more specific?

A fact is something presented as objectively real, such as the Ha-
waiian alphabet, which has twelve letters, or the percentage of wilder-
ness in North America, which is twenty-eight percent, ten percent
higher than Africa. An instance is a case in point, such as *àina kakahi-*

tional River wilderness area in the Arkansas Ozarks which is accessible only by foot, horseback, or canoe.

So based on induction, what kind of assumptions have you made of this world?

Life is hard. And very short. It goes by in a blink. Some people are born into wealth and some people are born into poverty. None of it makes much sense. Some people behave in a way that is caring and compassionate and some people behave in a way that is predatory and savage. Some people believe in an all-powerful entity called God and some people are convinced that there is no God. Some people believe that our destinies are predetermined and some people believe our circumstances are completely random. I could go on all day.

This is a problem with language.

Yes.

It never seems to end.

Have you ever tried to think without using words?

Yes, but I haven't been successful. Although there are probably times when an idea occurs with no words being involved.

Such as?

Such as ducking when there is a loud sound, or grabbing an apple if I'm hungry.

These are instinctive.

Yes.

What about more intricate ideas?

They require words.

Can a meaning be velvet?

I don't follow.

Can words produce a sensation that is secondary to their content?

Yes, I believe that words have qualities that overflow their boundaries. Colors, hues, textures. Shadows, halos, vibrations.

I hear a helicopter.

I wonder if one of the Blue Angels has crashed?

Doubt it. There would've been a big noise. It's probably the helicopter from one of the TV stations checking the flow of traffic, though it may also be that someone is preparing to jump to their death from the bridge.

Does that happen often?

Yes. A lot of people commit suicide there. They all jump facing west. Nobody jumps from the east side of the bridge. It must seem natural to people to jump in the direction that the sun sets. I can't imagine someone jumping to their death on the east side of the bridge as the sun is rising. That would be perverse indeed.

Isn't suicide perverse?

That's difficult to answer. Hurting other people is wrong. But if the only person you are hurting is yourself, is that wrong?

It is a blasphemy against the sanctity of life.

That's putting it pretty strongly.

It does seem a little heavy-handed.

Do you find suicide disturbing?

Very.

What do you imagine it is that leads people to take such drastic action?

I suppose the pain of existence becomes unbearable.

Yes. Accompanied by a complete loss of hope.

Hope is an enduring feeling. It must be very painful when it's gone.

This is getting depressing.

Think about something else.

Like what?

How about glamour.

Glamour is fascinating.

Who do you think has glamour?

Carla Bruni. Michelle Obama. Helen Mirren. Charlotte Gains-bourg. Catherine Deneuve. Cate Blanchett.

All women.

Yes. Glamour seems to be essentially feminine. But I can't say why.

There is perfume in the word.

Yes. There is perfume in the word.

I am the anti-Gary Snyder. This does not mean I do not like Gary Snyder, or the work of Gary Snyder, or the many wonderful things associated with Gary Snyder, thorny buckbrush and bears and manzanita and bees. No, I most emphatically do not mean that.

Here is what I mean: I go to a reading and talk by Gary Snyder. The auditorium seats 2,700 people and every seat is filled. People have arrived hours early. These are the people who got the cheaper center seats. The rows closer to the stage go for seventy-five bucks.

I am amazed. Stunned. Stupefied. I have never seen a poet draw this many people. Poets, evidently, are not always pariahs.

Why this man? I reflect on the qualities of Mr. Snyder. He cares about the planet. He cares about plants and animals. He enjoys life. His demeanor exclaims joyful balance and equanimity. It is these latter qualities that elude me. Balance and equanimity are not among my tools of trade. My adjustments to this planet have not gone entirely well. I languish like a sturgeon in the slough of despond. Weltschmerz is my home address. Vexation and wormwood are blood and nutrition. I am bitter like cider. Abrasive like a grinder. Nothing like cedar. Nothing like high still air.

Nothing like Gary Snyder.

I am, in fact, the anti-Gary Snyder. I am the reverse of his obverse. A cross-stitch to his box stitch. The west to his east. The push to his pull. The nib to his nub. The did to his does. The itch to his scratch. The ding to his dong. The ying to his yang. The doodle to his noodle.

Gary Snyder is wise. I am not wise. If the regrets in my life could be converted to dollars, they would pay off the national debt. If I had the capacity to learn from all these regrets, I would travel through life with enlightened discernment and the capacity to absorb life's blows with philosophical aplomb. But I do not learn. I follow my instincts. Which are not the animal intuitions of Gary Snyder. They are the deluded calculations of a destitute gambler.

Gary Snyder has respect for the inherent nobility of work, particularly for those early jobs he got as a merchant seaman, logger, and lookout on Sourdough Mountain.

I hate work. Loathe work. I avoid it whenever possible. That's why I became a poet. So that I would not have to work.

Gary Snyder has a soothing voice and a measured, warm, cadenced style of reading.

I read like a nuclear reactor having a meltdown.

Gary Snyder is calm and well-adjusted. He exudes assurance and hope.

I am choked with bile, crammed with envy, incontinent with castigation. I exude uric acid and black despair.

Gary Snyder writes in a style that is precise, immediate, and eminently accessible. It has all the play and clarity of a mountain brook.

My writing is grotesque and elliptical. It mangles syntax. It obscures its own meaning with the violence of virulence and the tinsel of ostentation.

Very early in life I wanted to be like Gary Snyder. I read all of Gary Snyder's books. I studied Zen. I practiced Zen. I did rugged things and thought rugged thoughts. I climbed mountain peaks. I got wet camping in the rain. I shopped at Goodwill. I hitchhiked on Highway 99. I used my bones as tools to get me to places I wanted to be and out of places that I did not want to be. I lived each day as a haiku. I listened to owls. I studied the coins in my pocket. I dashed icy water on my face from a stone bowl. I noticed the warmth in people's hands. But somehow it all backfired. I do not know why. I do not know what happened. Maybe it was the goofy logic of the kangaroo, the thousand glories of a chronic and purposeless agitation, or too much pepperoni and baking soda.

Maybe it was the flagrant rotundity of the watermelon, its absurd size and juices, its insidious black seeds, its sordid rinds and picnic Gothicism.

Maybe it was a bad case of hyperbole, an ungovernable pataphysical appetence, or a colorful and incorrigible misanthropy.

Maybe it was the bounce of perspective, the faucets of Finland, the strut of the peacock, or the inscrutable malaise of mayonnaise.

Maybe it was the miniature lips of vengeance singing songs between the pennies of old barnacled piers.

Or maybe it was the skeleton of a trumpet dancing in its cage of fire.

I don't know.

I don't know what it was.

But I did not become Gary Snyder.

I became the anti-Gary Snyder.

Which is silliness. Because existence precedes essence, and if I stick my finger into existence, it smells of nothing.

Said Søren Kierkegaard.

Who was Danish.

And lived in Copenhagen.

And whose early work was written under various pseudonyms.

None of which were Gary Snyder.

This is not a good time to be timid. The past is propelled into the future for a better comprehension of goggles. Meanwhile, the harmonica articulates a garden of sound and a black limousine answers the pavement with its wheels. Wheels which are round and rubber and full of tread. The kind of tread that mumbles insinuations of asphalt and brick.

The world is a book. Reading fulfills the light bulbs of baptism. The eyes come alive. Images form in the mind. Mahogany misinterprets gravity in the jungles of Borneo.

It must be obvious to everyone by now that there are too many snobs in the city. Living in gated communities as we slide into an era of neo-feudalism. Hence, the fragrance of a banana cake holds fourteen temptations and a metronome. The burning objective of our time is revelation. The eyeball is an example.

Does the halibut feel exaltation?

Yes. Of course it does. How could it not?

I hear the dogs of Bohemia. They are composed of congealed light. Each is an amalgam of bone and blood swarming with words.

We ride on the wheels of perturbation. Forty years ago men walked on the moon. We were provided with a map of the galaxy. Now, my shirt hangs in the window and I am too tired to iron it. The library communicates a feeling of transport but its books languish on the shelves. There is an insect stuck to the window. Light diffuses its wings, which are delicately veined. I would prefer to live on the moon. But I'm stuck in a store filled with parrots. Nevertheless, clouds are implicit in water, and the past is implicit in the future.

Acidity is literal. The calliope is dead. Our planet is black. But hope is enduring and copper. Ductile. The stars around our planet explode into heat and light calling us to a redemption in olive and raw sienna. Earth colors. Viridian. Celadon. Russet.

Amber. Emerald. Sicilian umber.

Their names are sprinkled on paper. Breath gives them life.

The airplane of poetry pulls itself through the air. The view is stupefying.

And really, nothing needs to be ironed.

Norma Cole was recently in town and I enjoyed her reading and bought her book, *Where Shadows Will: Selected Poems 1988–2008*. I have had a special fascination for Norma's work for some time now and this is why: the words have a shiny, tangible brilliance, like knives. Not ordinary knives or hunting knives or those bizarre commando knives I sometimes see in the windows of the Army Navy Surplus store downtown, but Japanese knives, those beautifully balanced knives with linen textured resin handles and blades sharp enough to cut a proton in two.

The key word is "tangible." There is a peculiar sense in reading some poems that the words have three-dimensions, like rocks or gems, and that the phrases have been soldered together, so that their structure resembles the filigree of brooches or pins. This is not new. There has been a notable drive toward this presentation of words since at least Chaucer, in the western world. Its most salient address appeared with Gertrude Stein's *Tender Buttons*, nearly a hundred years ago, in 1914, and Sherwood Anderson's famous description of their effect on him as "rattling words one can throw into a box and shake, making a sharp, jingling sound, words that, when seen on the printed page, have a distinct arresting effect upon the eye, words that when they jump out from under the pen one may feel with the fingers as one might caress the cheeks of his beloved."

I don't know how to describe this phenomenon neurologically — that would take the expertise of an Oliver Sacks — but the sensation is acute, quite real.

What is the importance of this? Does it have any importance? To this day, Gertrude Stein is not generally the part of any college curriculum. And poets who choose to focus on the materiality of the language as opposed to its emotional charge or ability to convey sentiments and ideas still find themselves marginalized in the hapless alleys and lonely shelves of the small press ghetto.

Words, like money, are intended to symbolize ideas and experience so that we don't have to lug around sacks or wagons full of objects we might want to assemble in order to make a sentence like "I want to marry you" or "I would like to eat that meat you are cooking." It would be a complication to try to communicate the beauty of a sunset with two shoes and a rabbit pelt. So what is the point of abstracting the medium we humans use to communicate a feeling or idea so that it assumes the palpability of stone or clay? What is grasped? What is illuminated? What is raised into being? What illness is cured? What burden is lifted?

I don't know. I just find it fascinating.

My real inquiry is focused on how poets like Cole are able to achieve this effect. In "Nano-Shades" the effect is apparent in her coupling of images and the way she delicately coerces attention on the individual words. It is pertinent that a "nano" means "extremely small." A nanosecond, for instance, is one billionth of a second. And we are talking shades here. The shade of a nano, which would not be sufficient to cool a Death Valley gnat, much less play in the retina of an attentive reader.

Or would it?

Here is the poem:

the male deliberately positions himself
over his lover's fangs

the key is gravity
blankets, personal items

and clothing, extra-solar planets (class M)
like our sun, the memory

of history, empty or full
scared the daylights out of the name

The extreme dissimilarity between the first pair of lines, the male poised over his lover's fangs, followed by the brusque non-sequitur (nano-sequitur?) "the key is gravity," which itself is followed by the illogical blankets and personal items, generates a circuitry of hectic and broad associations. The human mind craves meaning, and will look for meaning where none apparently exists. So that in a situation such as the one created here, where the circuit is not, and cannot, ultimately be completed in any way that would satisfy the tenets of math-

380

ematics or logic, the process is ongoing. It is a virtual perpetual motion machine.

It's important to point out that this would fizzle were it not for the artistry in its making. A lot of poetry I find online and in the few magazines and chapbooks that have made it to print attempts to imitate this structure, but is rarely successful, because it's either too affected and obvious, or too oblique to work. The reason "the key is gravity/ blankets, personal items" works is because we can immediately see the folds of blankets, have felt blankets when we folded or slept under them. Blankets have a strong association with gravity; we are generally supine in relation to them. "Personal items" is a little more teasing, a little less obvious, but here I see perfume bottles, a can of shaving lather, little handheld mirrors, a set of keys, pocket change and combs, all arranged on a bureau, or bathroom countertop. These things may not pop into Stephen Hawking's mind when he thinks about gravity, but I see a vivid relation there.

"The memory/ of history" is funny. Aren't history and memory pretty much the same thing? Or has history disappeared, leaving a nano-shade of itself in memory? What a peculiar thought.

"Scared the daylights out of the name" is pretty funny, too. Is a name alive? Is a name an organism? Does it have scales? Cells? Cytoplasm? Are syllables cilia? The cartoonish character of a name (and what name? Jim? Martha? Galicia? Clarksville?) having the daylights scared out of it adds a comical and hallucinatory dimension to this curious work.

Another poet who is superb at promoting the materiality of language is Joseph Ceravolo. I remember the intense joy I felt when I first read "Drunken Winter" sometime in the '70s.

Oak! oak! like like
it then
   cold some wild paddle
so sky then;
flea you say
"geese geese" the boy
June of winter
of again
Oak sky

What I like immediately about this poem was that it was just so completely GOOFY. It sounded like speech, but who would ever begin a statement by shouting oak! oak! and follow it with like, like. Oak is hard. "Like" has no substance whatever. And here there they are linked, as if there were an actual equivalence between the two.

And there is. They're both words. Oak (the sound of which is strangely compelling as it begins with the open-o and ends with the hard velar "k") is a sign, not the actual wood, though that is what immediately pops up in the mind, the weight of it, heft of it, smell of oak. It's grain. It's gnarly trunk and big star-like leaves. Then, "like." Which frequently has the habit of weakening a statement by comparison. "My heart is like a red red rose" is not as firm as "My heart is a rose." Or, as a predicate, "I like you" does not have the same force as "I love you."

"it then" is just plain silly.

As is "cold some wild paddle." And yet I see, feel, hear, a paddle smack the water in the wild woods of northern Ontario.

"so sky then." I would like to say that to someone sometime. "so sky then" you fool.

"flea you say" I hear in return, as if in some Dada-like fusion with Shakespeare.

"'geese geese' the boy" sounds like something out of a North American Indian tale.

"June of winter" could be a balmy day in mid-December.

"of again" makes sense but I could not tell you why.

"Oak sky" completes the ring cycle of this mini-opera.

I was not surprised when I discovered that Joseph Ceravolo had made a living as a civil engineer. Many of his poems, as Norma Cole's, feel constructed. Assembled. The syntax is always a bit off, or sometimes way off, as if the construction were not yet complete, or Ceravolo wanted us to feel the torque in the metal supports, the tensions and strains that exist in grammar. Added to this is an opposite effect, spontaneous, emotional outbursts, such as "O targets!" or "Yet prize!" or "conch of frolick!" Ceravolo's wikipedia entry links him to the conversational style of the New York poets, and there is some of that, certainly, but how many times do we say in conversation "Be world to any apples!" or "O candy for our sore" or "How many steps to take to mud around, across, Ixtapalapa green canal?" If we could enter into conversation with fire hydrants and dogs, I imagine that these are the kinds of sentences we would be examining in the parliaments of our minds.

Clark Coolidge is, perhaps, the Santa Claus of this genre, the ultimate cornucopia, horn of Amalthea. He is abundance personified. He mints words with the solid determination of the coin dies in the Denver mint. The words have the tangibility and beauty of bone. Yet they read smoothly. They do not have the delicacy of Cole, or the engineered torque of Ceravolo. Their energy is different, more like bebop, or drumming. In "How to Open," from *Own Face*, one of his earlier books, Coolidge cleverly reverses the usual "window to the world" quality of most writers who want us to see through the words to the adventure, the drama, as if transparency were greatest virtue writing could possess.

the twig has hug from the whole porch a season
a break in the bottle of amberhood sauce
a gleam without a cleavage or a typer to trammel it
here is the window that there are the words.

In the first line, Coolidge has robbed "hug" of its properties as a predicate and given it the quality of a noun. "Hug" is a pun on hung, but far more interesting than a mere pun because a literal hanging is not as metaphorically charged as feeling the energy of "hug" in that twig. It is not just hanging. One feels as if it has been fully and firmly encompassed by its surrounding on the porch.

"Typer" is redolent of "typewriter." *Own Face* was first published in 1978, when writers used typewriters. Those old enough to remember using typewriters remember how noisy they were, the clackety-clack-clack-clack of the metal keys striking the paper wrapped around the platen. Writing had real solidity then.

It astonishes and baffles me that the younger writers are content to read their work online. I'm slowly coming around to the idea that publication online is as meaningful as publication on paper, but the lack of tangibility is disturbing. I enjoy the fact that work is so much more readily accessed electronically, at least by those privileged enough to have access to computers, but I am able to see a linkage between the kind of unrealities our economy has taken with the pixilated giddiness of virtual reality. There is a potential for harm there.

I should be happy, too, that so many graduates of the MFA programs have chosen to go in the direction of Cole, Ceravolo, and Coolidge. Yet so much of it seems slipshod and precious when it should be hot with intention, as if the soldering iron had just been taken away and the sentences were still smoking.

What is the solution? Miners were able to distinguish true gold from fool's gold (iron pyrite) by biting it. True gold is malleable. A tooth will leave a dent. You can't bite words, but you can assay their quality in other ways. Have sex with them. Cook them. Eat them. Incorporate them into your living. It is a personal matter, not a science. Subjective, not objective. And therein lies the frustration: how to give palpability to what is essentially a mental, intellectual experience?

"There's no way out but in," writes Coolidge in "The Cave Remain," "Grunt and compare the stretched body to rock in its literal sluice."

Lou Reed and Edgar Allan Poe share a certain affinity. Not the obvious affinity one finds among leaves in a hedge hyssop, or the supercilious eccentricities one finds among poodle owners, but the more oblique variety, the kind of affinities we feel in ourselves with certain figures in history.

The affinity of spirits. Sympathies beyond the grave.

As if time were an accident. As if linear, chronological time did not exist. And it all collapsed. Centuries collapsed. The entire architecture of time melted into Dali watches. The scaffolding fell. And groggy and dazed Poe dusted himself off and stood before us. Impishly smiling. Displaying a preternatural mirth.

It's easy to imagine Poe hanging out at The Factory in the early days of the Velvet Underground. Warhol filming him for hours. Drugs. Parties. Dylan and Nico. And the sad-eyed lady of the lowlands.

I can imagine the two of them, Eddie and Lou, in various situations. Circumstances of a macabre nature. Adventures involving maelstroms, penguins, flares, and the piercing shriek of an epileptic sun.

I can see them as gravediggers, doing that scene in Hamlet with uncanny panache. Prodding bones. Holding skulls. Lowering a coffin into the ground with looks of knowing neutrality.

I can see them given to odd humors. Elfin provocations. Long, sinuous conversations that trail into the night leaving behind a chiaroscuro of ancient mythologies and exotic names.

I can see them on stage. Imagine them as musicians.

What kind of instrument would Poe play?

Poe would play a gigantic organ, a Romantic organ of the nineteenth century with five keyboards of Burmese ivory and pipes of silver and brass. It would have the fiery splendor of a chorus of trumpets and the deep somber tones of a Veronese crypt.

He would sway back and forth in a trance.

Wings would grow out of his back.

A phantom woman in diaphanous veils would swirl gracefully around him then fade back into the darkness.

He would fall silent, as if in deep contemplation.

Reed would enter the stage regal and eremitical and play his guitar.

He would lower his head, bring his mouth to the mic, and sing "Venus in Furs."

Shiny, shiny, shiny boots of leather.

And the world would make sense as moonlight slid over the walls like a squid and the corridors filled with moss and a reverence for the blue dials of the radio would turn solemn on the highways running to the end of time.

I don't remember a time of greater insecurity. The nation is founder-
ing in the wake of an economic catastrophe of a magnitude not seen
since the Great Depression of the 1930s. University of Massachusetts
Economics Professor Richard Wolff argues that government bailouts
and stimulus packages will not be enough to address the real causes
of the crisis or mend the "seismic failures within the structures of
American-style capitalism itself." While Wall Street has been re-
floated with staggering amounts of capital, the rest of the country
remains floundering on a dry, mud-caked riverbed. The passage of a
bailout package on October 3rd, 2008, proved grossly ineffective, and
staggeringly myopic. "The bailout package," observed Joseph Stiglitz in
a January, 2009, *Vanity Fair* essay appropriately titled "Capitalist
Fools," "was like a massive transfusion to a patient suffering from in-
ternal bleeding — and nothing was being done about the source of the
problem, namely all those foreclosures." According to the Center for
Responsible Lending (CRL) "a stunning 6,600 foreclosures are taking
place each day." Elsewhere, climate change is wreaking havoc among
the world's population. Australia, Argentina, India, Kenya and war-
torn Afghanistan are suffering unprecedented droughts, the polar ice
caps are melting at a much faster rate than scientists predicted, ty-
phoons, hurricanes, tornados and floods have increased in fury and
devastation, the Food and Agricultural Organization predicts that
370 million people could be facing famine by 2050 if food production
doesn't rise by at least seventy percent, and a series of wildfires have
left California, also drought-stricken and near bankruptcy, as black as
a handful of charcoal briquettes. Militants in Afghanistan spray acid
on the faces of girls walking on their way to school, hotline calls, shel-
ter visits, and domestic violence-related crimes are all up significantly
in the U.S., according to reports ranging from Wisconsin to Rhode
Island, 173 innocent people were killed and 308 wounded in the coor-
dinated shooting and bombing attacks on Mumbai, India, in Novem-
ber, 2008, and gang-related shootings and homicides have risen
dramatically worldwide. Hundreds of cars were burned in France a
few days ahead of Bastille Day in 2009, drug violence has killed over
5,000 people in Mexico in the last two years, and earlier this month

(October, 2009) a sixteen-year-old honors student in Chicago was beaten to death when he accidentally found himself in the middle of an altercation between two rival gangs.

Planet Earth is in traumatic turmoil. The combined services of Superman, Batman, Spider-Man and the Incredible Hulk could not put a dent in the problem. It would seem that anything more added to this hellishness would be lost in redundancy, but not so: one more item of astonishing freakishness is causing anxiety from, of all places, Switzerland. More specifically, a complex outside of Geneva known as CERN, the European Organization for Nuclear Research. There is the far-reaching yet very real apprehension that a black hole created in Switzerland could swallow the planet. Indeed, the entire universe.

At present, the world, and Switzerland, are still here. But that's because the $9 billion machine located outside Geneva has been riddled with problems and delays. On September 10th, 2008, a beam of protons were successfully circulated through the collider in stages, three kilometers at a time. A few days later, on September 19th, a quench (an abnormal termination of magnet operation) occurred in about one hundred bending magnets, causing a loss of approximately six tons of liquid helium, which are necessary to keep the collider cooled at a temperature of 1.9° Kelvin (-456° Fahrenheit). Later analysis revealed the problem to be bad electrical connections. A total of fifty-three magnets were damaged in the incident. The machine has been beset by problems of a less technical nature as well. On October 12th, 2009, in a scenario more redolent of a James Bond spy adventure, French investigators charged a physicist working at the LHC with having links to al-Qaida. One begins to wonder if all these delays and complications aren't owing to a more preordained cause. A pair of CERN physicists have somewhat whimsically suggested that the hypothesized Higgs Boson might be so abhorrent to nature that its creation would ripple backward through time and stop the collider before it could make one, like a time traveler who goes back in time to kill his grandfather. As of today (October 26th, 2009) BBC News announced that engineers working on the LHC have successfully injected beams of particles into two sections of the vast machine. This is not, however, the actual experiment, which will involve the *collision* of two beams, one running in a clockwise direction, the other running counter-clockwise. This experiment — the one intended to reveal the elusive Higgs Boson — is scheduled for December, 2009. If you happen to be reading this article past that date, it would be safe to assume that a particle with less mass than a second-generation quark has not swallowed our planet.

Not yet, anyway.

So what exactly is all this apprehension about, and how real is it? Predictions that the collision of subatomic particles at the Large Hadron Collider in the outlying region of Geneva might create a black hole and swallow our planet, if not the entire universe, owe more to hysteria than science. Black holes are created by the gravitational collapse of supermassive stars. Supermassive stars are rare and trillions of times the mass of earth. If a black hole were created at CERN it would be so tiny as it eradicate itself instantly.

Fears of creating a black hole are way overblown and easily dismissed. But fear has a way of expanding and exacerbating worst-case scenarios. Anxiety is exponential. Problems interact to compound into an ever broadening chain of unlooked-for consequences. There has also been some speculation that a peculiar set of entities called strangelets would turn our world inside out and make it look like a funhouse gone completely mad. A strangelet is a hypothetical object composed of a finite number of roughly equal "up, down, and strange quarks." This anxiety, however improbable, is not entirely void of validity, or charm. A strangelet, coming into contact with the familiar world, could convert ordinary matter into strange matter. As much as the current political milieu feels like some form of bizarre, parallel dimension where very little makes sense, the familiar world of nasturtiums, yo-yos, and lifeguards is still emphatically present. What would a world composed "up, down, and strange quarks" gone awry be like? Would everything be neatly reversed? Would up be down and down be up? Would backward go forward and forward go backward? Would tomorrow happen yesterday and yesterday happen tomorrow?

This is heady stuff. My understanding of quarks and relativity is pretty limited. My preferred domain is that of poetry, not physics. I also know that physicists tend to get irritated when poets attempt to turn their mathematical formulations into metaphors. Nevertheless, the two domains share similar appetites for knowledge: why are we here? How does something come from nothing? How did the universe begin? Is there a supreme intelligence behind creation?

Physicists may be ill at ease when poets and philosophers distort their precise mathematical constructions to illustrate a facet of metaphysical thought, but physicists themselves borrow heavily from poetry. Murray Gell-Mann borrowed the word "quark" from James Joyce to name an elementary particle (the quark is one of two basic constituents of matter, the other being the lepton). But the poetry doesn't stop there. There are six different types of quarks which physicists have chosen to describe as flavors: up, down, charm, strange, top, and bottom. This isn't just poetry, this is enchantment.

What intrigues me the most about the current state of physics isn't this strange sortie into the realm of literature to find language for their formulations, but their quest itself: the fundamental nature of reality. How does one go about finding a solution to a metaphysical problem using empirical methods and expensive machinery? Isn't this inherently flawed, doomed to flail about in blind alleys and dead ends, another waste of public funds and humongous resources? Did the universe pop out of a proton? Can God be discovered in a quark?

The Large Hadron Collider consists of 37,000 tons of equipment arranged in a vast ring of superconducting magnets housed in a seventeen-mile-long tunnel approximately 300 feet below the earth. The complex lies about ten miles west of Geneva. Portions of the tunnel pass under the Jura Mountains of France. This is some of the most beautiful country in the world, filled with luxurious wildflower meadows, craggy cascades, pine forests, and mossy rock walls dripping with delicate ferns. It was near here in the rainy summer of 1816 that Percy Bysshe Shelley and Lord Byron watched electric storms rage above the rocky summits and discuss Erasmus Darwin's experiments in galvanism. Mary Shelley participated in these discussions and she was especially intrigued by the prospect of reanimation. "Darwin kept a piece of vermicelli in a glass case," she wrote, "till by some extraordinary means it began to move with voluntary motion… Perhaps a corpse would be reanimated, galvanism has given token of such things, perhaps the component parts of a creature might be manufactured, brought together and endued with vital warmth." These speculations, of course, culminated in her novel *Frankenstein, Or The Modern Prometheus*, one of the world's first cautionary tales of about the dangers of science unchecked by judicious or ethical concerns.

The goal of the Large Hadron Collider is no less Promethean than the ambitions of Victor Frankenstein: to find the God Particle. The God Particle — or Higgs Boson as it is more secularly known — is a hypothetical massive scalar elementary particle predicted to exist by the Standard Model of particle physics. Its discovery would help to explain how otherwise massless elementary particles cause matter to have mass. That is to say, the Higgs Boson is a noun with a long string of adjectives. Adjectives, it must be said, which contradict one another. How can a particle be massive? If a particle is elementary, how can it also be hypothetical? One feels as disoriented as if one were in the realm of surrealist poetry, or the Zen Koan.

Mass is not what it seems. This is because we inhabit a world of weight, density, texture and tangibility. The realities produced by calculus and differential equations make no sense to us, literally. Our perceptions are keyed to specific sensations. Roughness, weightiness, smoothness, sharpness, dullness. Things taste sweet or bitter or a combination of the two. Some things are warm and dry, others cold and wet. We cannot conceive of a reality not immersed in these things. Not without faith in numbers. Trajectories and orbital mechanics. Energy and force. Momentum and inertia. Some of these things are available to our senses. We all know what velocity feels like. But when someone tells us that there is more space in an ingot of steel than there is steel we balk at the truthfulness of such a statement. We might readily agree, based on what we have learned in science. But it still seems beyond the reach of imagining. Because if there is more space than steel in an ingot of steel, what does that say about us? Are we ghosts? Clouds of atoms? Symphonies of molecules? Waves of light and radiant heat? All improbable, all incredible revelations. But the fact remains: a three-ton ingot of steel is mostly space. If an atom were the size of a fourteen-story building, the nucleus would be a grain of salt in the middle of the seventh floor.

Two things come to mind: Dr. Samuel Johnson dismissing George Berkeley's ideas of immaterialism with his famous "I refute Berkeley thus," and then kicking a rock, and Jack Kerouac addressing an audience at the Hunter College Playhouse on November 6th, 1958 during a symposium titled "Is There a Beat Generation?" "We should be wondering tonight, 'Is there a world?' But I could go and talk on 5, 10,

20 minutes about is there a world, because there is really no world, cause sometimes I'm walkin' on the ground and I see right through the ground. And there is no world. And you'll find out."

It is Kerouac and George Berkeley who were right. Johnson's rock was essentially phantasmal, a cloud of subatomic particles. He was kicking a dream.

Quarks and leptons are considered to be the fundamental particles that constitute all matter. A quark is an elementary fermion particle which interacts via the strong force. There are six different types of quarks, known as flavors: up, down, charm, strange, top, and bottom. Leptons are a family of fundamental subatomic particle, comprising the electron, the muon, and the tauon (or tau particle), as well as their associated neutrinos (electron neutrino, muon neutrino, and tau neutrino). Leptons are spin ½ particles, and as such are fermions. Leptons do not strongly interact, in contrast to the quarks.

The problem with these definitions, which I wicked from Wikipedia, is their circularity: one definition leads to another question, and another definition. It is a good thing Wikipedia's definitions are hyperlinked, because the process of discovering what goes on in high energy particle physics is unending. The end result of these quests is a little knowledge, a tiny bit of insight, and a whole lot of dizziness and confusion.

All this becomes even more intriguing when one begins to question what is meant by particle. It is apparent that physicists are not referring to dust motes or gains of sand. Dust motes and sand do not have spin, probability waves, or flavors like up and down.

Or do they?

In the realm of particle physics, the word "particle" is a misnomer. What is actually being referred to is a probability pattern, an abstract mathematical quantity which is related to the probabilities of finding particles in various places and with various properties. A particle is never present at a definite place, nor is it absent. It occupies a realm of transcended opposites mathematically sandwiched between existence and non-existence. One must learn to think outside the framework of classical logic.

Poets do this all the time. Charles Olson once referred to the poem as a "high energy construct." Words, feathered and smashed together, produce piquant contradictions: black light, civil disobedience, urban cowboy, act naturally, crash landing, jumbo shrimp, hollow point. One can easily imagine a poem as a word accelerator. A broth of verbal hardware bouncing through metaphysical problems like thunderous hues of afternoon reverie.

This is a charmingly deviant tangent, but the fact is the Large Hadron Collider near Geneva is neither a quatrain nor a sonnet. It is 38,000 tons of super conducting dipole magnets, blow valves, sleeper screws, bellow chambers, control racks, helium pipes, gauges, busbars, flow meters, pumps, storage tanks, electrical sensors and cryogenic fluids. All to answer a question: how does energy acquire mass?

Physicists hope that this perplexing problem will be answered by something called the Higgs Boson, a.k.a. the God Particle. They hope to achieve this by smashing protons together at a velocity within a millionth of a percent of the speed of light. In essence, they will be recreating conditions such as they existed at the birth of the universe, when the universe was an undifferentiated soup of matter and radiation, particles colliding rapidly with one another in a temperature of inconceivable strength, 100,000 million degrees Kelvin, too hot to sip from a tablespoon. Which doesn't really matter, as you would not be able to lift the spoon to your mouth: the mass density of the universe would be in the neighborhood of 3.8 thousand million kilograms per liter, or 3.8 thousand million times the density of water under normal terrestrial conditions.

If it exists, the Higgs Boson will prove itself to be an essential and universal component of the material world. Hence, its nickname God Particle. The Higgs Boson is an exchange particle that gives mass to other particles by causing them to cluster around it in much the same way a group of people may cluster around one another to hear a rumor, or bit of important news. Peter Higgs, for whom the particle is named, created a model in which particle masses arise from "fields" spread over space and time. In order to give particles mass, a background field (Higgs field) is invented which becomes locally distorted whenever a particle moves through it. The distortion — the clustering of the field around the particle — generates the particle's mass. Once the particle has mass, it interacts with other elementary particles, slowing them down and giving them mass as well. On the other hand, the Higgs Boson may turn out to be a neat mathematical trick, a form of quantum legerdemain, in which the rabbit and hat are nothing more than a vertiginous mass of numbers, much like the numbers that appear in the movie *The Matrix* when Neo finally penetrates the illusory nature of his world.

But what about that black hole? The LHC came online on September 10th, then shut down again for repair. Problems with a "magnetic quench" on September 19th, 2008, caused a leak of a ton of liquid helium. Particles will not collide again until spring, 2009. When it fires up again, is there still a chance we may all disappear into a black hole? Will a diluted public healthcare option and a hyperinflated American dollar really matter?

The answer may not be a flat-out absolute no (nothing in this universe is ever that certain) but it is extremely unlikely. For an LHC-style black hole, estimated to be only a billionth of a billionth of a meter across, the black hole would exist for a bit more than a few billion-billion-billionths of a second. It wouldn't be around long enough to swallow any nearby matter and would pose no danger to ordinary matter.

I think I'd rather be witness to those stranglets, rogue fragments of strange matter converting the earth to miracles of gold and beatitude, the dream of the alchemists proclaimed in ingots of joy. But this isn't physics. Just simple effervescence.

If the Higgs Boson is confirmed it will provide an answer to how things exist, but not why they exist. What is left out is our creative response to the things of this world, this universe, this dimension. Aristotle referred to matter as "stuff." Potential without actuality. It is essence that gives the potentiality of matter its ultimate design and purpose, its declamation and aspiration. Its character and value. Its genius, its gesture. The agitations that give it life. The intention behind it. Chopin, after all, is not just notes. Chopin is the glamour of yearning.

Each creative act we perform is a God particle. We are complicit in the creation of the universe. Matter without consciousness is raw ore. It is consciousness that smelts that ore into beams and bridges, enduring alloys that shine with an inner light.

What sort of laboratory would we need to fathom the mysteries of consciousness? How do we make sense of sense? Matter without thought is random matter, but thought without matter is empty as a parking lot on Christmas day. It is our perceptions and memories that give meaning to words, but the words themselves are representative of a higher order of being. They are the strange quarks of a giant quirk called Being.

Essence is an indissoluble kernel of inner principle, an inner grammar that gives shape and meaning to things. Anything in general, anything material, anything spiritual, anything living, is the product of a creative act on our part, our participation in its being. The discovery of a particle that allows energy to acquire mass is intrinsically exciting, but what it implies is staggering. What it implies is process. What it implies is a universe that is in a continual state of becoming. Not just expanding, but flowering, blossoming, revealing its mysteries to the pollination of our curiosity. Our involvement with it is immense; we stand at the end of a wharf gazing at the immensity of the horizon, knowing, in our deepest self, that horizon is within as well as without.

It is more than a little coincidental that the fall of our financial institutions and the illusory nature of our wealth has been revealed at the same time as the Large Hadron Collider came online. Money, like language, like up, down, top, bottom, strange and charmed flavors of quark, are interactions, not fully realized realities. As long as we deepen and honor our experiences in this world with an audacious creativity, and push our language to its utmost limits of possibility, we will keep those black holes and bankruptcies at bay. Language extends our ability to exist because not merely because it surrounds and envelops us, but because it is always in a state of potentiality. Reality may prove to be a probability pattern, but without anyone to perceive and give it value, it remains a pattern. It does not become a ship, an avocado, or a hand. It does not awaken. It does not shine.

What is visible before our eyes is there with or without us. It does not require our eyes and ears, the touch of our hands, the warmth of our bodies. But without that, without these things, without this involvement, it remains what it is in its barest sense: space, time, and probability patterns. A tendency to exist. It isn't so much that our involvement completes or fulfills its existence, but that we reciprocate its tendencies, and so become more fully alive ourselves. And if that isn't a particle of Godliness, I don't know what is.

✴

JOHN OLSON is the author eight collections of poetry including
Backscatter: New and Selected Poems from Black Widow Press in
2008. *Souls of Wind*, a novel about French poet Arthur Rimbaud in
the American West — which was shortlisted for a *Believer* magazine
book of the year award — was published by Quale Press in 2008.
The Nothing That Is, an autobiographical novel written from the 2nd
person point of view, was published by Ravenna Press in 2010. He is
the recipient of a Stranger genius award for literature and is a three-
time recipient of a Fund For Poetry Award. He recently finished a
novel about French painter Georges Braque, to be published by
Quale Press in 2012, titled *The Seeing Machine*.

TITLES FROM BLACK WIDOW PRESS

TRANSLATION SERIES

Approximate Man and Other Writings
by Tristan Tzara. Translated and edited
by Mary Ann Caws.

Art Poétique by Guillevic.
Translated by Maureen Smith.

The Big Game by Benjamin Péret.
Translated with an introduction by
Marilyn Kallet.

Capital of Pain by Paul Eluard.
Translated by Mary Ann Caws,
Patricia Terry, and Nancy Kline.

Chanson Dada: Selected Poems
by Tristan Tzara. Translated with an
introduction and essay by Lee Harwood.

*Essential Poems and Writings of Joyce Mansour:
A Bilingual Anthology*
Translated with an introduction by
Serge Gavronsky.

Essential Poems and Prose of Jules Laforgue
Translated and edited by Patricia Terry.

*Essential Poems and Writings of Robert Desnos:
A Bilingual Anthology*
Edited with an introduction and essay by
Mary Ann Caws.

EyeSeas (Les Ziaux) by Raymond Queneau.
Translated with an introduction by Daniela
Hurezanu and Stephen Kessler.

Furor and Mystery & Other Writings
by René Char. Edited and translated by
Mary Ann Caws and Nancy Kline.

The Inventor of Love & Other Writings
by Gherasim Luca. Translated by Julian and
Laura Semilian. Introduction by Andrei
Codrescu. Essay by Petre Răileanu.

La Fontaine's Bawdy by Jean de la Fontaine.
Translated with an introduction by
Norman R. Shapiro.

Last Love Poems of Paul Eluard
Translated with an introduction by
Marilyn Kallet.

Love, Poetry (L'amour la poésie) by Paul Eluard.
Translated with an essay by Stuart Kendall.

Poems of André Breton: A Bilingual Anthology
Translated with essays by Jean-Pierre Cauvin
and Mary Ann Caws.

Poems of A.O. Barnabooth by Valéry Larbaud.
Translated by Ron Padgett and Bill Zavatsky.

Preversities: A Jacques Prévert Sampler
Translated and edited by Norman R. Shapiro.

The Sea and Other Poems by Guillevic.
Translated by Patricia Terry. Introduction by
Monique Chefdor.

To Speak, to Tell You? Poems by Sabine Sicaud.
Translated by Norman R. Shapiro. Introduction
and notes by Odile Ayral-Clause.

forthcoming translations

A Life of Poems, Poems of a Life by Anna de
Noailles. Translated by Norman R. Shapiro.
Introduction by Catherine Perry.

Jules Choppin (1830-1914)
New Orleans Poems in Creole and French
Translated by Norman R. Shapiro

WWW.BLACKWIDOWPRESS.COM

This book was set primarily in Adobe Jenson Pro, with Dharma Gothic P for the poem titles, and Dada Antiquerist for the cover and sectionals.

Adobe Jenson is an old style serif typeface drawn by Robert Slimbach. It is an organic, somewhat idiosyncratic font, with a low x-height.

Dharma Gothic P by Ryoichi Tsunekawa is a distressed offshoot from the original Dharma Gothic.

Dada Antiquerist is a distorted font by "heyheydecay". While all caps, it has the look of hand-lettering.